Seeing Race in Modern America

Seeing Race

IN MODERN AMERICA

Matthew Pratt Guterl

The University of North Carolina Press   *Chapel Hill*

This book was published with the assistance of the Anniversary
Endowment Fund of the University of North Carolina Press.

The paper in this book meets the guidelines for
permanence and durability of the Committee on Production
Guidelines for Book Longevity of the Council on Library Resources.

The University of North Carolina Press has been
a member of the Green Press Initiative since 2003.

Library of Congress Cataloging-in-Publication Data
Guterl, Matthew Pratt, 1970–
Seeing race in modern America / Matthew Pratt Guterl.
p. cm.
Includes bibliographical references and index.
ISBN 978-1-4696-1068-9 (hardback)
1. Race discrimination—United States. 2. Race discrimination—
United States—Psychological aspects. 3. Race awareness—United States.
4. Ethnicity—United States—Public opinion. I. Title.
E184.A1G963 2013
305.800973—dc23
2013015590

17 16 15 14 13   5 4 3 2 1

THIS BOOK WAS DIGITALLY PRINTED.

For Sandi, of course

Contents

Acknowledgments

Good ideas come from everywhere. I could trace the conception of this book back to an academic idyll, to an ideal classroom exchange with a student, or to some high-minded kaffeeklatsch with a generous colleague. Its emergence could be rooted in the rich soil of interlocking interdisciplinary fields, as if it were the hybrid by-product of a comingling of American Studies, History, and Ethnic Studies, to name just three. *Seeing Race in Modern America* could have its origins in a story of abuse at the hands of a policeman or a TSA agent, or a micro-aggressive joke told at the office. It could flow downhill from a childhood memory of some acutely recalled encounter.

But the catalytic, generative truth is more commonplace, more everyday, and perhaps, as a consequence, it creates a stronger foundation for the consideration of "discrimination" as a visual practice with astonishing, awesome reach. I went to Kroger one day with my son and daughter, then about three years and one year old, roughly, and the cashier, a kindly old woman, asked me if they were "Hispanic." Her words registered at a deeper level, as an eerily too familiar reminder that I'd heard many other people ask that question, or some version of it. In that instant of recognition, it didn't matter whether my kids were or weren't Mexican, or Latino, or Hispanic; what mattered was that they were being interpreted—or read, like a text—routinely, regularly, and everywhere. And so, on the short, quotidian drive home from the banal surrounds of my local grocery store, I began to think about how the world was reading my children, and through them my wife, my family, my friends and colleagues, and all of us. At a basic level, the idea for this book emerged from that short trip to Kroger.

The book might have died right at the Kroger exit, though, were it not for five people. Matthew Frye Jacobson, the genius who has fathered a thousand dissertations, made an offhand remark during a long-ago breakfast at EJ's on the Upper West Side about race and sight, a remark that stuck with me as a great idea for a book. "How would you tell the story," he asked, "of what people saw?" Editor

Sian Hunter took a casual, "thinking-out-loud" phone call, and during a conversation about John Singleton Copley's painting *Watson and the Shark* laid out the idea for a picture-rich book with UNC Press. From the very start, Sian was an indefatigable advocate for this book. Caroline Field Levander, my boon compañera, gave me a semester at Rice, and shared beer, ribs, and ambiance with me as I composed the most emotionally challenging part of this book. CFL is the very soul of disco cool. Before and after she left Bloomington, Katie Lofton was game for anything—even if that meant watching *Rambo* at a near-midnight showing at the local multiplex. Her passion for the broadest conception of intellectual life—and her refusal to fear the popular—is infectious and inspiring. She is, in many ways, my teacher. And, finally, Rosanne Currarino patiently read every word of this book a hundred times, and wrote detailed replies about everything. If the prose is at all conversational, it is a consequence of our endless back and forth. She remains my ideal, and much beloved, reader. Without this gang of five, there is no book.

Bloomington, Indiana, was fertile ground for the bulk of the writing and thinking. Deborah Cohn and Vivian Halloran pressed me to keep writing when I should have been filling out e-docs or handling administrative paperwork. Carol Glaze and Paula Cotner and Sean McGuire kept that paperwork—and the unscheduled visitors to our office—away when they knew I was writing. Jason McGraw and Kevin O'Neill and Stephen Selka entertained conversations about *Predator* that went on for way too long. With just twenty-four-hour's notice, Denise Cruz read the first draft of an introduction, and the second, and the third, and so on. Michael McGerr, my guide to absolutely everything, reminded me over lunch one day that while good writing was important, no one reads the prose if the book doesn't get finished. There is no way, finally, that this book could have been written without the generous institutional support of IU's College Arts and Humanities Institute, then directed by Andrea Ciccarelli, and the New Frontiers grant competition.

After Bloomington, in the very final stages, Tony Bogues, Bob Lee, Susan Smulyan, and Corey Walker welcomed me back to Providence and made sure I had the time to finish. My colleagues in Africana Studies and American Studies made the transition to a new home easier than I'd ever imagined it could be.

Students at three very different institutions made great readers.

The section of the book on "Code Red" began as a seminar discussion with Brown students in the early 2000s, at which we all consumed way too much of the drink. Rice students eagerly listened to me talk about *Rambo* and adoption more than I care to admit, and welcomed "Brangelina" as a subject worthy of serious inquiry. And my former IU students have heard all of this before, albeit in rougher form, as I worked through some of these close readings in lecture. My senior seminar students thought it was hilarious that we should be talking about *Tropic Thunder*, but that hilarity, I reminded them, is the very mortar of American Studies. Liz Ericson at Rice and Danille Christensen and Holly Mayne at IU were excellent research assistants. Rita Kelly and Elizabeth Warren—two of the very best undergraduates I'd ever had in the classroom—kept asking about the book, long after they'd left IU.

This is a "UNC" book, for sure. In the early days, Sian Hunter was an extraordinary editor. I drafted and redrafted the original proposal a half dozen times for her, and every time we worked through it, it was substantially improved. After her departure, Mark Simpson-Vos stepped right into her shoes and cheered me on, from first submission through final revisions. Mark is the man. His faith in this book was sustaining. The readers of the original proposal and the complete manuscript—the incomparable Erika Doss and Joy Kasson—were wonderfully constructive and engaged. I hope they find in the book proof that their hard work was, in the end, worth it.

For casual conversations about everything—but especially about the dark and sometimes offbeat subject of this book—I owe some serious thanks to Sarika Chandra, Stephanie Camp, Deborah Cohn, Finis Dunaway, Hugh and Indira Hamilton, Scott Herring and Shane Vogel, Vivian and David Halloran, David Levering Lewis and Ruth Ann Stewart, Jason McGraw and Ellen Wu, Khalil Muhammad and Stephanie Lawson-Muhammad, Marissa Moorman, Ralph Rodriguez, Steve Selka, Micol Seigel and Sarah Zanti, Tim and Angie Sledd, Christine Skwiot, Christina Snyder, Todd Uhlman and Anne Dobmeyer, Drew and Melissa Watters, Kelly Compton and Frankie Price-Presslaff, and David Wall. Gracias, all y'all.

More intimately, my mother, Sheryl, has been—and always will be—supportive of projects that should mystify or trouble her. She does what she can, we joke. In truth, she does far more than that. Robert and Maya, my companions on that fateful trip to Kroger, are now six and eight, and, though they are patient, they are also tired of the watching me type on the laptop.

The first conversation I had about the subject of this book was with Sandra Latcha, my co-parent, life coach, toughest critic, and wife/partner of twenty years, who received me (and the bags of groceries from Kroger) with a raised eyebrow six years ago, on the day when everything clicked. In a classic style, her response was, in just the right sequence, practical ("Can we get the groceries in first?") and philosophical ("So, do *you* think our kids look Mexican?") and instrumental ("What does this do for you?"). She was a supportive skeptic from the start. And in the years that have followed, right up through the copy edits, she has routinely insisted that I persuade her, that I make the book clearer and more convincing, that I not write only for boring, stuffy academics. There is no universe of possibility in which this book could have been written without Sandi's famous candor and her legendary and exacting standards for real life outside of the false world of academe. I owe her everything. Including this book.

Matthew Pratt Guterl
Providence, Rhode Island

Seeing Race in Modern America

Introduction

Discrimination, 1a. The action of discriminating;
the perceiving, noting, or making a distinction or difference between
things; a distinction (made with the mind, or in action).
FROM *THE OXFORD ENGLISH DICTIONARY*

I n the early 1920s, young Langston Hughes was an avant-garde
New Negro poet, a conduit for both white and black audiences to
a racially authentic aesthetic emerging from Harlem's cobblestone
streets (plate 1). As young crewman on the S.S. *Malone*, Hughes had
left New York for Europe's postwar possibilities, but the route took
him to the western edge of Africa first. He had hopeful expectations
of a spiritual connection with his ancestral continent.[1] Arriving at
the "long sandy coastline, gleaming in the sun" after transatlantic
passage aboard the tramp steamer, he watched as the men, their
"rippling muscles" on display, off-loaded the stuff of modernity—
"machinery and tools," he remembered, "canned goods and Hollywood films"—and then loaded the belly of the ship with the spoils of
empire. Embittered by his encounters with prejudice in the United
States, and moved by the busy drama of imperial exchange below
the ship's deck, Hughes sought out and spoke to the dockhands,
and expressed his commitment to racial solidarity. "Our problems
in America are very much like yours," he stressed. "I am a Negro,
too." Looking him up and down, they merely laughed, insisting, "You,
white man!"[2]

Africa, Hughes mused in 1940, "was the only place in the world
where I've been called a white man." Thinking back on it, he emphasized the way he appeared to the stevedores and wharfies, and
not the uneven power dynamic between First and Third Worlds.
"They looked at my copper-brown skin and straight black hair—like
my grandmother's Indian hair, except a little curly—and they said:
You—white man." It was such a mystery, this abrupt reclassification
of a man who was undeniably "Negro" in Harlem but indisputably

"white" in western Africa. A Liberian crewmate familiar with the physical signposts helpfully had translated the local understanding. Any visible mixture, he told Hughes, made one white; and the public absence of mixture, in turn, made one black. As proof, Hughes's guide cut across the obvious geopolitical division and pointed to "George," a kitchen worker on the *Malone*, saying, "You black." The guide had seen in George's body the indicators of pure blackness that were absent, he thought, in the skin and hair of Hughes. So it was left to George, in defiant response, to reinscribe the First World location of African Americans, invoking his home in Lexington, Kentucky, insisting that he had "no African blood anywhere," and then concluding, "I can part my hair and it ain't nappy."[3]

Historian James T. Campbell, in his wonderful account of black travel, begins with this same famous vignette because it reveals "Africa's persistent hold on the African American imagination."[4] And so it does. I begin with it for a different reason, though. For me, it tells us something about seeing race. Hughes and his African interlocutors, I note, all used the same visual practice—a way of looking for distinctions—to read these little details, but they came to different conclusions. The back and forth on the docks and on board the ship highlights a clash between fundamentally different ways of reading race into the many distinctions grafted onto the body. Race—construed in this exchange as color, and more narrowly as blackness and whiteness—is marked by little details, by skin tone, by hair texture, by anything that might reveal mixture or its absence, a shared catalog of clues read differently. The two men debating Hughes's racial character emerged from two different historical contexts, two different symbolic surrounds. Their irreconcilable readings suggest perpendicular viewings of the same body through different sightlines, with shared attention to the same details producing different results. And that resulting, jarring clash between ways of looking at the racialized body highlights not just Hughes's "wonderment" when confronted with "that other taxonomy," and not merely "the exotic charm of another system of thought," but also "the limitation of [his] own, the stark impossibility of thinking that."[5]

Race, as Langston Hughes would tell us, begins with a discriminating look, a calculated assessment of the tone of the skin, or the texture of the hair, or the shape of the face. That racial look, globally speaking, has a long history. Within the modern age, faith in the eye's capacity to discern racial difference can be traced to the beginning of contact between Europe, Africa, and Asia, if not before. One could follow it forward, through the first fantastic travelogues, into the human sciences, into art, lithography, printing, illustration, filmmaking, and still photography. It looms large in the conquest of the New World, in the establishment of African slavery and Asian indenture, in the age of empires, in Jim Crow and apartheid, in the Holocaust, and in the genocides of Rwanda and Yugoslavia. There is no moment in this long history when the certainty of the official racial look to reveal the truth was troubled, when doubt crept into the dominant racial language, since even the most mysterious bodies revealed race eventually. Now as then, most people today believe that they can see something that can be named "race," even if they disagree—like Hughes and his West African wharfies—over the basic nomenclature.

Seeing Race in Modern America is an exploration of this racial sight in the modern United States, from the early nineteenth century to the very recent present. Limiting its purview to one national context, it is an illumination of the long-term popular reliance on observable details and racial biometrics to classify, organize, and arrange different kinds of bodies, and the enrollment and imprinting of individual bodies with multiple markers that match a particular template, stereotype, or stock representation. It is a history of the discriminating gaze, of racial taste, which sometimes becomes a part of public policy, and just as often becomes a feature of high fashion, or popular culture, or political movements, or the quotidian interaction. The breadth of this story is important. The story of race, I argue here, is not just the story of the social construction of color in recent policing strategies, rarified legal decisions, obscure scientific findings, public discourse, and literature; it is also the story of the everyday assessment, or scan, of the body as text, and the culturally informed interpretation of the signs and symbols seen in the profile, the posture, and the comportment of a person's carriage. It is, too, the story of visual habits, sightlines that allow the national popular to prescribe common sight. And it is a story of persistence and consistency, of less change over time than we might expect or hope for, of taxonomies that endure beyond their expected lifespan, and of representations that repeat, that recirculate, and that don't die off.

Discrimination is a deeply disciplined, popular practice. Informed by supposedly shared experience and invested in the national popular as a shared civic space, the everyday person draws upon a common set of conventions in interpreting the physical world, even as artists, filmmakers, advertising agents, and other producers of visual culture rely on the idea of "the public's visual capacity" to understand these same conventions in their color-filled representations of our material conditions.[6] This disciplining of the American eye happens slowly, as the builders of racial difference are also built within it, as the rich symbolic surround related to race becomes a part of the nation's cultural education. Racism and racial thinking are enduring aspects of the modern experience, and have been consistently featured in U.S. history. Situated within national popular culture, Americans learn to see the details of race over time, and are obligated, by their commitment to the national consensus, to agree, generally, that race can be seen, can be tracked, can be verified, in most cases, on the body. As unofficial agents of this verification, they interpret the available signs, give them publicity, and conclude with as much certainty as can be mustered about categories and definitions, classifications and fit. They repeat those certainties over lunch, or at dinner. Policies are based on their efficacy, and people are hired or fired because of what their bodies tell us. Big, durable institutions are created to support this practice.

Ways of looking usually change over time, and images might, under normal circumstances, be read differently as their meaning becomes fluid and inconsistent from generation to generation. The aesthetics of feminine beauty, of a pleasing landscape, have a history pockmarked with alteration. But the persistence of racism in American culture and society gives sightlines some longevity as well-circulated images acquire—by virtue of their usefulness—something close to a permanent meaning. Sightlines thus seem more durable because racism is longer-lived. Seeing race is making race, an act of mutual construction that makes common sight possible, and that ensures that sightlines last longer than they should.[7] For much of the past five hundred years, here and around the world, people have performed this act of mutual reinforcement every day, without a thought, simply by saying—to themselves or to others, and no matter their politics—"he is a Negro," or "she looks Mexican," or "he looks Asian."

Because of its ubiquity and vast utility, the practice of racial looking has, though, a surprising orderliness to it. It works as technique, as practice, shaped by repetition and consensus. The repetition of certain themes and patterns over time indicates that the conclusions drawn from racial sight are persistent and durable, reflecting grooves in the visual landscape. These grooves, or sightlines, lead us back to consolidated representations, a feature of common racial sight, and evidence, as W. J. T. Mitchell might say, that race is now a mediating feature of the national popular, that we see *through* it.[8] They make it easier, or more likely, to see some features as evidence of race, and harder to see others as proof of the same. In the same way that certain well-known literary genres shape our reading of mass culture, sightlines structure our encounter with the visual world. In the moment the sightlines emerge, what is built and constructed is generally durable and powerful, and aims to be prescriptive and constraining. A sightline is, then, a persistent and prescribed reading of an image, or of images related to each other, sustained by the history of racism and race relations. As such, sightlines haunt the eyes.

My interest in line of sight as a metaphor for techniques of racial sight isn't chiefly about the meanings attached to various representations; it is also about the work of sightlines in making certain things legible and readable. In each sightline, the emphasis is on a specific disciplining of the eye, and on the creation of a conventional, commonly accessible "political anatomy of detail."[9] Some sightlines focus on a single body, weighed down with meaning. These make the racialized body visible in tight focus, like the literal reading of a racial profile. Other sightlines consider a matched racial set, complementary or antagonistic but still bound and defined together, so that the body can be compared, or juxtaposed, with an opposite, with its natural complement, or with the full array of types. Still other sightlines engage an imprecise object, nearly impossible to snap into focus but alluring in its imprecision, its blurriness calling the eye to focus, even if it cannot, because the object of its consideration is thought to be ambiguous, or hybrid, or passing. "Races," philosopher Linda Martín Alcoff notes, "may have indeterminate borders, and some individuals may appear ambiguous, but many people believe that (a) there exists a fact of the matter about one's racial identity, usually determined by ancestry, and (b) that identity is discernable if one peers long enough at, or observes carefully enough, the person's physical features and practiced mannerisms."[10] Sightlines organize the production of racial knowledge—the thousands of details we see and watch and study in order to realize the "fact of the matter"—into predictable conclusions.

They are visual shorthand, with an obvious familiarity that makes it possible to name them, to list them, and to clarify their function. As the media noted in 2008, when LeBron James clutches Gisele Bündchen on the cover of *Vogue*, his mouth open in an angry scream, the image isn't just a reference to the early *King Kong* (1933) movie posters; it is also embedded (as was *King Kong*) in a very specific, recycled pairing—that of the brutish beast and the white woman—that forces attention to specific, memorable details (size, color, sex, emotion) and that allows us to align LeBron and Gisele with Kong and Ann Darrow, with Gus and Flora from *Birth of a Nation* (1915), and with the angry, simian Hun of the 1917 U.S. Army recruitment poster.[11] The sense of repetition and remediation found in the details announces a working sightline, drawing together the reader and the read. Such a sightline makes it easier to see a band of disparate young men as potential rapists, and to see every white woman as a potential victim of their predations. It makes it possible for a lynch mob to see a black man as a "beast," to hang him from a tree, and to smile as a local photographer snaps a picture. Any immediate, direct threat to the virtue of white womanhood is darkened, racialized, visualized as "black," not strictly by the terms of ancestry and descent but by the broader conventions of racial thinking and racial sight.

The photograph of James and Bündchen, one might suggest, calls for an ironic reading. The repetitive circulation of racial stereotypes is plain to see, but Leibovitz seems keen to draw on these stereotypes only to disrupt them: James is depicted as a heroic star athlete, holding a basketball not a club, with a feral expression that references his command of the court, not his inner nature. Bündchen, in turn, has a slight smile, not a frozen scream. The photographer, some might argue, could be repeating the sightline, but she is also challenging its valuations of black and white. I read this image a little more cynically, though. That is, I recognize that Leibovitz may well have intended to play with the representation of Kong ironically, but I don't believe that the playfulness actually transforms meaning. By shifting our attention to sightlines, we see that such a transformation—which can't be fully successful until racism is no longer—requires more than irony. Disrupting the workings of a sightline,

A reproduction of the original *King Kong* movie poster, issued c. 1933. A classic metaphor for the danger posed by "the Negro," who, like Kong, is brought from savagery to civilization, and, once relocated, poses a threat to white womanhood. Note that here, as in the *Vogue* image and the army recruitment poster, the "black beast" is an outsized threat. From author's collection.

even if temporarily and incompletely, requires unmanageable "clutter," or the presence of objects and details that are foreign, weird, or inexplicable, that distract the eye. Simply ironic interpretations cannot be transgressive. For far too many sets of eyes, and for all the wrong reasons, that basketball just seems like a "natural" object in the hands of the dark-skinned James. (And, indeed, *Vogue*'s unwillingness to release the image for this book and others suggests that their PR people, too, have come to similar conclusions).

My point here, again, isn't to worry too much about how this image represents blackness along stereotypical lines, or whether or not it should be seen as transgressive. Instead, I want to change the terms of our reading and acknowledge that the scandalous portrait of James and Bündchen does something else very clearly: it relies on stark juxtaposition—on the close proximity of established and detailed points of difference—to reveal race. When I talk about ways of looking, or ways of seeing race, it is, for me and in this case, the

H. R. Hopps, "Destroy this Mad Brute. Enlist—US Army," c. 1917. Here, importantly, the savage threat is posed as the mad Hun, transformed into a wild beast not unlike Kong. During the Great War, the Hun was often imagined as a distinct race, with dangerously primitive qualities. Blackness here is a precise synonym not for "the Negro" but for sexual predation and brutality. The website gawker.com, seeing the parallel to the Leibovitz photo, called on the photographer to confess that she had produced an "homage to a xenophobic wartime poster" ("Time for Leibovitz to Confess," http://twoguyswhoneveragree.blogspot.com/2008/03/exhibit.html [accessed August 15, 2012]). Library of Congress, Prints and Photographs Division.

juxtaposition that matters, that makes the image complicit. Complicit, that is, not with a particular politics, but with the sightline that makes it possible for us to look at all black/white pairings the same way, with a focus on a specific, agreed-upon set of details.

Race relies on the endless circulation and mediation of representation through these very comfortable, historically repeating perspectives. A cue for the eye, these sightlines ensure—or are designed to ensure—that the eye finds the center of attraction, that it sees race, and that we all see the same thing, generally, when we look. They guide our sight along familiar trajectories. They have established contours that close off other ways of seeing race, other possible ways of knowing and thinking about color, difference, and the body. With an end point that is obvious, they presume a specific focus on a certain, recognizable, even predictable object. Their potency and endurance are the reason we see so many repeating representations, over such a wide swath of time, and across so many different contexts.

But they are many, not one. They can converge and intersect with each other, complement or clash.

As I wrote earlier, these sightlines also endure. Much historical work emphasizes change over time, but *Seeing Race in Modern America* does not—or at least, not in the same fashion. Often, the historiographical emphasis on change carries with it a liberal teleology—things change, and generally things improve, to match the expansion of rights in U.S. history, and along with the expansion the reform of patriarchy, the protection of the young and the old, the bestowal of rights on the working class, and the abolition of indenture, slavery, and Jim Crow. Just as often, there is a declension storyline, in which things suddenly, or unexpectedly get worse, and in which options for improvement are increasingly constrained, and human progress now seems doomed to fail, or at least to take a step backward. These two plotlines are sometimes messy, and the narratives might be marked by ups and downs, but their emphasis on change—for good or for bad—is undeniable.

In *Seeing Race in Modern America*, then, I argue that visual culture—and especially that featuring race—supplies a useful public archive, and resists the conventional emphasis on change. Current debates about border controls, for instance, rely on the visual signifiers of illegality and inferiority, but those signifiers repeat, sometimes detail for detail, older debates and frameworks. Historic representations and sightlines are so repeatedly recycled, so frequently brought back to the surface, and so constantly in mediation and circulation, that it can seem as if they were never truly "old." Despite extraordinary and historic transformations in the material and political "relations" of the races over five centuries of American history, we have seen race, in short, through stylistic sightlines that are fairly stable, a stability that makes public certainty and common sight possible. I am less interested, here, in political narratives of triumph and retrenchment, or of equality and justice, because I worry that those narratives do dangerous work to hide what has remained essentially unchanged. I want, as Coco Fusco instructs, to make a distinction between "racialization as a visual process, and racism as an ethical and political dilemma."[12] And my emphasis here is on the former.

These different processes demand different histories, I believe. That *Vanity Fair* cover provocatively pushes back against racism, putting a smile on Gisele's face and reminding us that yesterday's "black beasts" are today's multimillionaires, but it also wholeheartedly confirms the crispness of the line dividing black from white. Within the context of U.S. history, the pairing on the cover of *Vogue*—the black beast and his white female victim—is ancient. So, too, is our way of seeing that pair.

If, however, this coupling is ancient, that doesn't mean it is timeless or eternal. The beginnings of these sightlines are available for scrutiny, even if, once established, they don't necessarily transform, or shift, with the passage of social movements and political periodizations. The search for the passing body, to choose one example, might begin with the Great Migration, conceived ambitiously enough to include the earlier movements to cities after slavery and the current return to the New South by large numbers of African Americans. The official mapping of the racial profile for the purpose of "better policing" began in the early nineteenth century, with urbanization and immigration, and with a concern over crime, danger, and alienation. The multiracial platoon was produced in the midst of the early twentieth century's wars, when such a vision of the nation-in-action was politically expedient and meaningful. Over time, old sightlines endure, and new sightlines are opened up, always without a discernable author, or the trace of individual construction. They emerge, alongside visual culture itself, and they establish shape and strength out of what would otherwise be chaos and random representation.

Such a useful public archive is organized, like most archives, to also serve local and global interests. Wherever there is race, surely there are sightlines. And these sightlines are just as certainly portable and durable and, indeed, on occasion, transnational. There are local and regional inflections, and ways of seeing and making sense of race that work on the ground in cultural microclimates. There are racial looks that emerge from historical contexts dating back to medieval constructs, to contact with the New World, to slavery and anti-Semitism. Some ways of seeing race spring from specific psychologies and biographies; and some represent counterpolitics, or the persistence of the subaltern or the subversive. Indeed, for as long as there have been efforts to describe, in words or in pictures, human difference through a consideration of the surface, there have been myriad ways of seeing race.

But the notion of sightlines as an ideal of the national popular—reflecting the interests of people within the borders of the nation to create temporal simultaneity and shared space—is still critically important. Indeed, establishing a belief in common racial sight is a critically important project of the nation-state, its citizens, and its denizens, especially in an age of terror. My aim in this book is thus focused on one context—that of the United States. I'm not attempting to track the global influence of American racial sightlines, though I do want to acknowledge a wider, worldly practice of seeing race, and of creating sightlines, that is far bigger than the nation-state. Nor am I mapping the routes of other ways of seeing race, rooted outside of the United States and carried across the border. Instead, I want simply to catalog some of the more revealing sightlines in the national popular and to explore the productive, working myth of national sight. I want to highlight the meaning and significance of sightlines, and this desire compels a singular focus on the nation as a case study. So, then, Seeing Race in Modern America is a demonstration of a theory about daily life in the United States, and about the unreflective way that people caught up in the national popular (across well-demarcated divisions of region, race, ethnicity, and class) make discerning choices each and every day about taxonomy and classification and meaning.

To organize this book, I've chosen to focus on three basic kinds, or genres, of sightlines. Part I includes a series of short chapters on the close reading of the individual body in American culture, on topics ranging from racial profiling to silhouetting to commodification. Part II dwells on a few of those sightlines that rely on the public presentation of diversity in ensemble, from the various black and white pairings, to adoptive families, to competing visions of multiculturalism, to the establishment of multiethnic platoons in war films, Westerns, and action movies. Part III considers those sightlines that make it possible to see—or to strive to see—what is difficult to mark, including the body that passes in literature, that deliberately shrouds itself in ethnic ambiguity in film, that presents itself, through an actor's unusual surrogacy, as a stand-in for another race, or that engages, across all media, in self-conscious racial masquerades. The point here isn't to definitively trace all specific sightlines but to illustratively demonstrate, in three larger groupings, how we see race, essentially, through sightline, and by doing that, to call our attention to the varieties of such things in mass culture.[13]

In using such a focus, my writing of Seeing Race in Modern America is meant to subtly disconnect the history of racial sight from the dominant categories of color, and instead suggest a mediating emphasis on theme, genre, and pattern. There is much rich work on the great representational categories of complexion, but I don't assume here that color is the visual sine qua non of race, or that a theory of racial looking must necessarily be a history of blackness or whiteness or brownness. Instead, I step back and consider the practices of looking that make, shape, and reinforce color. Coming at this differently, I conclude that race emerges when the body is scanned in profile, in silhouette, or in relation, or in a set series of assemblages and juxtapositions, or when a form is marked by hybridity, ambiguity, subterfuge, and masquerade. It is within these sightlines—and others—that evidence of color, so eagerly sought by the eye, is found. It is this set of sightlines that signals visual convention, that reveals the national interest in common sight. And so, I attend here to these sightlines, and not to color, as illustrations of how we—scholars of race, interested readers, and practitioners of racial looking—might come to make sense of the nearly unchanging sameness of race and representation.

How we look at the body, I believe, is as important as what we think we see. When it comes to race, there is nothing we trust as much as sight. "What you see is what you get," we like to say. Or, "Seeing is believing." But when such trust allows us to "see" a specific racial object, it also creates the conditions for us to see any racial object. When we see—and love—race in one context, we make it possible to see—and loathe—race in another. If, as scholars and citizens concerned about civil society, all we do is focus on the worst aspects of visual culture—negative stereotypes and racist representations— we miss the overall significance of racial sight itself: the "logic" of the system of classification—the trust in the eye to see and discern race—makes all forms of sight possible, the good and the bad and the benign. So, with that caution in mind, I am trying to break down the various ways of seeing race here, to explain that we see what we want to see, what we've been built to see, what we have to see, and not what actually is.

Though the book strays far and wide over American visual culture, its greater significance is revealed in small, dense, complicated stories. As I write these words, the New York Police Department stands accused of encouraging its officers to "stop and frisk" a very singular, bodily category: "male blacks 14 to 20, 21."[14] An Academy Award–winning actor, Forest Whitaker, was patted down at a Morningside Heights deli, simply because of his skin tone. The racial look can seem trivial, or depoliticized, until you remember that the common ways of looking for, at, and through race described throughout this book also make it possible for a police inspector to insist that a young officer ought to know which bodies to seize on behalf of the state. They make it possible for a celebrity to be seen as a thief. They make it possible for the leather of a wallet to look, under the night sky, like gunmetal. Recognizing this, a friend once told me that my project was akin to a broad history of racial profiling. And so, in some very unhappy way, it is.

PART I

Close-Ups

The Devil in the Details

I have blond hair, blue eyes, and fair skin. My brother however
is the exact opposite. Basically what I'm asking is if someone who
has blond hair and blue eyes and fair skin, if they were to tan and
get dark and dye there hair black would they look Mexican[?]

"WHAT MAKES A MEXICAN LOOK LIKE A MEXICAN?," YAHOO ANSWERS

When an anonymous young woman posted her question on Yahoo—"What makes a Mexican look like a Mexican?"—she asked for "serious and kind answers only." "You know," she explained, "when you look at a person, and automatically know that they are most likely Mexican, not by the way they dress or language there [sic] talking, but there [sic] characteristics like dark hair, dark skin, etc?"[1] Her request for thoughtful responses didn't stop one respondent from suggesting that she look for "a really big Sombrero." She also got a long answer describing the mix of peoples and races that went into the Olmec civilizations, a response with three links to a flickr account corresponding to the three racial types supposedly found in Mexico, and still another from someone who began by noting that "many Mexicans do have black or dark brown hair, brown eyes and dark skin" before continuing on to say that "I had a neighbor who was Mexican as well, with blonde hair and green eyes. Her skin was lighter than mine. I didn't believe her until she held her arm next to mine—and I'm not dark-skinned at all." Still, despite the anecdotal diversity, the author of the post was satisfied enough with their collective confirmation that the right answer was written on the body somewhere to mark the question as "resolved."

Here, I want to explore the workings of three sightlines—those related to racial profiling, to silhouetting, and to racial commodification. I do so without, by and large, a straightforward chronological orientation because I am interested in a specific way of seeing. All three of these examples, I argue, depend on very close readings of the familiar racialized body alone, typically without ensemble and accompaniment, emphasizing the sorts of minutiae critically engaged by racial sight. All three are thus illustrative of the sorts of close readings done regularly, in these and other parallel sightlines, and in any focused consideration of the single body, where microscopic detail is mined from the singular, racialized physique for proof of origins.

These close readings present themselves as unconscious, or instinctual, and not as manifestations of a specific, practiced technique. On an episode of *Identity*, a now defunct game show on NBC hosted by comedian Penn Jillette in 2006 and 2007, a contestant surveyed the body of "person No. 8." The premise of the show was that contestants would look over the body of a different person each week and rely on their instincts to make snap judgments about the character, personality, and identity of the numbered person before them. On this particular episode, "No. 8" was wearing very little—only a black bikini top, denim shorts, and a jeweled halter collar. She stood alone on the stage, waiting for her identification. With heightened gravitas, Jillette asked the female contestant, "Is she Haitian?" For a minute, against the stressful background of dramatic music, the woman nervously surveyed the body and face of No. 8. At one point, she complained that No. 8 didn't look like "the textbooks [she'd] read." Finally, she guessed: "Yes, I think she is." "Well, I live in LA," No. 8 replied blithely, "but I was born in Haiti." The crowd cheered.

Like the young woman seeking to know what it means to look "Mexican," *Identity* capitalized on the craze for subconscious, unprocessed visual interpretation—epitomized by the publication of Malcolm Gladwell's *Blink* in 2005. But in this episode, and in others, *Identity* also depended on a kind of encyclopedic, collective memory about race, and encouraged the supposedly careful scrutiny of the face and the body to find and interpret a curl of hair, or shade of skin color, or shape of a chin to mark one as "Haitian" and not, say, "Jamaican." Or to see Haiti as an imprecise synonym for "black." This dependence and its particular manifestation here—seeing "Haiti" in No. 8—suggests, in the end, that racial sight isn't truly instinctual, and that human beings aren't driven by nature to search for these markings, but that these distinctions emerge to serve and are given greater meaning by recent historical context. In the modern age, they have been formed and structured by the modern institutions of slavery and empire, nationalism and internationalism, among others. As ways of looking, they are constituted by—and in turn constitute—other structures of power, other manifestations of difference.

The complete cataloging of No. 8 is one example of something we do every day—something we don't often think about or analyze carefully. We narrowly focus on what we assume is self-evident and obvious: the skin color divide between black and white. We set aside the smaller, easily synthesized "facts" that make that narrower focus possible. And in doing so, we utterly fail to properly understand exactly how race gets seen, how it is made, and how it has changed—and not changed—over time. The seeing of No. 8, then, is not the just the story of social construction of color; it is also the story of the eye in context, schooled to see the same thing in the face and on the body, to see a panoply of overdetermined details, brimming with public importance. The contestant didn't merely see what she thought was black skin; she also saw other subcutaneous specifics. And the audience's applause was confirmation that she attended to what was imagined as the right details, and reached what was seen as a logical conclusion.

A critique of the discriminating look should have, at the very beginning, a discussion of the body without relation, of the body alone, on a dais and under a spotlight, like No. 8. Unattached bodies like that of No. 8 are viewed outside of an ensemble or partnership, and thus require different techniques of sight. But they are still very easily seen within the racial landscape—more easily seen, for example, than the passing figure, or the ambiguous physique, both of which I will consider later. These singular, easily discerned bodies become, for instance, fixtures of state policy through racial profiling and other criminal and anti-terror initiatives. Or they become silhouettes whose certain edges present themselves as "obvious," defying debate. Or they become biopolitical metaphors for consumer goods and for the dazzling world of services and servants. Their most important shared quality, however, is that they are seen primarily alone, without relation or juxtaposition or comparison, and that their proper identification is determined by the structured body, by the slope of the brow, by the flare of the nose, by the length of the fingers and the shape of the lips, by the shape of the breast, or by the texture of the hair. Absent larger comparison and contrast, the devil is in the very finest details.

CHAPTER ONE

Profiles

"There are 16 million eyes in the city," the poster reads, "[and] we're counting on all of them." An array of twelve sets of eyes, each marked with racial and ethnic distinctions, stares outward at the reader. A part of the "See Something, Say Something" sloganeering effort of the Metropolitan Transportation Agency in New York City, the poster was framed by stainless steel and encased in one of the official protective frames found on most of the city's subway trains. The MTA's use of this imperative axiom was a by-product of the attacks on September 11, 2001, and the image on the poster conveyed what was a standard response of the cosmopolitan metropolis to the threat posed by global terrorism. The array of different faces and eyes communicated a common cause, with the larger, polyglot group self-interestedly guarding a generally shared and collected interests. The thing to be seen was, of course, the "terrorist," inevitably construed as brown, as Arab, and as Muslim. The entire city, MTA spokesman Kevin Ortiz remarked, would be "the eyes and ears of our system."[1] Establishing a commonplace practice of racial profiling by a multicultural community, the image offered up a militarized world city, populated by myriad and discrete racial types, searching for those who were easily identifiable, and who would destroy the uniform fabric of twenty-first-century America.

By the spring of 2010, "See Something, Say Something" had become a national campaign. Dan Fanelli, an insurgent Republican candidate for a seat in the House of Representatives, asked television viewers in central Florida to trust their eyes. In the commercial, he stood between an elderly man presented as "white," with light skin, white hair, glasses, and a tie, and a younger, muscled man with dark hair, wearing a black t-shirt, with a scowl and a menacing, hunched-over posture. Fanelli gestured to the bespectacled white face and, with heavy sarcasm, asked his potential constituents, "Does this

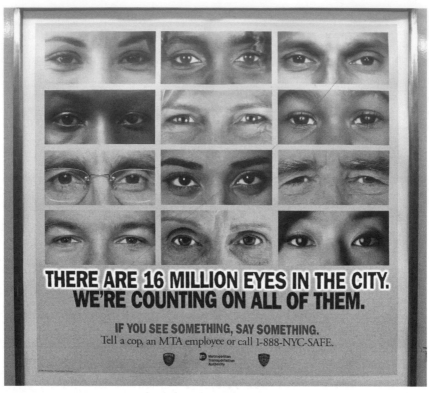

The public eye, as conceived by the "See Something, Say Something" campaign, here broadcast on a subway. David Goehring/Flickr/Creative Commons.

look like a terrorist?" Laughingly, he then turned to "this guy"—the man we are meant to see as dark, as foreign, as Islamic—and asked the same question. Railing against "political correctness" and speaking over the theme music from the classic 1971 "tough cop" film *Dirty Harry*, the would-be congressman suggested that racial profiling was a necessarily logical antiterrorism strategy, and that, by forsaking it, the nation-state was making a critical mistake that would cost lives. People from the Middle East could be more closely watched, he told the *Washington Post*, because "you can't be light and from those countries." Linking race to place, and skin color to climate and geopolitical location, Fanelli's "common sense" split apart those who "look like" Americans from those who "look like" they could be terrorists, a division that made sense only if one agreed that "an Arab" was a singular thing, identifiable with a brief look.[2] Later that week, comedian Jon Stewart, poking fun at the presumption of the look on his

The obvious Arab, otherwise known as "this guy," from Dan Fanelli's campaign commercial.

Comedy Central "news" show, reversed the valance, and wondered if the older, lighter man was "Dr. Kevorkian," the much-maligned proponent of assisted suicide, and if the younger, darker man was a comparatively harmless, well-suntanned "Guido" cast member from the reality television show *The Jersey Shore*.

Fanelli's campaign, likewise, assumed that viewers would see things through a common logic, without explanation or interpretation. The MTA poster—and the campaign it reflected—suggested that common cause, especially in the service of the nation-state, could produce common sight, that shared vision could conjure up a single enemy, and that the single enemy could be identified, by those dozen uncommon eyes, as a verifiable racial and religious type. Both confirmed the practice of establishing a common sight around the relation of race and crime (commonly called racial profiling, but now a feature of antiterrorism campaigns) that has long been one of the most prominent sightlines in contemporary American political culture. "See Something, Say Something" was not merely a slogan but also a call to articulate the specifics of race as a part of shared public policing of bodies marked as brown, or Arab, or Muslim.

Before 9/11, the concept of racial profiling had been most closely associated with domestic concerns: the overpolicing of African Americans in the 1980s and 1990s, or the intense surveillance of Central American gangs in the broader American Southwest. A feature of the American racial landscape for two generations, and a component of the "broken windows" theory of urban policing, the tactic's foundational assumption was that attention to little things could make a big difference, or that a black man out of place—in a white neighborhood, driving an expensive car, or entering an exclusive boutique—was quite likely in the midst of making trouble. The "common sense" of the practice was, then, a matter of assigning a criminal identity based on surface physical characteristics and performative markers that were easily racialized and historicized. Fanelli's commitment to that discriminating look was, in the wake of 9/11, standard-issue, hard-right boilerplate, applicable to myriad social concerns, many of them outside of major cities. It was as common with Republicans as with many conservative Democrats, all of whom were interested in firming up the border between the United States and Mexico, in seeming tough on national security, or in preventing the ingress of radicals and terrorists and "illegals." As Arizona congressional candidate Gabriella Saucedo Mercer put it, most of the world's dangerous populations "look Mexican, or they look like a lot of people from South America—dark hair, brown eyes. And they mix."[3]

With its tactical emphasis on bodies out of place—in the wrong neighborhood, driving the wrong car, or in the wrong store—racial profiling has a stark geographic quality, an emphasis on ideal, racially ordered space. In an age of widening socioeconomic divergence for everyone, its emphasis on race, and not class, seems quintessentially American, reflecting the way that diminishing chances for poor white progress get translated into shared white concern about the spatial transgressions of people of color. Contrarily, with its reliance on surveillance and authoritarian action, racial profiling would also seem to be a desperate creation of the supposedly un-American tropics, a reflex of effete colonial powers and juntas, anxious to retain control, turning loose the police function of the nation-state. In these iterations and others, the first assumption of racial profiling is that we know race. That we, as a social body, can see race well enough, clearly enough, and intelligently enough to make an assessment about who is most certainly a criminal and who is most certainly not. What interests me about racial profiling, then, is not its political function but its social function, not its claims to be a part of "good policing" but its older, less understood role as a way to see the foreign body in contrast with the ideal social body.

That first assumption—that we can police what we see—isn't new, and it deserves a history of its own. In 1854, the Mobile, Alabama, physician Josiah C. Nott and the former U.S. Consul in Cairo, George Glidden, published a massive ethnological survey, *Types of Mankind*. The work was nominally derived from the craniometric examinations conducted by the recently deceased Samuel George Morton, a renowned figure in American ethnology, and the man who, as Ann Fabian puts it, "defined" scientific racism.[4] It drew deeply from Morton's own conclusions to show that racial differences were profoundly speciated—that is, that skin color and other physical and mental indicators of difference marked the borders of distinct species, or "types." To make this point clear, Nott and Glidden included a foldout array of the world's various racial types, drawn by Harvard paleontologist Louis Agassiz, and surrounded by different animal species. Arranged in a grid, the races of the world—captured in profile—ran across the very top of the array. Beneath the top row, Agassiz provided the skull of each race, also arranged in profile. And beneath that row were six more rows, each filled with different animal species. The tableau's algebra was obvious: a "Mongol" was a different species from a "Negro" and so, too, was a giraffe a different species from a llama. Speciation was captured, in the end, in the racial profile, and in the slope, shape, and size of the skull.[5]

Types of Mankind was a sequel, of sorts, to Morton's *Crania Aegyptiaca* (1844), which established the ancient Egyptians as Caucasian, and *Crania Americana* (1839), which stressed the eternal inferiority of African and Indigenous peoples in the Americas. But Nott and Glidden, deeply sympathetic to the Southern proslavery argument and committed to a scientific justification for chattel bondage, expanded upon Morton's earlier conclusions and assembled *Types of Mankind* as more muscular proof of racial polygenism and white perfection. To the type named as "the Caucasian," the authors ascribed a nearly godly physique: "To them have been assigned, in all ages, the largest brains and the most powerful intellect; *theirs* is the mission of extending and perfecting civilization."[6]

The image of this physical type standing at the apex of civilization is ubiquitous across the nineteenth century. "Typical America," one late-nineteenth-century representation was labeled, as if the nation and the body were one and the same. "American Flower," read another. Both emphasized not merely a rosy skin tone, indicating health and vigor, but also a high brow, a direct, level gaze, an erect carriage, and a strong chin. And both were commonplace,

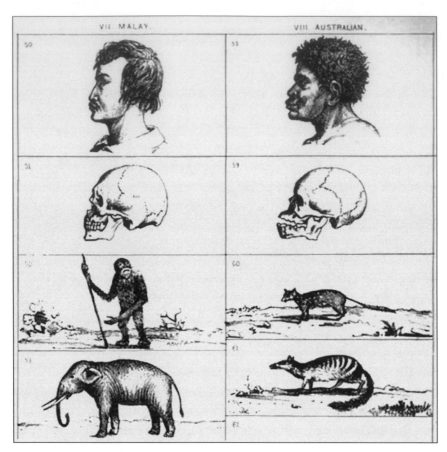

A detail from Agassiz's chart, with a taxonomy that includes everything from the profile, to the skull, to associated animal types, from Nott and Glidden, *Types of Mankind* (Philadelphia: Lippincott, Grambo, 1855), 44.

even disposable images, merely labels on cigar boxes, repeating lessons learned across the wider landscape of American visual culture. Their disposable ubiquity is evidence of their broadcast function. By offering a singular whitened American type, these images also cut through the messiness of nineteenth-century racial thinking, in which whiteness functioned as a larger category fractured into smaller, and only slightly less significant racial groups. Still, they also confirmed the relevance of the face, and the profile, in revealing the facts of race, however race may have been defined.

Despite its pronounced white supremacist sentiments, Nott and Glidden's *Types of Mankind* proved to be less popular than the au-

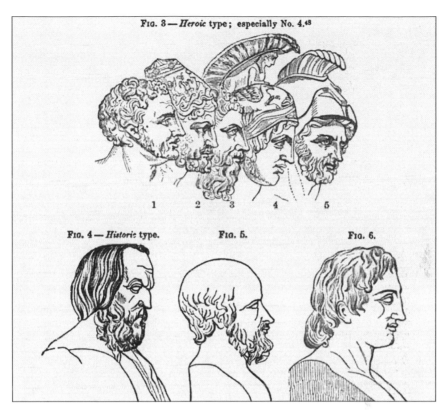

FIG. 3 — *Heroic* type; especially No. 4.⁴⁸

1 2 3 4 5

FIG. 4 — *Historic* type.   FIG. 5.   FIG. 6.

"Heroic" and "historic" types of whiteness, from Nott and Glidden, *Types of Mankind*, 104.

thors might have hoped. In an era dominated by Christian genealogies, its rejection of biblical explanations for the Negro's inferiority was, in the end, too radical. As a rich text in the history of physiognomic thought, though, *Types of Mankind* illustrated the power of the informed eye to make more precise sense of a tangled bodily landscape. Like many others in the nineteenth century, Nott and Glidden stressed that the shape of the skull could be divined from the features of the face, and that the structure of the face and body — the profile, cheekbones, and jawline, to name three aspects — offered evidence of inner character. "One might," the authors proffered, "describe an Indian's skull by saying, it is the opposite in every respect from that of the Negro; as much as the brown complexion of the Red-man is instantly distinguishable from the Black's; or the long hair of the former differs in substance from the short wool of the latter."[7] The book is ribboned with charts, lithographs, and tableaus,

"Typical America," detail from a cigar box label. Warshaw Collection of Business Americana, Series: TT & I, Archives Center, National Museum of American History, Smithsonian Institution.

literal illustrations of the surface manifestations of inner distinction. *Types of Mankind* was, then, a profiler's handbook, written to facilitate better and more accurate racial assessments.

Some physical evidence was, however, unavailable. After noting the absence of "Mongolian skulls," Nott and Glidden turned to what they described as "Chinese iconography" for proof of the primitive. Their first portrait—taken, they assure us, from a certifiably Chinese volume kept in Holland—shows a man from "the unsubdued and aboriginal savage tribes of China," with a pronounced ridge on his lower brow, shuttered eyes, and a downturned face. Such peoples, Nott and Glidden conclude, are "untameable," along the very same lines as "the aborigines of America." The second portrait, in unquiet contrast, is that of the philosopher Confucius. In this case, the authors call attention to "the massive lineaments of a great man." The authors close their discussion of this "type" by offering a trio of "authentic Chinese portraits," dating back to the ancient past, along the bottom of the same page, concluding that "the Chinese have not altered in the 4000 years for which we possess their records." Through their simply rendered physiognomy, this sequential arrangement of Chinese profiles communicated the truth of race, as Nott and Gliddon saw it, in three dimensions. And the repeated use of the present tense by the authors—when discussing woodcuts

THE PRIDE OF THE HOUSEHOLD.

LEFT An ad from Buffalo Soap Company connecting cleanliness to whiteness and the idealized white physique. Note the presence of rosy cheeks, fair hair, and a direct, level gaze. Warshaw Collection of Business Americana, Series: Soap, Archives Center, National Museum of American History, Smithsonian Institution. RIGHT Another example of idealized whiteness, set apart and privileged. Warshaw Collection of Business Americana, Series: Soap, Archives Center, National Museum of American History, Smithsonian Institution.

and paintings thousands of years old—confirmed the permanence of those prominent slopes and massive lineaments, the diversity within the unchanging Chinese "type," carried forward in time from 4,000 years earlier.[8]

A racial profile is an instrument of policy. But it can also be a representation of the head or the face. It can be a sidelong view of the sort used in Nott and Gliddon's tableau, or it can be a straightforward, framed face, like the portrait of Confucius or the array of criminal types presented in Cesare Lombroso's famous deviant typology. It can show the body in full, or it can assess the body in context. But no matter how it is presented to the public, it is a puzzle of details, each a series of imaginative impressions, arranged for a political viewing and labeled as facts. As consequence of its roots in science, and its usefulness in public policy, it has a powerfully truthful resonance.

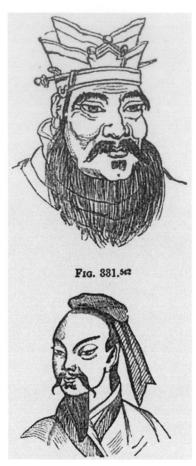

Fig. 331.⁵⁴²

"Authentic Chinese Portraits," frozen in the ancient past, from Nott and Glidden, *Types of Mankind*, 449.

In scrutinizing the body and establishing the visual details of difference, Nott and Glidden aimed to make an impact on the national scene. They aspired to document the array of supposedly inferior bodies, each used to establish the superiority of whiteness. They wanted to shape the conversation about Asian immigration, and the expanding "celestial horde" on the West Coast. Most of all, they wanted to end debate over "Negro inferiority," and thus to provide support for the proslavery argument. These goals, as Najia Aarim-Heriot suggests, were collaborative and intertwined.[9] But, after the Civil War, the firmest link between the science of racial profiles and public policy would be forged through the development of on-the-ground policing strategies for those particular bodies marked as both free and unequal, through the creation of the black codes and the legal framework that came to be called Jim Crow, or the overpolicing of Asian immigrants and Irish toughs. In a mixed postemancipation world, with regionally variable racial "problems," it fell to law enforcement—and popular surveillance—to make practical, enforceable distinctions between the good and the bad, between those capable of self-governance and those in need of more scrupulous policing. Still, despite the concern with demographic factors, the prevailing representation of "problems" and "hordes" and "beasts" almost invariably emphasized the individual type, presenting the threat—any racial threat—through the singular image of one body closely examined, and not through a motley crew or consolidated proletariat.

The ubiquitous "mugshot" was one particularly useful assessment tool. Emerging in this same moment, the famous two-part portrait of the criminal face—one shot head-on, and one shot in profile—was the creation of Allan Pinkerton, onetime Civil War spy

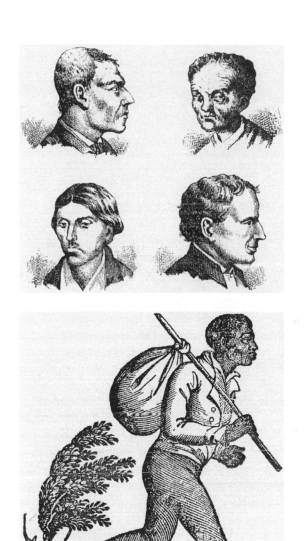

TOP One of the arrays from Cesare Lombroso's "Criminal Faces," from *L'homme Criminel* (Paris: Alcan, 1895), 43. BOTTOM A depiction of a fugitive slave, common in early-nineteenth- century advertisements for runaways. Such advertisements—precursors to mugshots, and relying on an ethnology of the slave—often referred to physical marks, bodily distinctions, skin colorations, and attitudes. This one appeared in the July 1837 issue of *The Anti-Slavery Record*. Image courtesy of the Ohio Historical Society.

Minnie Bradley, arrested in Omaha, Nebraska, 1902, for prostitution. Special Collections Division of the Nebraska State Historical Association.

and counterinsurgent, and then, in the postwar era, the enterprising head of a widely used private security and investigation firm, the Pinkerton Detective Agency, now famous for its role in Gilded Age strike-breaking. It was Pinkerton, concerned about flight before prosecution, who emphasized the taking of these images at the moment of arrest, rather than conviction. A collector and innovator, he built the first database of criminal profiles, including a vast collection of mugshots and more general photographs of the nation's most unsavory types, as he literally saw them. He then cleverly used the arrest photos as the centerpiece of more accurate and scientific "Wanted" posters. The ubiquity of these images served as a widely circulating composite impression of the generically unlawful face. Of course, this mugshot was not a theoretical imagining of the criminal type but a snapshot of an already confirmed deviant. It offered proof of the eye's predictive suspicions and stressed a powerful, damning sameness across individual facial features.[10]

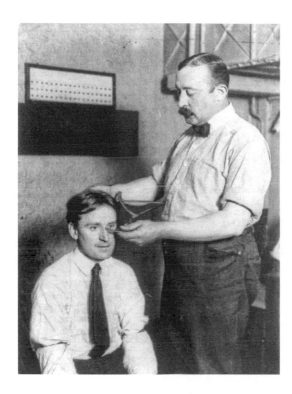

The physical science of crime. "New York City Police Dept. activities: taking Bertillon measurements—cranium," ca. 1908. Prints and Photographs Division, Library of Congress.

These assessments were greatly aided by the science of ethnology, which encouraged a similar attention to the little things, and a related understanding that the individual body could represent a type. Ethnology was a skillful mode of racial sight that anyone could master. "I passed along by one of those monster American tea stores in New York," Mark Twain wrote in 1870. "I found a Chinaman sitting before it acting in the capacity of a sign. Everybody that passed by gave him a steady stare as long as their heads would twist over their shoulders without dislocating their necks, and a large group had stopped to stare deliberately." "Men calling themselves the superior race," Twain continued, "scanned his quaint Chinese hat, with peaked roof and ball on top; and his long queue dangling down his back; his short silken blouse, curiously frogged and figured (and, like the rest of his raiment, rusty, dilapidated, and awkwardly put on); his blue cotton, tight-legged pants tied close around the ankles, and his clumsy, blunt-toed shoes with thick cork soles; and having so scanned him from head to foot, cracked some unseemly joke about his outlandish attire or his melancholy face, and passed on." Twain's brief mention of this public looking—at the very beginning of a longer essay on the Chinese—stresses the importance of the actual encounter and of the public gaze. "The Chinaman" is, in this case, a literal and figurative "sign."[11] Something to be read, in other words, full of surface facts.

In the nineteenth century, this close reading of "John Chinaman" or "the Negro" was informed by a deep fear of "the foreign" and the non-Christian, a fear that links these early practices of racial looking and public policing and the present-day concept of racial profiling. The "yellow peril" of Twain's era was a profoundly significant moral and political panic, tightly intertwined with the creation of an industrial color bar, and with the parallel steps taken to ensure and then to enact immigration restriction.[12] But it was also a part of—and enabled by—the debate over "Negro" suffrage, the confinement of Native peoples, and, more generally, the expansion of visual culture, which provided enhanced signposting for ordinary citizens enlisted in a Gilded Age campaign of racial profiling, to "see something," as Twain did, and to "say something." These were the defining political concerns of the day, and the pattern set in the debate—to stress the unique capacities of white people for self-governance, and to render the image of nonwhite peoples as impossibly alien—was deeply significant. Indeed, the public viewing of such finely drawn human signposts became, through this extended debate, a necessary precondition of the establishment of a herrenvolk republic, making it possible for people separated by thousands of miles and dozens of ancestral homelands to mark difference with greater clarity on the body politic, and to find comfort in a newly constituted, increasingly uniform whiteness.

As an example, a set of advertising cards for the Empire Wringer Company was a part of this great sifting and sorting of humankind. In the first of several images, Uncle Sam stands up straight, turning the handle on his new device, and smiling at its technological advancements. The scene is clean of detritus, and the room is well organized and nicely appointed. In the back, a banded box marked "U.S. Treasury" suggests an overflowing surplus, a nice complement to the material sophistication of the wringer. Whiteness, here, meant control of technology—and control through technology—and the consequent command of the material world, along with what was

Uncle Sam enthusing over the new technology. Warshaw Collection of Business Americana, Series: Laundry Machinery, Archives Center, National Museum of American History, Smithsonian Institution.

construed as an orderly domestic environment and rational gender relations.

These representations—inscribed onto a small surface roughly the size of a business card—are supposed to get us to linger on the little things. The Chinese, for instance, were meant to look, or be seen as, different. On another small advertising card in the same series, the typical cork shoes, the queue, and the pajamas are all present, as is the gentle sloping brow. There is a male and a female present in the frame—she is absentmindedly turning the wringer, unaware that his queue is caught up—but the common costume of the Chinese confuses male with female, a central feature of the representation of the Chinese as either nonhuman machines or effeminate beasts. Indeed, the tangle of the queue and the wringer, a metaphor for the place of the Chinese in modern America, is at the center. Note, too, the prominence of the hands, bookending the comedic center point:

The same technology proves to be too much for "John Chinaman." Warshaw Collection of Business Americana, Series: Laundry Machinery, Archives Center, National Museum of American History, Smithsonian Institution.

hers turning the wringer easily, while his are wickedly sharp and clawlike. As Twain's own cataloging suggests, the "racial sign" is a richly coded thing, with multiple matching points. The truth of John Chinaman's quality was found not just in his skin color but in the closer correlation of that dusky hue with other, equally significant markers, especially the hands and the costume, and in the fumbling misuse of the wringer.[13] And Twain, despite his role as a satirist and cultural critic, writes as a common man functioning as a working ethnologist, seeing something racial and saying something about it, as the MTA might put it.

Beyond the cruel comedy of these distinctions, John Chinaman's essential character was troublesome because it was inherently criminal, and some of that trouble was resolve by making him more visible. In one turn-of-the-century rendering of the Chinese in San Fran-

"Chinamen confined to their quarters, cooking their meals," *Harper's Weekly*, June 2, 1900. Prints and Photographs Division, Library of Congress.

cisco, echoing concern over the Opium trade, we find a group confined belowground, huddled over a long workbench, their faces lit from below by the open flames. Sequestered in this fashion because of an outbreak of bubonic plague on the surface, they are creatures of Hell—surrounded by smoke, flames, and darkness, and entirely without joy or even contentment. The literal center of the portrait is a long, elegant pair of Chinese hands—emphasizing, again, the core of the debate about the Chinese. Those troublesome hands are carefully adding a pinch of some unknown substance to an Oriental concoction that is brewing on the workbench. Despite the darkness of their subterranean prison, the Chinese here have no eyes, only closed slits, forbidding access to the soul. These "celestial" figures are impenetrable, unknowable. Even the face of the cherubic child in the foreground—wearing the classic silk "pajamas" and the cork shoes—is enigmatic and emotionless, supernaturally wise and untrustworthy. These representations are a part of a long-standing public scrutiny of the details—the cork shoes, the queue, the long fingernails, the shape of the eyes, and the slope of the forehead—that has persisted right up to the present as central features in what Robert Lee has called our tradition of the "racial grotesque." If criminality is racialized, it is also specifically attentive.

In the postemancipation context, the newly enfranchised population of former slaves also required special, discerning attention. Freedmen and freedwomen took advantage of the aftermath of the Civil War to move, sometimes locally and sometimes nationally, searching for lost loved ones or a better life. The response, south and north, was to build into the juridical landscape a series of forbidding impediments to this movement, from the Jim Crow legislation of cities, with restrictions on housing and employment and expectations of deferential performance, to the informal black codes of the agricultural countryside. Potent ideas—the discourse of the "negro rapist," or the complaints about "the lazy Negro," or assumptions of a baseline of black criminality released by emancipation—emerged rapidly, becoming a part of the political landscape, and calling attention to every black body encountered outside of the comfortable confines of the cotton field or the canebrake. Nostalgic commemorations of the Old South, in turn, celebrated the certainties of race and place before the surrender at Appomattox. In what seems like the blink of an eye, plantations became prisons, places where that same certainty could be restored. Not surprisingly, given its outsized place in American history writing, the restoration of white supremacy in the postemancipation South and the concomitant struggle over black citizenship seem like the logical antecedents to the post–civil rights era urban policing strategies. But it is important to remember that the attention to racial profiles was a nationally aimed phenomenon, as useful in California as it was in New Orleans, as applicable to "the Negro" as it was to "John Chinaman."

The late nineteenth century, then, is the moment where the great racial assumption—that every black body is a potential criminal body, for instance, or that every brown body is likely illegal—became a widespread policing strategy. It is the moment, as well, where the profile acquired its powerful double meaning, linking the presumed ethnological texture of the single body with the supposed character of an entire race, and reading the latter into the former over and over again. The assumption here is visually prescriptive, because

Here, in an ad featuring a purportedly comedic "darky" family, the mother is uncertain how to use the iron and decides to use it simply as a means of punishment. Such an image, of course, confirms the differential threat assessment of the day, in which the Chinese were a danger by virtue of their numbers and work habits and "the Negro" was a threat for very different reasons. Warshaw Collection of Business Americana, Series: Laundry Machinery, Archives Center, National Museum of American History, Smithsonian Institution.

the enforceable (and always temporary) distinction between "white" and "black" or between "Caucasian" and the slit-eyed beasts of the Opium den can only be made through line of sight, whether that means looking across the street, staring through the window of a patrol car, or simply watching a movie. To enact policy, one needed first to be able to rely on common sight, a visual technique that needed to be established scientifically, with a taxonomy of racial details carefully mapped. The establishment of that common sight is captured in Twain's simple assertion: "I found a Chinaman . . . acting in the capacity of a sign." And that same great racial assumption, of course, is what makes it possible to find reason in the firing of forty-one shots when a black body reaches for a wallet. In the moment of the look, such a thing—a quartet of officers, targeting a black outline, a presumed rapist—makes perfect, logical sense.

The contemporary practice of racial profiling relies on the same regular confusion of race and nation, and of darker color and foreignness. In the summer of 2010, for instance, the state of Arizona, where a supposed uptick in illegal immigration had enabled a fresher, firmer linkage of terrorism, nativism, and border control, debated the power of the discriminating look. Despite no measurable statewide uptick in crime, a war between the Mexican state and that country's major narco-traffickers had given the very idea of the border an even more surreal, apocalyptic texture. A Republican candidate for the House from Iowa, worrying over the spread of "illegals," urged that they be "microchipped" for easier tracking and capture, "like we do with dogs." A rancher murdered on his property in the Southwest was thought to be the victim of a smuggler. There were rumors of raids into the United States, and of "headless corpses" left in the wake of assaults against American citizens by migrant drug gangs. "Our law enforcement agencies," Governor Jan Brewer announced, apparently without evidence, "have found bodies in the desert either buried or just lying out there that have been beheaded." "Our border," she summed in another press conference, "is being erased," pointedly ignoring the massive walls and fences, guarded checkpoints, and militarized police zones that mark the difference between Sonora and Arizona. "Ay Caramba!" joked *Washington Post* columnist Dana Milbank, "those dark-skinned foreigners are now severing the heads of fair-skinned Americans? Maybe they're also scalping them or shrinking them or putting them on a spike."[14] A pseudonymous critic, commenting on conservative senatorial candidate Sharron Angle's supportive reference to the same story, joked that there were so many "headless corpses littering the Arizona desert" that one could "walk from Flagstaff all the way to the border without ever touching the ground."[15]

Concerned about declining poll numbers and confronted with what she viewed as a growing security crisis, Brewer signed new, potent legislation authorizing new local anti-immigration policing tactics. The "Support Our Law Enforcement and Safe Neighborhoods Act"—or SB 1070—gestured to the prevailing national standards of "reasonable suspicion" and "probable cause," but it also shifted the focus of state and local law enforcement onto a new class of criminal: illegal immigrants. The law empowered police to arrest and detain without a warrant if there was the mere appearance of foreignness, to confirm identity and residence, and to export all those identified as "aliens." It relied on the common sense of the officer to see difference, but it also explicitly rejected race. Defending the ideals of the bill, California's Brian Bilbray suggested that the enactment of

The metrics of racial profiling: "The Skin Tone Color Chart," from the *Minneapolis Star-Tribune*, May 6, 2010. Courtesy of the artist, Steve Sack.

SB 1070 would not have to rely on race, and that "trained professionals" could identify illegal immigrants based on their dress and demeanor.[16] Brewer, signing the bill into law on April 23, indicated that police officers could consider race, so long as it was accompanied by other, complementary factors. In its quickly revised training materials, the Arizona Peace Officer Standards and Training Board added a range of other markers, including "difficulty communicating in English," proximity to other illegal aliens, and physical location in neighborhoods known to be populated with troublesome bodies.[17]

Arizona's new policing tactics seemed, from the very first, to be an engineered farce. Comedian Jon Stewart rechristened SB 1070 the "Round Up the Browns Law." Steve Sack, the editorial cartoonist of the *Minneapolis Star Tribune*, laid out the "Traffic Stop Policing Tools" of Arizona's law enforcement community: a standard breathalyzer and an "Illegal Alienyzer," which was really a "Skin Tone Color Chart," ranging from pale white to darkest brown. Such parodies reveal how the racial profile of a single body, marked as yellow, brown, or black, can be an instrument of many different agendas. But they also highlight the challenge of making sure-footed racial identifications in an age of dramatic demographic transformations and in wake of national yearnings to be "postracial." In a landscape arranged to make diversity hypervisible, how, many wondered, could "reasonable suspicion" not emerge from racial looking?

Only a few years after the presidential election of 2008, it is striking to note how the postracial sensibility was so quickly and seam-

The police sketch of Harold and Kumar—twenty-first-century stoners as nineteenth-century stereotypes. *Harold and Kumar Go to White Castle*, dir. Danny Leiner (Endgame, 2004).

lessly related to the rapid expansion of racial profiling. "No one in real life can say definitively what an American looks like," writes movie critic Stephanie Zacharek, inspired by the phenomenon of Barack Obama, and enthusing over *Harold and Kumar Go to White Castle*, "[so] why can't it be that way in the movies too?"[18] But Zacharek gets it wrong. Harold Lee and Kumar Patel—the erstwhile protagonists of the original 2004 film—move through a country defined by acute racial surveillance, and though they ultimately manage to get their "sliders" and (in the second film) to get to Amsterdam, they are repeatedly impounded and overpoliced by the power of racial sight. Harold cannot get out of his own workplace parking lot without being persistently profiled. At a local hospital, Kumar is mistaken for his father—who is at least thirty years older, is bald, wears glasses, and is a doctor—and performs surgery on a critically injured man as a consequence. Harold jaywalks into an empty street and is immediately confronted by an angry police officer materializing out of the dark of night. Indeed, when they finally sit down at White Castle for the "perfect meal," they are fugitives. And within twelve hours (according to the "real time" chronology of the two films), both men will be imprisoned in Guantanamo. Indeed, to stress the centrality of racial profiling, as the credits roll in the first film, we see the visage of each as conceived by a police sketch artist. And Harold has been drawn as a coolie, bucktoothed, slant-eyed, and wearing a straw hat, a time-traveler from another day and age. The politics of the Harold and Kumar films might be revolutionary satire, but the humor isn't post-anything.[19]

There is, I hasten to add, no "real" thing to be seen here, no deeper racial truth to be brought into the light. With an irony that Harold Lee and Kumar Patel might have enjoyed, the overheated debate about racial profiling in the summer of 2010 also drew attention to what was imagined to be a set of racial misidentifications, those extraordinary moments where one person's perceptions suddenly clash with what the larger social frame insists, in more powerful terms, is true. Some of these misidentifications were ironic. Brian Sandoval, then a Republican candidate for governor of Nevada, pushed aside a question about the chance that his children could be pulled over by police by noting that they "don't look Hispanic." That is, they would profit from their misidentification, being truthfully (as Sandoval knew) Hispanic but visually (as Sandoval saw) Anglo. Later, when confronted with a brief media firestorm, Sandoval offered a cryptic admission of political miscalculation that left open whether he still believed that his children had a certain racially tinged look about them. "If I did say those words," he hedged, "it was wrong and I sincerely regret it."[20]

More famously, Sharron Angle, a candidate for one of Arizona's senate seats, while defending a campaign advertisement that featured scenes of illegal border-crossing and Mexican peasants, admitted to the Hispanic Student Union of Rancho High School in Las Vegas that "I don't know that all of you are Latino. Some of you look a little more Asian to me." In a video of the gathering that was replayed repeatedly and parodied relentlessly, the Rancho students begin to murmur uneasily, while Angle confesses that she has been called "the first Asian legislator" from Nevada because, presumably, like the students, she resembles a different racial type. A *Washington Post* reader, poking fun at the confluence of these stories, wondered if Sandoval's children might "look Filipino or Pakistani" to Angle.[21]

The humor of such "misidentifications" is, in the end, a consequence of their perverse connection to working systems of domination and authority. In *Harold and Kumar Escape from Guantanamo Bay*, the 2008 sequel to the original epic, the pair is wrongly confined, redacted to a military prison, and chased, after an escape, through Miami, to the deep South. In the first film, their intersections with the police were dramatic but not globally significant, but in the sequel, they are fleeing the entire national security apparatus. Though the film pretends to be a stoner comedy, it is, more deeply, a serious critique of the Bush administration's domestic antiterrorism strategies, many of which relied on racial profiling. At a flag-draped airport, Kumar protests a proposed search of his bags and threatens to call an ACLU attorney. In the very next scene, he is mistaken for a Muslim terrorist and his "smokeless bong" is thought to be bomb; Harold, in turn, is thought to be a North Korean. On the lam, they encounter a Klan drinking party in the woods but are greeted with the finger-pointing assessment of "Mexicans!" When the parents of the two boys are interrogated, their misidentification is so pronounced that the interpreter assigned to translate simply cannot understand the crystalline English spoken by Harold's father and dismisses it as "gibberish." The special agent in charge of finding the escaped proto-terrorists, when confronted with a black witness talking on his cell phone, instinctively draws his firearm and is just barely prevented from shooting him. Noticing Kumar in the next row on the airplane, a fellow traveler sees only his brown skin and dark hair, and mis-hears "bong" as "bomb," with darkly comic results. In these fictions, every consequence is a near miss, a potential disaster just barely averted.

Like the too-glib miscues of Sharron Angle and Brian Sandoval, these "comic" moments are reminiscent of the well-documented power of the state to make serious mistakes, with profound, tragic consequences, when it trusts what it sees. Fictional satire isn't necessary for this reminiscence. Real life is enough. On September 12, 2001, emboldened by their confidence in racial sight, armed police boarded an Amtrak train in Providence, Rhode Island, after rumors circulated that the planners of the previous day's catastrophic destruction were somewhere between Boston and New York. Roving "news choppers" captured the scene as FBI agents clad in bullet-proof vests entered the station with weapons drawn and emerged from the train with a brown-skinned man wearing a turban in handcuffs who was quickly tucked into the back of a police car. An angry crowd hurled insults and chased behind the car as it sped away. Confusing skin color with foreign status and a headdress with radical theology, the police had arrested Sher J. B. Singh, a South Asian Sikh and American citizen, for carrying a concealed weapon—his kirpan, a three-inch-long ceremonial knife carried by many Sikh men. His only connection to what is now universally called "9/11" were the untrustworthy visual cues of skin color, facial features, and dress.

Sikh temple members bring in a casket for the funeral and memorial service for the six victims of the mass shooting at the Sikh Temple of Wisconsin in Oak Creek, Wisconsin, Friday, August 10, 2012. The public service was held in the Oak Creek High School. Three other people were wounded in the shooting. Jeffrey Phelps/ Associated Press.

Singh's mistaken identification was not an exception or an unusual example. Indeed, in the days after the events of September 11, 2001, several other Sikh men and women were beaten, stabbed, burned, or murdered, in Seattle, San Diego, and Phoenix, all in presumed retaliation for the still unfolding national tragedy. Included among them was Balbir Singh Sodhi, gunned down because he "looked Muslim." In donning a traditional turban, Sher J. B. Singh, Balbir Singh Sodhi, and their disparate coreligionists had become racial signs.[22]

These are racial looks that can kill. And they are learned at home and abroad, in the quite comfort of an evening watching a movie, or in the hot, dusty theater of war. One thinks of former army soldier Michael Page—inked with white supremacist tattoos, behind on the rent, angry about the presence of so many brown-skinned peoples, and drummed out of military for boozing—perhaps confusing a local Sikh temple just outside of Milwaukee for an Islamic mosque. Hoping to "end apathy" (the name of his skinhead band), Page used his Springfield 9mm semiautomatic to murder seven members of the local Sikh community before killing himself. No "suicide" note was found, and Page's precise motives were unclear. Still, nearly every news story covering the tragedy mentioned that Sikhs have been routinely confused for Muslims, as if this were an explanation for the shooting. And nearly all of them mentioned Page's military service, though it wasn't clear that he had served in the Near East at all, and it was even less clear how that service—if it had happened—might have prejudiced him against Muslims. Still, the reading of the event was scripted as if Page had hoped to kill Muslims and not, more generally, "browns," and as if the shooting deaths were somehow, in the strange calculus of these things, less rational precisely because they rested on a misidentification.

Racial misidentifications are not mistakes. Page's rampage and Sodhi's murder and Singh's improvident day on the Northeast Corridor line were the predictable results of the way we see race. Police tactics like racial profiling reflect the long-standing popular faith in—and knowledge of—the supposedly stable visual signs of race, and rely on some fairly common historical stereotypes about minority populations. The popular presumption of profiling—that difference is everywhere, to be seen and cataloged—reinforces the power of those signs and stereotypes, enhancing their durability over time, and ensuring that the image moves easily from the squad car to our living room sofa to the internet and onto the silver screen. It makes the mugshot not an individual portrait but an image of a racial type, a proof of a racial pattern. Frank Silva Roque, driving around in his black pickup truck, *saw* a man—Balbir Singh Sodhi—he thought *looked* "Muslim," sized him up and shot him dead. Identifying the hapless Sher J. B. Singh as a threat to national security, everyone involved—the passengers on Amtrak, the FBI agents, the news reporters, and the angry mob—scanned his entire body, cataloged a lengthy list of surface features, and translated them into a simpler, well-established racial template: the brown-skinned Muslim terrorist. Michael Page, bitter and angry, hunted down people who looked vaguely, imprecisely, Arab.

And racial identifications are not truths: there is no right way to see race, and therefore no certainty to those bodies that have been racially profiled. Sightlines establish supposedly factual conventions—what is "right" and what is a "mistake"—and those conventions become, in racial profiling, operationalized. When a Sikh is seen as a Muslim, the supposed mistake is acknowledged, but the mechanism that allowed it to happen—the visual habit of racial recognition—remains in working order. Reforms always address diversity training and the education of the public, but that merely fine-tunes the system of racial sight, keeping it in working order. There is, then, always the certainty of cataclysmic, unlucky misidentifications, some of which result in death, or incarceration, some of which provoke laughter, and the rest of which are just accepted as the unremarkable truth.

CHAPTER TWO

Silhouettes

O n the eve of the Great Depression, a trio of European eugenicists, eager to more accurately identify race and to provide the common public with easy-to-use tools, suggested that the practice of silhouetting offered some startling new data points. Working in the Anthropometric Department of the Galton Laboratory, a genetics research facility in London, they devised an "apparatus" to "draw life sized silhouettes." Writing with urgency, they stressed that their findings were revelatory, that "[t]here are several points on the silhouette not available on the skull, or not corresponding to the definite points on the skull."[1] After giving new scientific names to each point, the authors proposed that the simple silhouette was a more reliable way to see race.

To represent whiteness, they used their apparatus to capture the profiles of fifty current English undergraduates at the laboratory and then created a composite. To represent blackness, they created a similar composite image from a series of ethnological photos taken of West African prisoners of war—French colonials captured by the Germans, and photographed randomly, regardless of "tribal differences"—and then compared them to a "living subject." Concluding that they had captured in monochrome "a truly typical West African Negro," they noted the myriad points of divergence on the silhouette from the standard, Caucasian type, calling attention to particularities on the chin, the neck, the forehead, and the nose. Typical of the racial science of the day, these men saw nothing wrong—morally or scientifically—with their "comparison" of POWs culled from across a wide swath of nations and tribal territories on the African continent with a parochial group of English schoolboys. They were driven, in the end, by the hope that silhouetting might prove to be a more reliable scientific practice in the field, where amateurs, unfamiliar with the guild secrets and specialized tools of skull measurements, might

The composite silhouette based on a survey of fifty British students (left) and the supposed opposite—a composite silhouette based on an ethnographic survey of one hundred imprisoned West Africans. From *Biometrika* 20B, no. 3/4 (December 1928).

be prone to make mistakes.[2] They thought that their new equipment, and the useful way of seeing it enabled, could be popularly deployed.

A silhouette is a profile set in contrast, a dark outline against a light backdrop. As a keepsake work of portraiture, the art form dates back to the middle of the eighteenth century, and to the first great burst of consumer culture, when such things became fashionable. It is thought to be so easy to capture the truth of the profile in silhouette that children often make them. More recent innovations in the genre—for instance, the work of Kara Walker—have tried to upturn this notion of simplicity, but still, the general and historic point of the silhouette, literally, was to focus on the trace outline of the face or the body, and to force the eye to attend to the edge. And through that concentrated focus to reveal, with an authority derived from our confidence in sight, the objectively revealed inner character of the subject, stripped of emotion and adornment. This thing is, then, a set of fixed bumps and slopes, stripped of tone and color, scale and physical context, revealing only the most essential, elemen-

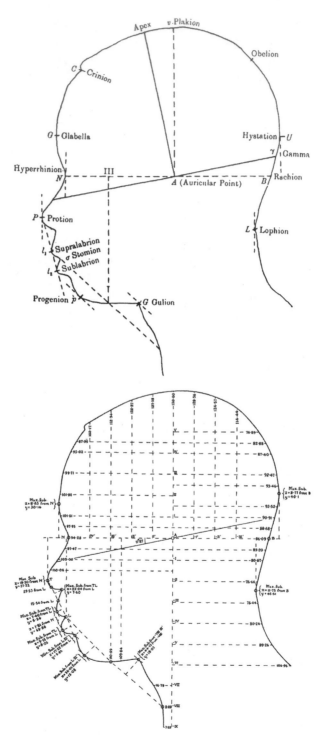

The metrics of the silhouette, revealed. From *Biometrika* 20B, no. 3/4 (December 1928).

tal details. And so, when and where complex physical objects are scrutinized, racial sight turns to the silhouette to reveal the desired truth to help establish clear identifications where confusion would otherwise reign. Just as that trio of craniometricians had desired, the silhouette is understood to be a reliable, honest piece of evidence, easily read and understood. In a set of bumps and ridges, peaks and swells, it reveals the outline of whiteness, or blackness, or brownness, and of race more generally.

In contemporary popular culture, the silhouette is a sort of mathematical proof for what the eye suspects. "I am black and white, biracial," Jenna says, "but I only claim the white side." Tyra Banks, the African American model-cum-talk-show-host, wearing a long, flowing, blond wig, asks, "You only claim the white side?" The audience at this 2008 taping of *The Tyra Banks Show*, is, like the host, incredulous. A disbelieving, low murmur gets louder and louder until the host asks someone nearby for an explanation of the dissent. "She looks black," one woman in the audience offers straightforwardly, as if the obviousness of this point were hardly worth the effort of speaking the words aloud. Jenna is an ordinary person, brought to the show not because of her fame but because she fit the theme. Her life as a biracial woman, Tyra and her supportive audience soon learn, is complicated by her disgust with black popular culture, which she derides as "low" and vulgar, and by her physical presentation, which seems, to the studio crowd, so obviously black. She likes the rodeo. She carries a rebel flag. She has posed in Klan garb. Each admission, each declaration of love for whiteness, provokes a sharper, more anguished response from the audience. "What color do you see when you look in the mirror," Tyra wonders, pressing the therapeutic point, trying to get to the root of what she has defined as self-hate. "I don't see a color," Jenna responds. "No, Jenna," Tyra corrects, admonishing her, "you aren't colorblind." "I would love to see white," Jenna offers. "But what color do you see?" Tyra asks, pressing relentlessly. With a voice that gets softer over three syllables, Jenna confesses, "I see black."

"Most people," Tyra offered at the very start of the show, "think that they can tell what race somebody is just by looking at them." "They look them head up and head down," the host offered, in a less polished, informal accent, giving voice to her imagined typical person. "I know she black, I know she white, I know she Asian." Banks's fame was a by-product of a particular historical confluence; famous,

Jenna, a guest on Tyra Banks's talk show.

beloved, and beautiful, her adoration of blackness, her ubiquity, and her "street smart" public voice reflect the extraordinary, durable political achievements of the civil rights movement and Black Power, the deeper cultural shifts that have emerged in the wake of the seeming end of empire and global white supremacy, the rise of a liberal consensus against racism, and even the fundamental impacts of the telecommunications revolution and the democratization of popular culture. Her show often dwells on race and race relations, especially when and where those subjects touch on the lives of women, and it often cuts against convention. This particular episode of *The Tyra Banks Show*, she announces, will feature women who try to defy the racial look.

There was nothing unusual in this focus. "Biracial" women have been a constant topic of interest for Banks. Her rhetorical engagement with Jenna, and her subsequent unveiling of the "truth" of racial identity, repeated itself on later episodes of her talk show, and on *America's Next Top Model*, which she also hosted. She also routinely "experimented" with racial silhouettes, in an effort to capitalize on the recent craze for subconscious, unprocessed visual interpretation—the sort of impulsive insight celebrated in Malcolm Gladwell's popular book *Blink* (2005)—or to steal from the vogue in DNA testing and racial ancestry, as dramatized in Henry Louis Gates Jr.'s *Faces of America*. This specific episode, though, also depended on a collective memory about race—on the idea that "everyone" knows where to look and what to see—and encouraged the supposedly careful scrutiny of a person's physical appearance for indicators that defined one as "black" and not "white." A thousand common articles of faith are exposed in the audience's scandalized reaction to Jenna's effort at self-definition. "I see black," said Jenna. And by saying it just like that, a whole history is revealed. Tyra Banks, despite the social forces that made her incorporation as a celebrity possible, and despite the transformation of the world around her, sees black too.

The show drifts, slowly and inexorably, testing audience's racial sight. Before the start of the program, the studio audience had been instructed by Banks to look over this quartet and to assess their racial background. Most, Tyra insists, had guessed that Jenna was black, a fact we learn just as the camera pauses over Jenna's face. And we—the television viewer—are thus asked in that instant to grade the studio audience's assessment. Is it accurate? Is she black? Can we trust what we see? The subsequent intervention with Jenna, focused largely on correcting her desire to see white when she looks in the mirror, confirms that what you see is what you get. Every participant in the chain of assessment—the fellow panelists, the audience, the host, the producers, and, one supposes, the viewers—is supposed to see the same thing: a black woman in racial denial.

The rest of the episode features other women who "hate" one part of themselves, who are regularly confused for another "nationality," or who look, in shape or in outline, like they belong to another race. But Jenna's opening affiliation with whiteness is marked as uniquely strange or odd. When Giselle, "black and Puerto Rican," says that she considers herself "black," the audience is still surprised—"Wow," Tyra says, laughingly. "OK, I don't necessarily think the audience sees that"—but the overall reaction is more positive, less critical, in part because her choice seems, on the surface, less racist. Giselle has no thirst for white company, no rebel flag. She just thinks that Puerto Ricans dress "trashy." Likewise, if the bulk of the studio gaggle sees Candice, featured on a later segment, as a mixture of "Hispanic" and "black," she describes herself as "100% African American." After complaining that too many people think she is some exotic type based on her hair, her face, and her skin color, Candice suggests that she has had a tough life, caught up in other people's fantasies of the tropics. Tyra, no stranger to such fantasies, seems unimpressed. And one audience member stands up to suggest that a woman who, like herself, is "slave black"—too dark, with "bad" skin and "bad" hair, and this with the worst stereotypes attached to her body—walks a far tougher road than Candice. But here, too, a debate over the algebra of oppression ends in an embrace, staged by Tyra as an effort to recognize the solidarities of blackness. At the conclusion of the show, only Jenna's racial provocations are deemed pathological. All the other "sisters" just need to reconnect to the cohesive category "of color."

In the final and most unusual "experimental" segment of the show, two women stand behind a white screen with just their silhouettes available for a public viewing. Here is an opportunity, we are told, for more guesswork. When the women step out from behind the screen and the host asks coyly, "Confused, audience?," we are meant to look at their bodies in wonderment, searching for some correspondence between the silhouette, and what it was supposed to reveal, and what stands in front of us. After Taralynn, the first of the silhouettes, confesses that she is "100% Caucasian," she is greeted with a surprised chorus of "Wow!" The camera cuts to a single woman in the crowd, her brow furrowed in bemusement. A cheerful, brightly dressed woman takes the microphone from Tyra and admits that she had marked Taralynn's silhouette as "black" and not "white." "Even standing in front of us," Tyra follows, eyeing the woman up and down, "I see a black woman." "Just a European mixture," Taralynn responds, clearly displeased at this supposedly deep misreading. When, a few seconds later, Tyra mistakenly refers to Taralynn as a "contestant," we are reminded about the stakes of this "game," and about the nature of the prize: everyone wins when the power of the eye to see race—and the certainty of race itself—is confirmed. The silhouette, in the end, is invoked as the final proof of our capacity to see racial difference. For Tyra, and for the audience, it confirms the deeper truth. Taralynn's refusal to accept that truth, documented in outline on a silk screen, lets the host resume her therapeutic assault.

The racial politics of silhouettes appear surprisingly—evenly strangely—static. Emphasizing the relationship between racial descents and physical outlines, they are dominant, controlling, and generally white supremacist. As a racial proof, silhouettes have no transgressive tendencies, but they are not devoid, as some might have it, of racial content. Art critics, for example, often take note of the use of black paper and find deeper meaning, or irony, in the production of white profiles in dark tones. Through the creation of "black" silhouettes, the argument goes, white subjects undergo a racial reversal, expressing both desire for and fear of difference. This is the art critic's approach—to preserve the form as a vessel for color. In this way of thinking, to think of silhouetting as a visual practice, as a way of manufacturing racial certainty on the page, would be a corruption.

Literary historian Samuel Otter, likewise, contrasts the silhouettes produced for Charles Willson Peale's early-nineteenth-century museum by the "physiognotrace"—a mechanical tracing device—with the racial caricatures of contemporary newspapers. The former, Otter suggests, emphasizes a common set of themes or a shared condition, while the latter seems more directly aimed at the satirical reinforcement of racial hierarchy. Looking closely at two silhouettes of African Americans, Otter notes a certain "fullness of lip" (among other features) in both, but he stresses the "void" in the middle of the representation. "Individual character," he writes, "is located on the edge, in slight inflections," while the great bulk of the portrait is "without color of feature." For Otter, the political freight of the silhouette is in the center of the image. But the silhouette isn't so much a contrasting worldview, emphasizing that "void," as it is a different sightline, expanding the significance of those "slight inflections" at the edge of the outline, and offering those up as better, cheaper, easier-to-locate racial indicators.[3] This is how Tyra Banks, like those Galton scientists, imagines it. Her use of the silhouette isn't a return to a race-free medium, so that her audience can avoid the distractions of tone and twirl, but a switch to a different—and related—mode of sight.

Banks, of course, imagines herself as the bringer of truth, and not as someone actively engaged in reproducing old-fashioned racial sight. Even where the outlines of silhouettes are unconventional, though, their political transgressions rely on (and often satirize) the unchanging power of the outline to convey racial truth. Banks's reproduction of Taralynn's shadow against a white silk screen is meant to be disruptive, even therapeutic. Philippe Derome's *Black Head Paris* (1971), for instance, couples a primitive, colonial profile with modernist geometrical shapes, emphasizing a race out of place and out of time, not so much adrift as resettled and comfortable in cosmopolitan Paris. Such an image doesn't fog up the racial sightline, even if it does challenge conventions about time, space, and race. To understand the sightline, then, is not to concentrate on the specific details of the outlines—a full lip, a wide nose, or whatever—but to propose, more basically, that it is that edge that is doing the work.

Kara Walker's life-sized silhouettes have been routinely described as controversial, unconventional, and provocative, generally because

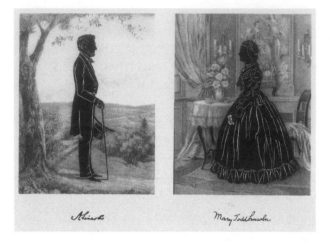

Detail from Morris
& Bendien, Inc.,
silhouette portrait of
Abraham and Mary
Todd Lincoln, c. 1900–
1925. The Alfred Whital
Stern Collection of
Lincolniana, Library of
Congress, Rare Book
and Special Collections
Division.

of their relative candor about the relationship of sex and rape to racial domination and resistance, but also because she warps, or perverts, the supposed accuracy of the form. "Walker," critic Jerry Saltz wrote in 1998, "gets the wimpy, unassuming, long dead medium of cut-paper silhouette to sing the hymn of the divided self and take on vast paranoiac histories."[4] In Walker's hands, the gentlemanly, Bible-thumping South is reimagined as a ghastly playground filled with white serial rapists and pedophiles, and the meek Negress becomes suicidal, vengeful, or dangerous. Slaves and masters, rather than mutually contented and peaceably engaged, carve each other up, or pleasure each other cruelly, demonically. Instead of moonlight and magnolias, the roiling landscape of Dixie is hellish, littered with body parts and blood, penetrating and painful, and devoid of innocence. The confused reaction to such necessary work, art historian Gwendolyn DuBois Shaw concludes, illuminates the long troubled relationship between white patrons, the museum establishment, and avant-garde African American artists.[5]

Walker's silhouettes trouble and confirm the form's role as a racial sightline. *After the Deluge*, her response to the disaster of Hurricane Katrina, was a 2006 mixed media exhibit at the Metropolitan Museum of Art in New York City. "I was tired of seeing news images of (Black) people suffering," Walker remembered, "presented as though it were a fresh, new thrilling subject." Watching the melodrama unfold, she was drawn not merely to study the abnegation of official responsibilities once the levees broke, but also to dispute the media's

Kara Walker's *Deadbrook After the Battle of Ezra's Church* (2005), which plays with the lithography of *Harper's Pictorial History of the Civil War*. Image courtesy of Sikkema Jenkins & Co., New York.

corresponding sanctimony. She wanted, as she put it, "to understand the subconscious narratives at work when we talk about such an event."[6] Combing through the Met's collections, and revisiting her own materials, Walker curated a vast, ambitious project, drawing together major works across genres and formats and assembling them in small pairings or clusters.

In *Deadbrook After the Battle of Ezra's Church*, a mix of old and new typical of the *After the Deluge* exhibit, Walker reversed the story of Katrina as popularly told, with its emphasis on black suffering. The taunting silhouette of black woman, her hair twisted into tendrils, looms over a Confederate soldier, frozen in death or near-death, and lying on his back in a shallow riverbed. He holds his cutlass aloft, thin and white, at the ready. Crouched on top of another nearby white soldier—this one surely dead—she has her hands extended, as if ready to strike the Confederate. Seeing his weakness, and sensing her opportunity, she is, perhaps, ready to bring him to a quick, undignified end. Or maybe she is just there to watch him die. In any case, she appears to be defecating on the dead solider who serves as her perch, while her opposite's sword appears as a phallus, erect and dangerous. The mix of genre—Walker's unusual stereotypically shaped silhouette pressed onto a nineteenth-century lithograph, with an equally clichéd vision of white manliness lost in battle—is a part of Walker's technique in the exhibit, suggesting visual constancy across two centuries even in the midst of political change, and lingering resentment and anger.

Walker's provocation relies on the silhouette's explicit clarification of racial difference. Indeed, one direct purpose of the exhibition (beyond its angry, didactic function in the wake of a national tragedy) was to call attention to the function of the racial silhouette in American visual culture. The reviewer for the New York Times, Roberta Smith, opined that Walker wanted to literally turn every figure black, and so her use of more conventional silhouettes by well-known European and American artists was a racial recontextualization, through which figures once thought to be white were now assumed to be black.[7] But this was a misreading. Walker's use of silhouettes—like her use of more colorful stereotype in lithography and collage—relies on the clarity of racial content within the format for its provocative punch. The anonymously produced nineteenth-century image Two Men, One Cutting a Silhouette features a wall of silhouettes in the background, and two men, marked as white, in the foreground. The man on the left is not merely "cutting" a silhouette; he is engaged, Walker wants us to know, in the act of creating a racial representation, one easily seen and made. To make this point plain, Walker assembled the edited volume that followed the exhibit so that another nineteenth-century construction—portraits of the self-emancipated former slaves who dramatically overthrew their captors aboard the Amistad in 1839—was facing Two Men, One Cutting a Silhouette. With the exception of their leader, Cinqué, those "Amistad captives," as they were known, were drawn only in profile and in silhouette, reduced to a racial type, their individual details lost to history.[8] "One theme of my artwork," Walker noted, "is the idea that the Black subject in the present tense is a container for specific pathologies from the past, and is continually growing and feeding off those maladies."[9] One cannot critique this phenomenon, as Walker does, without the use of a racial form that is quickly recognizable.

Walker first became interested in silhouettes after growing disenchanted with formal techniques, which she imagined were in-

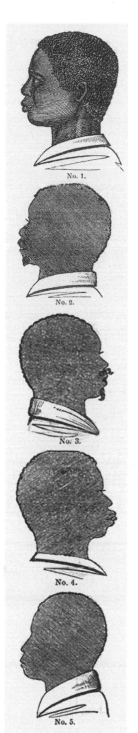

No. 1, No. 2, No. 3, No.4, and No.5. From John Walker Barber, *A History of the Amistad Captives: Being a Circumstantial Account of the Capture of the Spanish Schooner Amistad, by the Africans on Board; Their Voyage, and Capture near Long Island, New York; with Biographical Sketches of Each of the Surviving Africans Also, an Account of the Trials Had on Their Case, Before the District and Circuit Courts of the United States, for the District of Connecticut.* (New Haven, Conn.: E. L. & J. W. Barber, 1840), 9–10.

vested with "patriarchal authority." Trolling through popular works of early-American portraiture, she found that silhouettes were "devoid of any nuance or color," expressing a "desire for clarity" without "texture or subtlety."[10] "I was really searching for a format to sort of encapsulate, to simplify complicated things," she said in a 1998 interview. The silhouette, she continued, "spoke to me in the same way that the minstrel show does."[11] That is, it carried within itself the same racial sensibilities. Before Walker, Jerry Saltz wrote, the silhouette was "a genre of portraiture, caricature, idyllic landscape and decorative craft. In her hands, it becomes a deadly weapon and she an avenging angel. Her use of it as a material metaphor for stereotype is inventive and devastating."[12] Art critics have an interest in making such claims. But it is precisely the simplicity and commonality of the form—its capacity to be produced idly, and accurately, we assume, by anyone with scissors, black paper, and a discerning eye—that makes it possible for Walker to pervert the saccharine fantasy of "the South." And it is just as certainly true that the continuity of the form over time—its function as a well-established racial sightline, educating the eye, fostering that same discernment—is something that she plays with mercilessly in her *ouvre*.

The common racial silhouette—a simple and disposable thing, de-spite its revision by Kara Walker—provides reinforcement for other sightlines even as it gives us a confident racial identification. Apple's early advertisements for the iPod in the mid-2000s were thought to be daring precisely because they featured a variety of body types dancing alone and in silhouette. Set to popular music with a heavy base line, the official storyline was that anyone anywhere could lis-ten to all of their music and dance happily. But to make this point about the widespread usefulness of the iPod, the silhouettes them-selves—all young, all vibrantly in motion—placed a great stress on racial difference, emphasizing all of the finer particulars, and espe-cially hair and dress, so that viewers could understand, implicitly, that these recklessly twirling figures weren't listening to the same music, or even dancing in the same space. We see dreadlocks and long straight hair and "natural" short hair and muscle-bound frames and thin bodies, and we attend, as the sightline requires, to these things along the outer edge as racial markers. We see age, too, along with the outlines of cool. We don't see a jumble of bodies in the throws of a multiracial party but a segregated set of private spaces, full of young people passionately captured in the midst of a solipsis-tic silent rave (plate 2).

The bodies in these advertisements, though, do more than merely corroborate the biometrics of shadows and outlines. They remind us, as well, that objects have politics. And in this case, the object here—the iPod, inevitably rendered bright white in contrast to the dark sil-houette—is rendered "cool" or "hip" largely because it is attached in a series of repeating frames to what we are meant to see as the spectacular black body, hat pulled low and baggy shirt drawn over a powerful frame, Afro in place or locked hair twirling. If the gen-eral function of this array of silhouettes is to dramatize the youth-ful, hip pleasure of music and dance, and to remind us that many people from all walks of life like to dance, the specific purpose of the black body—easily seen with a discriminating gaze—is to confuse the sense of what, exactly, is being sold or advertised, and what, pre-cisely, we are meant to desire. Why, one wonders, is the black body, identified by its silhouette, such an alluring feature of Apple's adver-tising strategy?

It is tempting to celebrate these images as ironic, or to believe that their self-mocking use of race disrupts hierarchy or challenges racism, an approach that forces us to focus on the relations of discrete groups, rather than the constitution of categories through sight. I can't agree with that reading. Yes, Kara Walker is a provocateur, troubling the values attached to race, messing around with the storylines attached to black and white bodies. But her provocations—as clever and as shocking as they are—are still utterly dependent on our capacity to recognize a black nose, or a white mouth, at first glance, without thinking too much about what it means that such a form, or such a detail, is so singularly identifiable. The Apple advertisement, less transgressive by design, attaches "cool" to blackness and asks us to want the result, but it also requires that both things be seen clearly and easily. Even if its tongue-in-cheek message is, "Don't we all love music?," it wants us to parse the "we" by race. In the logic of this book, irony only reifies racial stereotypes, broadcasting them, neutralizing only their most obviously offensive "racial content," and leaving their deeper role in promoting racial sight unchallenged. A silhouette is a silhouette is a silhouette, and it doesn't matter that one makes us laugh and one makes us cry. If it confirms the outlines of the racial body, then it works within—and not against—a sightline.

Sightlines don't determine everything, though. When and where we trouble them, or "disrupt" or "challenge" them, we do so not by spotlighting race but by cluttering the viewing lane, loading it up with mismatched materials and dissonant details that don't make sense, that distract the eye from the spectacular object at the sightline's terminus. And in its awful, dangerous simplicity, the grayscale silhouette doesn't leave much room for such distractions.

CHAPTER THREE

Bought and Sold

O n his tour of the slave states, James Silk Buckingham went
to New Orleans and stopped in the Rotunda of the St. Louis
Hotel to watch a slave auction. For the sojourning British abo-
litionist and temperance advocate, the dramatic bidding for human
flesh at the rotunda was a version of something he'd seen across the
South and the slaveholding Americas. Indeed, his description of the
auction of Africans was meant to outrage the reader. "There were a
half a dozen auctioneers, he wrote, "each endeavoring to drown out
every voice but his own, and all straining their lungs, and distorting
their countenances in a hideous manner." Invoking the "unhappy
negro family" at the center of this bazaar, Buckingham noted that
"their good qualities were enumerated in English and in French, and
their persons were carefully examined by intending purchasers."[1]
Positioned on top of wooden boxes so that the audience might get a
better look, the slaves were the centerpiece of this market exchange.
If Harriet Jacobs, while enslaved, "never dreamed she was a piece
of merchandise," the same could not be said at the St. Louis Hotel's
Rotunda, where the eager consumer dreamed the opposite. To see
blackness in the age of slaveholding was to see a commodity, to see
no difference between "estates, pictures, and slaves." But it was also,
as Buckingham noted, to see the slave, a subject and an object, ele-
vated above the ordinary goods offered up by the caterwauling auc-
tioneer.[2]

This link between the black body and commerce endures. Long
after slavery, it is common to see the black body not merely as evidence of humanity but also as an object, and as a metaphor for other
objects, so that the desirable and raced body is densely related to
the symbolic surround of American consumer culture. To visualize
blackness, then, is to strangely conflate blackness and a product, a
bauble, or an object that we desperately desire. Indeed, inasmuch

The frontispiece to the first volume of Buckingham's travelogue, titled "Sale of Estates, Pictures, and Slaves in the Rotunda." From James Silk Buckingham, *The Slave States of America* (London: Fisher, Son, & Co., 1842).

as the postemancipation desire for the black body connoted—and continues to connote—a desire for the presumably stable relations of slavery, the love of blackness as a medium for advertisement also breathes life, as we understand it, into the otherwise static and disembodied world of things. To see the black body as a commodity, then, is to see race in a very particular way, to make use of a very unusual, very long lived sightline.

Consumer capitalism has, today, transformed every distinctive type of body into an object for sale, or a signpost for a product, so within the world of advertisements and sloganeering, there are other complementary sightlines. There is that which joins the representations of the skin and the hair and the face of white women (or all women) to the aesthetics of fashion or beauty. And there is the association of white masculinity (or masculinity generally) to the rugged outdoors, emergent in the images of Marlboro Men, the Brawny Towel Man, and Paul Bunyan. There are pale bodies and dark bodies, male bodies and female bodies, perfect bodies and bodies in need of improvement; all are for sale, at least metaphorically. As

marketing strategies become increasingly aimed at microcommuni-
ties, and as the consumer base of the nation becomes slightly more
diverse and complex, an ever-wider range of body types can be deployed in the service of profit. The state and society make an effort,
then, to alert the viewer to their presence, to call attention to their
race, their gender, their age, and to all of the identifying inflections
on their surfaces.

But the black body—and especially the black male body—is different. Those other mythic representations emphasize, first and foremost, the individuality of the consumer. A real man wants to smoke
Marlboros. A real woman hopes for flawless skin. To create "want"
and "need," such representations are meant to spark recognition of
sameness, or at least similarity, in the mind of the viewer. They create a web of positive associations, and attempt to compel a specific
action—a purchase or investment of some kind—as a consequence.
The black body, in contrast, has an opposite affect. It generates distance and difference and want, all at once. Other bodies "of color"—
inscribed with a past as coolies and braceros—do similar work in
modern visual culture, though none have the same ubiquity, or the
exact same historic density and weight. And the white body, to be
glib, does not have this function. It may have a history—as Marx
would say—of being figured as labor, but only black bodies know the
auction block as a literal marketing of their physicality. For white
bodies, the history of their pricing is a more ephemeral and euphe-
mistic, enclosed in the rich language of dowries and inheritances;
only the black body was parsed for literal marketing, making its
present circulation more representative, more referential of what
was once a ghastly trade in real men and women. To understand the
commodification of the black body, we need to attend to a sightline
rooted in the history of the chattel slave market, and depend on a
practice of seeing the black body as an object for sale, greased up to
show physical detail, and mounted for better viewing. The history of
this black body, transformed from flesh to capital, makes the contemporary visual link between darker skin tones and consumer culture particularly confounding, perverse, and important.

This link is significant, in part, because it was reproduced everywhere, and stands as a common feature of American—if not global—
culture for the past two hundred years. In 1885, roughly forty years
after Buckingham's survey of the New Orleans slave market, Wil-

GROWN WITH
WILLIAMS, CLARK & CO'S
High Grade Bone Fertilizers.

The black body and the cotton boll. Warshaw Collection of Business Americana, Series: Fertilizer, Archives Center, National Museum of American History, Smithsonian Institution.

liams, Clark & Company produced a small, disposable advertising card. The company manufactured "high grade bone fertilizer," a valuable additive to the soil for planters and farmers. Not unusually, then, it chose to feature a lush specimen plant—in this case, a tall cotton plant—on the front of its card, an inevitable consequence, the reader was meant to understand, of the proper application of the product. The branches of the plant are heavy with cotton, bursting from the bolls and ready for picking. In the background, other plants can be seen, their branches turned downward, straining with the weight of that profitable, soft fiber. And in the foreground, a bin, already overflowing, stands ready to be removed to the market. At the very top of the central plant is a head, crowned with cotton, the smiling visage of "the Negro," reduced once again, twenty-five years after the end of the Civil War, to the status of commodity.

Here, embedded in the image of a cotton plant topped off with the head of "the Negro," is the image of the black body as a thing, and a referent for other things, a doubled quality that centers it at the symbolic surround of consumer culture. The central feature of this way of seeing blackness is the confusion of body with the product or products for sale, the utter lack of daylight between that jaunty, smiling black face and the stalk of cotton growing skyward. Such confusion allows the viewer to see, paraphrasing historian M. M. Manring, the slaves on the box as a happy euphemism for the "slaves in a box."[3] Beyond its metaphorical qualities, such a sightline also makes it possible to recall in half-consciously nostalgic tones the older image of the black body as desirable merchandise.

An icon that needed no explanation, "the Negro" was an all-purpose referent for conspicuous consumption, used to sell just about everything. Nineteenth-century advertisements for foodstuffs, soap, and just about everything relied on the comical black figure, narrowly deploying "the Negro" as humorous proof of the audience's whiteness. In older form, smiling and welcoming, versions of Uncle Tom and Mammy served as mascots of sorts for the full, rich table, appearing on coffee cans, bags and boxes of rice, and pitchers of syrup. (In England and in France and much of the white world, there were Golliwoggs, a somewhat parallel figure.) Iconic representations like these were deeply etched into the cultural landscape for most of the nineteenth and twentieth centuries, and it is tempting to see their transformation into black collectibles as proof that the world has changed, but the "surrogacy" they enacted—standing in for black folks who were either a figment of the historical imagination or far, far away—has been surprisingly consistent.[4] By the start of the twenty-first century, the black body was still attached to a far wider spectrum of products, in campaigns for consumer dollars that relied on humor, magic, and chic, along with everything in between. Long after the civil rights movement, the black body is a soothingly familiar feature of the consumer landscape, easy, it seems, to read, draw, and copy, connoting desire for purchase, status advancement, and personal transformation. Even more broadly, the black body has long been featured in worldwide art, in political discourse, and in literature, and stands as perhaps the single most important nationally and globally recognized referent.

The abolition of slavery and the emancipation of captive Africans

LEFT A black man with a corncob body. Warshaw Collection of Business Americana, Series: Fertilizer, Archives Center, National Museum of American History, Smithsonian Institution. RIGHT A black man with a cotton ball head. Warshaw Collection of Business Americana, Series: Fertilizer, Archives Center, National Museum of American History, Smithsonian Institution.

did not, of course, end the confusion of blackness and the desirable commodity. The advertisement by Williams, Clark & Company rested on the serious presumption that cotton was a product best picked by its logical and customary attendants. Parallel advertisements made the same presumption and included the same odd marriage of blackness and the natural world. But there was more going on here than merely a romantic commemoration of a time when African Americans understood and accepted "their place." Another series, produced by a rival fertilizer company, replaced the black body with a corncob, leaving the head free to blow a trumpet. A field of corn is the background, and a trio of raccoons dances below. "There's a new coon in town," reads the banner draped across the length of the trumpet. Still another promotional card, labeled "A Cotton Ball," features a small, ambiguously gendered black body, dancing, wearing a brightly colored yellow dress, with an outsized cotton ball on its head. The utter collapse of the gap between the black body and the cotton plant, or the ear of corn, is a reflection of *both* the lingering status of African Americans as past commodities themselves, once traded in an open market like animals, and the contemporary urge to make sense of a world and a nation in transition.

"Bro-ing" is a recently coined name for this old corporate practice of deliberately mistaking black bodies for the products they endorse. The term—derisively applied by Naomi Klein, a critic of American consumer culture, to Nike's deployment of Michael Jordan—suggests that the physical proximity of the black body to a product is a reflection of a kindred metaphorical parallelism, in which the repeated association of black bodies with plain, presumably nonracial products may well suggest marketing savvy, but it also surfaces the history of the black body as commodity, as product, as owned slave and leased convict. Jordan, the logic goes, was a talented athlete, but he was available for purchase, literally, by fans in the seats, and, metaphorically, through his endorsement of everything from Nike shoes to Hanes underwear. Bro-ing calls our attention to the unique ease with which the bodies marked as black—more than those marked as yellow or brown or red—are affiliated with all manner of things domestic and material, an affiliation that indicates their lingering and special closeness, in the American imagination, to the historic experience of slave purchase and ownership. Our lusty hunt for products that have been "bro-ed" is, in part, a memory project, an effort to obliquely reconstruct, through the shadows and the distance, an act that approximates the survey of the glistening goods of the chattel market, in which some measure of psychological benefit is derived from the surplus value of black bodies. Through the iconography of consumer culture, and through the sightline that merges blackness with an object of desire, one surveys and measures the black body, and expresses the wish to own it through the purchase of an affiliated product.

A black head on a cotton plant sways, smiling happily. A young, dark-skinned man stands on a basketball court, holding a cold soft drink, a joyful smile hinting at his impending refreshment. A round-faced, caramel-colored woman, her hair bound up in a handkerchief, smiles from the label on a syrup bottle. We often see black bodies in direct association to commerce. That is, we see the black body in obvious relation, in tandem, for instance, with a product, an object, a service, or a transaction. The white body—and the male, hetero-sexed body more specifically—can be imagined alone, without clear referent, and unbound by affiliation. In these instances, blackness is always drawing our attention, obviously or obliquely, to something else. As such, it is both the conduit to commodification, and also a commodity in and of itself. But, again, the commodity fetish for blackness can also bridge the gap between the body and the product, so that it can be literally impossible to tell the difference between the medium and the mediated.

Often, the commodity in question is not merely the product itself, but the service it provides, happily, and without complaint. In the early-twentieth-century advertisements featuring the Gold Dust twins, the pitch-black pair, clad only in skirts labeled "Gold Dust," scrub their way through a dirty house, leaving it perfect. "The Boys Who Took the Work Out of Housework," the narrative proclaims at the end, offering up Gold Dust washing powder as the literal equiva-lent of two small "black" children. The twins are so dark-skinned that their features and expressions cannot be easily seen. And they are forever estranged from the nation. Their only clothing is a brand label. In another image, the company celebrated former president Teddy Roosevelt's safari in Africa by suggesting that the twins had come to make up the difference. Balancing boxes of Gold Dust pow-der on their heads, they are also each carrying a hunting rifle and wearing a tiger pelt. They do not merely bring the soap—they *are* Gold Dust powder. And the work they/it does in your home is per-manently joined to empire, to slavery, and to white supremacy. Their twinning allows them to be seen as one thing copied once over, as a single body providing twice the service, so that the master of the house can enjoy the fuller labors of his or her metaphorical slave.

In more recent times, the link between the historic commodifi-cation of chattel and the contemporary conflation of blackness and commodities is often found in critiques of professional sport, where African Americans are imaged as "Forty Million Dollar Slaves." For columnist William Rhoden, the expanding reputation of black ath-letes over the past 150 years has been increasingly defined by the needs of white spectators and consumers. Along the way, black ath-letes have lost their sense of "mission," their moral compass alerting them to the need to represent the race well.[5] Rhoden's portrait of the perils attending black athleticism, though discomforting, is easy to

dishes, crockery, glassware, pots and pans.

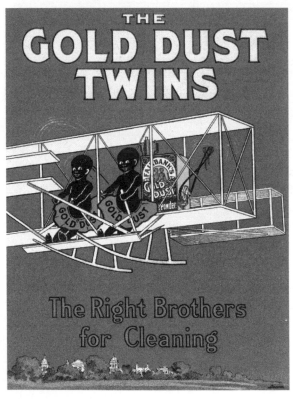

ABOVE The "Gold Dust Twins," always ready to work and work and work. Warshaw Collection of Business Americana, Series: Soap, Archives Center, National Museum of American History, Smithsonian Institution. BELOW And always willing to travel to wherever their services are required. Warshaw Collection of Business Americana, Series: Soap, Archives Center, National Museum of American History, Smithsonian Institution.

digest, because resolving it is ultimately a matter of choice: if black athletes recommit themselves to a vision of community, and to self-sacrifice in the service of the race, the damage can be partly undone and the struggle for equality can be reengaged.

For artist Hank Willis Thomas, though, the present-day symbolic surround seems engineered to eliminate such opportunities. In *Branded*, a sequence of digitally altered photographs, Thomas plays with the "idiom" of advertisement in order to satirically stress the connections between the black body and "the cotton and slave trade." A bloodstain on the ground pools into the shape of an Absolut vodka bottle. A lynched body hangs from the branches of the Timberland tree. An old request to buy slaves is altered to include the logo of the National Basketball Association. The sequence's most powerful pair of images is a black-and-white photograph of a black man's head with the Nike "swoosh" branded into its side, and the chest and rib-cage of an African American man with a group of "swooshes" burned into the flesh. In these cases, the branding of the body is synony-mous with the branding of the product. The black body, shilling for Nike, becomes a product offered for sale, desired by white men for purchase, and permanently scarred to reflect the transformation.[6] To see it is to want it—to want it in all of its myriad meanings and materialities.

Critics might cavil about the dangers of "thug" culture, and cele-brants might enthuse over the entrepreneurial radicalism of an as-sertive, strong black male image, but the emphasis on strength and athleticism marshaled for the entertainment of a larger, generally nonblack audience is easily dated back to slavery. When William Rhoden writes about wealthy black athletes—millionaires and celeb-rities—being "slaves," this is what he means. And when Hank Willis Thomas suggestively plays with the double meaning of "branded," he is asking us to attend to the same thing: to recognize in the Nike advertisement for Air Jordans the old-fashioned, slaveholding em-phasis on the "natural" strength of "the Negro" in circumstances that would have wasted the white body, and to recall that this empha-sis was quickly transformed, in the postbellum age, into the fear of the "black buck," whose strength was matched by his rapacious appetites.

As commodity marked for sale, the contemporary commercial-ized black male body is subject to a deep ethnography, a parallel to

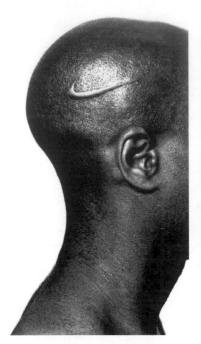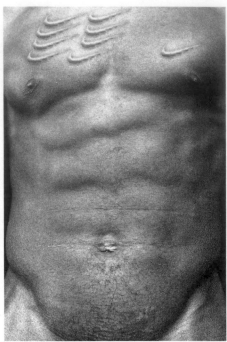

LEFT Hank Willis Thomas, *Branded Head* (2003), Lambda photograph, from the series *Branded*. Courtesy of the artist and Jack Shainman Gallery, New York. RIGHT Hank Willis Thomas, *Scarred Chest* (2003), Lambda photograph, from the series *Branded*. Courtesy of the artist and Jack Shainman Gallery, New York.

the police practice of racial profiling. The West Fourth Street basketball court in New York City, for instance, is known as "the Cage." The blacktop surface is smaller than usual, and a tall chain-link fence surrounds the playing area, making the play physically intense, intimate, and rough. There is a major subway confluence belowground, so the site is also a switching point for human traffic. "Pressed against the 20-foot-high fence that surrounds the Cage is the usual collection of foreign tourists who flock to the Village," one *Village Voice* profile summed; "[t]he courtside chatter is just as likely to be in French or German or Chinese as in English." The court's location in a popular tourist neighborhood generates crowds of people who cling to the chain-link, snap photographs and videos, and gaze anthropologically at the hard bodies on the asphalt. On weekends and during tournament play, "the Cage" locks the black players in combat in front of an attentive audience, as if it were staged diorama of life

The "bro-ed," or black-infused, Rocawear-designed Cherry Coke can, distributed in virtual form as a part of the public relations campaign. From author's collection.

and basketball in the South Bronx offered up for white and worldly consumption.[7]

All of this was well known when, in 2001, the advertising firm BBDO set out to make a commercial for a new soft drink created by Mountain Dew and called "Code Red." Hoping to link Code Red to blackness and to basketball—a perfect example of "bro-ing"—they dispatched ten members of a film production company to the Cage. Some were dressed as Con Ed repairmen. Others appeared as tourists. All carried small handheld cameras. Once the video team was in place, NBA superstars Chris Webber and Tracy McGrady appeared, and, semi-anonymously, joined the game in progress. The use of handheld video recording equipment heightened the documentary feel of the commercial. If the audience appeared surprised, excited, or enthusiastic, the grainy, rapid-cut commercial lent those emotions an air of authenticity. The narration for the video, in turn, was provided by an anonymous spectator at the Cage—named by BBDO as "Cell Phone Guy"—who had called a friend and was colorfully describing the action; his phone call was overheard and recorded. The commercial concluded, of course, with the gracious, restorative consumption of the bright red beverage itself, caught, as if surreptitiously, on a shaky handheld camera. The whole thing, one BBDO executive said, was "like an FBI operation."[8]

The BBDO Code Red campaign went to great lengths to establish the link between blackness and the soft drink. Code Red was supposed to be a sort of souped-up Mountain Dew, another Pepsico drink already well known for its heightened levels of caffeine and sugar. Initial advertising campaigns offered it up as the drink of choice for computer programmers and video gamers, but such "geek chic" had limited market appeal.[9] Attaching the product to African Americans and blackness, in contrast, offered double or triple penetration. Recent research by Pepsico had revealed, incredibly, that African Americans preferred fruit-flavored beverages and that His-

Tracy McGrady takes a drink of Code Red in "the Cage." The grainy image, taken with handheld cameras, lends the advertisement an authentic, unstaged quality.

panic consumers like the color red. And soft-drink companies had long recognized that young white suburban consumers would buy just about anything if it were affiliated with a black male body. The video shoot at the Cage, with its hardcore faux documentary style (one market critic called it "roundball verite"), seemed designed to reassure all viewers—white, black, brown, and otherwise—that "real" black basketball players, when they were off the hardwood and away from their mansions and the NBA's professional photographers, played rough, and then, with a smile on their face, they inevitably downed a bottle of icy Code Red, which illicitly promised, the hushed voice-over assured, "a rush as real as the street."[10]

Beyond the television advertisement filmed at the Cage, Pepsico pushed the "bro-ing" of Code Red to new levels. Busta Rhymes and Fatman Scoop endorsed it in trade jingles. The BBDO ads—another, shot in the same manner, featured singer Macy Gray singing in Washington Square Park—were slotted for BET, WB, MTV, and other television networks that presumably accessed black households. At the Mall of America, BBDO "lured" people to sample the drink with break-dancers and hip-hop.[11] The ad company also forged a new alliance (in search of a "multicultural marketing strategy") with Uni-World Group, "an urban marketing shop" specializing in the interests of minority communities.[12] Conveniently, research produced to show a racialized taste for fruit flavors assigned an urban tropical quality to the proposed clientele. A "graffiti-style cartoon ad" was featured in hip-hop magazines. Radio ads increased when research revealed that minority communities were more intense and committed listeners than whites. Finally, Code Red was initially released in single-serving twenty-ounce bottles and sold only in gas stations and convenience stores, sites, one trade publication noted, that were "frequented by the soft drink's core market: young, primarily teen-age, males."[13] In this fashion, BBDO and Pepsico created the black male consumer—his tastes, his needs, and his procurement zones.

But the desire to cater to a minority consumer was, in the end, merely a cover for something bigger. By placing those malt-liquor-sized bottles of Code Red in the hands of young black men in urban environments, BBDO created the conditions for a thousand micro-documentaries like the one shot at the Cage, featuring unwitting dark-skinned subjects clutching clear bottles filled with a mysteriously bright, scarlet drink. White consumers thus became, quite literally, amateur anthropologists, scrutinizing black thirst and divining the future of cool. Financially speaking, this "urban push" for Code Red was enormously successful, at least in the short term: in June and July of 2001, when the BBDO ad campaign was in full swing, sales of Mountain Dew products were up by over 25 percent, an increase attributed to Code Red "guerilla marketing" tactics. On cultural terms, though, it was merely a single feature of a mosaic of parallel attachments in which the proximate black figure signaled a desirable, hip abundance.

Cultural critic Douglas Rushkoff, paralleling the early work of Malcolm Gladwell in the *New Yorker*, has suggested that black urban culture is useful to marketers because it seems durably "cool" in a way that other cultural forms do not. Eager to capture the disposable income of young people, corporations rely on a "coolhunt" engineered by various marketing firms, knowing that what is appealing today will be trite, or even clichéd, tomorrow. Like amateur explorers armed with recorders and cameras, agents of the firms tour the campuses, street corners, and clubs, hoping to discern what is cutting-edge in time to use it in some series of advertisements. What they find is usually ephemeral, rapidly aging into uselessness. Focusing on the regular abundance of the Coca-Cola product Sprite at concerts and events—and abundance that seems "natural," even if it isn't—Rushkoff suggests that the hip-hop aesthetic has an unusually long life as a powerfully marketing device, which makes it quite appealing.

Code Red may not have sold well, but what *worked* was the obliteration of the difference between Chris Webber, an authenticated black man, and that bright red soft drink. For, to be seen as black is to be seen as a thing, and there is enormous profit potential in just that. Theorizing this relation, Kathryn Lofton, writing of Oprah Winfrey, takes note of the celebrity's capacity to be "a person who is also a product." For Lofton, the thing about Oprah is that she embodies a deep, rich, mesmeric intertwining of practice and performance and product, and a stark blending of the secular and the religious. She is Oprah Winfrey, Lofton reminds us, but also "Harpo, Inc.," and O, and a thousand other things—things that carry weight and meaning, and that do work. And she is a singularly dense knot, without parallel or precedent or, perhaps, heir. "No longer merely a therapeutic idiom," she writes, "Oprah has become an insignia, supplying a stylized economy," a "brand [that] supersedes her biography," and "a product that possesses acclaimed omnipotence and proclaimed omniscience."[14] It is Winfrey's blackness—as much a heavy motif of her self-representation as anything else—that makes this embodiment possible, and that enables her audience to see her as someone to love and something to own. A gifted performer of the commodified self, Winfrey makes this troubling pas de deux seem effortless and natural.

When this sightline is perfectly executed, if you can see the product, you can see the hidden black body behind it. An obvious physical presence is not necessary. When, for instance, the entrepreneurial hip-hop ambassador Jay-Z set out to create a "lifestyle" fashion line, the result—Rocawear, founded in 1999—clothed the black body in advertisement, and transformed every item of clothing into a cross-referent to the celebrity who presided over the company. As Nicole Fleetwood has shown, Jay-Z's efforts were a part of a broader "outreach" by hip-hop performers and producers (among them Russell Simmons and Sean Combs) who hoped to expand their market penetration by linking the mythic "urban street" to nationalist narratives and creating a "Hip Hop Americana."[15] By the mid-2000s, Rocawear was a widely popular brand, providing an ostensibly hip and urban "cool" for anyone and disseminating a verified black aesthetic through fashion. At its most provocative, the wearing of such a brand, and the display of black "cool," reverses the usual assumption—that the consumer endorses the brand—and gives anyone the right to claim, by the proxy of a fur-lined hoodie, the subaltern status of African Americans and the endorsement of Jay-Z himself.

Having produced a new thoroughly "black" skin for the body, Jay-Z and Rocawear set out to perform the same crossover maneuver once executed by the BBDO campaign for Code Red. At a New York Fashion Week party in 2007, Jay-Z revealed a Rocawear-designed Cherry Coke can, featuring a city skyline and a clutch of fruit floating in the sky. Katie Bayne, an executive for Coca-Cola, hoped for "an energetic new look and feel," something "hot," and a fusion of "design, fashion, and music." Only Jay-Z could make it work, she intimated. Rocawear's chief marketing officer, Jameel Spencer, felt that that "urban landscape" would help to "reinvent the Cherry Coke brand in a stylish, hip, and youthful new way."[16] As Spin magazine enthusiastically hinted, "an unspecified Jay-Z tune will serve as the official soundtrack for the fruit-flavored soda's TV advertisements."[17] The event at Fashion Week, complete with dozens of African American artists endorsing the synergy of the can/product/artist, captured by "Street Knowledge TV" in the same low-budget streetwise format as the Code Red ethnographies, provided certification that the new Cherry Coke was authentically, certifiably black.[18] The first-order goal, here, was to offer up a simple soda can, and to make it possible for consumers to see the tall, confident, smooth figure of Jay-Z. But beneath that, the Cherry Coke can offered exactly what Code Red promised: personal transformation, aided and abetted by the magical power of blackness. Buy the soda, and buy the man standing behind it. Be cured by his magical service. "Jay-Z," one online critic lamented, coining a new term, "is the perfect negrifier."[19]

In the symbolic surround of American consumer culture, the black body rarely slips loose of its visual status as a permanent commodity. In promotional music videos created at great cost by artists, the black body and voice often serves as a form of instrumentation paired with the white voice, replacing the guitar solo with the spoken-word poetry of rap and rhyme. The video is both a performance of the music and an advertisement for it. Every sparkling sequin, designer shirt, and sexy car is, too, a product, placed where the eye can see it. In another version of the Code Red promotion, at some well-timed break, an older, more authoritative voice "of the street" joins the music and the video and offers up something that is meant to be heard and seen as insurgent, and that is meant to inflect what would otherwise be dismissed as a market-tested, auto-tuned piece of corporately created merengue with the "gritty" look and sound of black truth and honesty. In these cases, where pop music scrambles desperately to make a case for its coolness, blackness becomes, once again, an aesthetic function of market capital-ism, a parallel to the claim of "new and improved" or "cutting edge." And the black voice and body, visually and aurally separated into the background, is mistaken for a guitar solo, taken as an endorsement, and reduced, once more, to service, all for the enjoyment of a pre-sumed white audience.

There is room, though, for this sightline and its accompanying soundscapes to be something more than mere exploitation, haunted by the slave market. Transgressions come in the form of well-placed clutter, troubling a sightline meant for one kind of body, adding de-tails that challenge what is supposed to be viewed, and altering the politics—or the work—of it. Blackness, we are repeatedly reminded, can also be a universal signifier of discontent with the West and alienation from the supposed mainstream. It is a variegated, com-plex, circulating thing, not the product or possession of any one place, one people, or one politics. Sightlines, then, may focus our vision in a particular way, but that vision can also make it possible to emphasize meaningful, two-way connection and collaboration, in which the attachment of blackness to a product is, despite the usual saturation with the ethos of consumer satisfaction, politically sub-versive.

Such subversions are hard to trace, because they necessarily rely on the unexpected, the illegible, and the hidden. In the summer of 1998, Rajinder Rai, a twenty-two-year-old living in Coventry, released a bhangra single titled "Mundian To Bach Ke." Rai's grandfather had emigrated from India after the Second World War. And bhangra, a form of Punjabi folk music, features the sitar and booming drums that, as music critic Sasha Frere-Jones describes, "could be a march-ing band."[20] Rai issued the song under a stage name, "Panjabi MC," a name given to him by a "crew of black rappers." In the background, beyond the sitar and the beat, Panjabi MC sampled the theme from a once-popular American television show, "Knight Rider"—a synthe-sized medley sounding like bits and bytes of information processed in a mechanical rhythm. He had heard this same track sampled once before, by Busta Rhymes on the 1997 song "Fire It Up."

Already a product of transatlantic flows, "Mundian" circulated across Europe in its original form and through a set of remixes as a kind of hip disco/folk rhythm, with just enough speed and bass and soul for the frenetic nightclub dance scene. Then, not long after its initial release, American hip-hop "godfather," Jay-Z, caught the song in a Swiss dance hall and "freaked out." This intersection of aesthetics and cultures—Jay-Z, in northern Europe, listening to "Mundian," composed by a Punjabi-speaking cosmopolite influenced by black British hip-hop and Busta Rhymes—resulted in a new remix of the original single, now with a heavier bass track, fresh lyrics by Jay-Z, and a new title, "Beware of the Boys," loosely translated from the original. Panjabi MC then reissued an album for a U.S. audience, featuring both the Jay-Z remix and the original version of "Mundian." On the cover of the CD *Beware* (2003), the artist is framed by an Islamic true arch, and he wears a stylized hip-hop ensemble, complete with grey pullover, fur-lined parka, and impenetrably dark sunglasses.

"This," as one Indian immigrant put it, "is called reverse colonialism." Or, as Indian American producer DJ Rekha argued, "We're trying to make 'world hip hop.'"[21] It was inevitable that some things would be lost in the transatlantic translation—Rai's lyrics stress the dangers of sex and love to young women, while Jay-Z urges his "mami" to "Move your body like a snake/Make me want to put that snake on ya."[22] But the overall effect—vocal tracks intertwined and racial politics affiliated—stresses the solidarities, complementarities, and mutual attraction of brown and black. And yet, without a doubt, the song is a product, a thing for sale, marketed chiefly on the basis of its connection to blackness.

The fame of "Beware of the Boys" can be traced backward to the bestowal of the sobriquet "Punjabi MC" or forward to the summer of 2003, when the song seemed to be everywhere. It can be traced outward to that Swiss nightclub, or inward, to the moving parts of Rai's rich and personal weltanschauung. These multiple, crossed-over arcs remind us that the appropriation, commodification, and appreciation of blackness cannot be limited only to the study of the African diaspora—that is, to communities of descent. The movement and transfer of blackness depends on the simultaneous creation of multiple singularities and networks across race, parallel communities and diasporas, and tangled exchanges within and around recognized language groups, cultural clusters, and geographical regions. What happens at the place where all this comes together, and where the marking of bodies, artifacts, and performances as black resonates locally, nationally, and globally? If "Mundian To Bach Ke" sampled American television themes, hip-hop beats, and Punjabi instrumentation, it was also true that bhangra, as Rai reminded one interviewer, was the "reggae of India." And by claiming both hip-hop and reggae as "influences," Rai inserts himself, his music, and his subsequently adopted persona—Panjabi MC—into the undulating, fractured singularity of black internationalism *and* links that diasporic formation to other parallel and intersecting cultures and communities.[23] And by doing that, he reminds us that markings are polymorphous, intimate adornments of the surface—"act[s] of representation," to borrow a phrase from Thomas Holt, linking the "micro local" with myriad globals.[24] These sorts of transnational connections steeped in a postcolonial politics that refuses to be reduced to a service function trouble what would otherwise merely be yet another act of "bro-ing," attaching the black body to the twang of bhangra.

"World hip-hop," broadly conceived, is more than a parallel expression of shared politics. It is both a product of meaningful exchange and appropriation *and* an extension of the sightline under consideration here. When Snoop Dogg collaborated with Akshay Kumar on the song and video for "Singh Is Kinng," the directors chose to feature his "ghetto" toughness but also to reimagine him as Indian. "Singh Is Kinng" isn't a bhangra tune, and the video for the song is classic Bollywood sublime. Legions of female dancers twirl richly colored scarves on hilltops and across a range of natural vistas or in front of an *Arabian Nights*–style backdrop. At the start, Snoop is wearing an oversized varsity letter jacket. Dressed in this American fashion, he appears against this stylized backdrop or behind a screen of undulating women. Kumar, in turn, wears a Sikh headdress, black leather pants, a sleeveless shirt, and a provocatively overdetermined Palestinian neck scarf. Their solidarity is, at first blush, simply a powerfully gendered, fantasy about the virtues of shared darkness and maleness.

What would typically be clichéd stereotype becomes, over time, an exchange and a transformation. As the video draws to a close, Snoop reappears in a crimson headdress and red robes. The two men trade dance moves. Kumar consumes fried chicken and waffles, while Snoop is given saag paneer and naan. As the song comes to a close, they two men recline while a smiling, curvaceous woman feeds Snoop grapes; Kumar, seated to his right, eats a banana. In this bewildering juxtaposition of foodstuffs there is an exchange of some sort, a blurring of the earlier divide, when Snoop was dressed in "gansta" fashion, and Kumar seemed to be an Oriental stereotype.

The collaborative affect of "Singh Is Kinng." From *Singh Is Kinng*, dir. Anees Bazmee (Reliance Entertainment, 2008).

To simultaneously raise and elide this exchange—this "browning" of Snoop Dog—the video also features a convenient minstrel stereotype: a short, rotund, loud and comedic dark-skinned man, clad in a bright red shirt, who pretends to "direct" Snoop and Kumar and who stands in for the backward-looking politics outside of their collaboration.

Like "Mundian," "Singh Is Kinng" perfectly expresses an "Urban Desi" diasporic politics that rests on the presumed association of blackness and brownness outside of sub-Saharan Africa and Southeast Asia. And there is here, too, a clever gambit to expand audience share, and to encourage consumers to cross the line between American hip-hop and world music. If the political affiliations seem potentially radical and progressive, capable of eroding the cultural capital of white world supremacy, they are also quite purposeful and well-calibrated efforts at cross-marketing. As always, the "cool" black body is offered up in the service of someone else's advancement. As always, the black body is product and personality. Not surprisingly, as Nicole Fleetwood might remind us, the alliance forged is male. But, in this case, viewers might also note that Snoop Dogg is reordering the world *and* lining his own pockets, a challenging reversal of Cecil Rhodes's doctrine of "philanthropy plus five percent" in the service of white civilization.

Sightlines make it easier for difference to be visualized in a particular way, but they also make it possible, in this case, for bodies marked as black to mobilize and challenge the structures of an authority just as well-marked as white. Snoop Dogg is, here, a performer, offered up as desirable object, as an advertisement or endorsement, as a feature of the black aesthetic, and as a radical, if commodified, politics. His power to alter, if slightly, the practice of "bro-ing"—to clutter the sightline—is a reflection of his ingenuity and a reminder that even in the long shameful history of racialized advertisement, there is the chance that the product will come alive and stake its own, additional claim for attention. It might very well, that is, unexpectedly affiliate itself with something else, something decidedly different. And the affiliation, in turn, might well make it possible to see the black body as more than a mere "slave in the box," and to thus complicate the racial content of what is seen.

PART II

Group Portraits

Looking for Contrast

A growing awareness among marketers of the
diversity of American consumers encourages them to pay
attention to ethnic, racial, and cultural differences. Multiculturalism
has emerged as one of America's most important social agendas in
the 21st century. In advertising and marketing, it simply makes good
business sense to take the culture of the consumer into account.
WILLIAM M. O'BARR, "MULTICULTURALISM IN THE MARKETPLACE,"
ADVERTISING AND SOCIETY REVIEW (2007)

The famous Italian clothier Benetton is renowned for a clothing line that is famously bright and cheerful, full of the lollipop colors of a cartoon rainbow. In its accompanying advertisements, the full spectrum of colors gets applied to the full spectrum of racial possibilities, once again with an emphasis on unexpected juxtaposition and self-styled random assignments. In one example, over a dozen young men and woman—once again, all roughly the same age, equally thin, and offered up as universally handsome—stand shirtless in a row. All of the women, no matter their skin tone, wear the same gray bra, so our eyes are once again drawn to their shared common womanhood. But the bodies are also paired and entangled across races and sexes, illuminating the self-conscious transgressive politics of the scene and calling attention to the possibilities of same-sex and cross-racial partnerships. Along the bottom half, we

The United Colors of Benetton. The mismatched clothing calls our attention to the disorganized physical rainbow, and vice versa. From the spring 2012 collection, in author's collection.

see that everyone is wearing differently colored versions of the same pants. The racially utopian romance is supported, then, by a rainbow of tangerine, pink, teal, and lime green.

In its spring 2010 catalog, Benetton's emphasis on "undercolor" relied on the same parallelism. In one image, a trio of models—the standard white, black, and yellow—press into each other. They wear mismatched, jewel-toned undergarments. The chief function of the advertisement is to sell clothing to women, but the second-order purpose, at a deeper level, is to deploy and affirm race to sell those bras. The overall effect, once again, is to call attention to—and sharply define—racial difference, and to positively emphasize the public disorderly mixture of varied bodies and distinctively private garments. The models appear chosen for the diversity of their skin tones, facial features, and hair colors, styles, and textures. They are arranged randomly, disorderly—not, that is, from "light" to "dark." They are jumbled by gender. And yet they are also all roughly the same age. Their clothing—which might further differentiate them, or locate them geopolitically, socioeconomically, or racially—is not visible. They are shot in the same lighting against a stark white backdrop. They share the same slightly bemused expression. All appear

The "Undercolor" array. From the spring 2012 collection, in author's collection.

to be roughly the same age, each an exemplar of youthful beauty. Presented with the ensemble, we are encouraged to see diversity and common humanity at once, in a single jarring look. If there is a Benetton aesthetic, this—this juxtapositioning of seemingly random but distinct racial types—is it (plate 3).

"Undercolor" here has two meanings, at least. Formally—and most obviously—it refers to the candy-colored undergarments produced as part of Benetton's fashion line. But it also gestures to skin color, one level "below" those undergarments, one level, as it were, closer to the racial truth. A typically clever play on words, Benetton wants to create a focus on both levels at once, emphasizing those complementary diversities through a focus on range and spectrum, on a clearly marked range of types and shades and tones. The "undercolors" on display have to be very distinctive for the advertisement to do their work, to teach the eye to see, or to cultivate want and desire by emphasizing the differences that are already understood to exist—as true things—in the real world. They aren't necessarily hierarchical; they don't have to be organized to mimic the rainbow; they merely awaken the senses to difference.

The search for contrast is a foundational element of the racially discriminating look. Seeing a single body in an array of dissimilar physiques, the eye constructs a system of differences and opposites, similarities and equivalences. In short, the look requires the invention, or assemblage, of an array as a tangible thing, or as an expression of a diversity of naturalized distinctions. That assemblage can take many forms—from a large family to a military platoon. Such contrasting ensembles make race visible, but they also place greater stress on skin tone than on any other feature. Within this larger genre, there are finer thematic distinctions that matter, too. The racially polyglot family, brought together under the benevolent stewardship of the white father and mother, is evidence of a future not quite attained but looming on the horizon. The mixed platoon, laboring on behalf of the nation, is a structured, authoritarian, and masculinist imagining of what that future might look like, and a test of the present commitment to positive harmony and interaction. And as we sit and watch the future play out, we learn to see, in those multicolored textures, the broader brush strokes of difference. Acknowledging their popularity and their great significance as national and global metaphors, Part II considers these examples, or case studies, of the racialized array (plate 4).

CHAPTER FOUR

The Domestic Ensemble

One striking expression of racial contrast comes through the representation of transnational and multiracial adoptive families. American visual culture is rich with images of stable, contented families, their comity and sameness a metaphor for national harmony. This imagined family has a long history. It is the primary social unit in civil society and a cornerstone of American citizenship, but also the nation-state in miniature. As such, it is typically imagined as racially homogenous and linguistically consistent, with carefully drawn lineages of descent and inheritance, and with easy-to-see markers of sameness, reflecting the mother or the father, the grandparents, and the siblings. In the nation and in the home, then, family resemblance is naturalized. Cross-racial and transnational adoptions add wrinkles that are hard to smooth out.

Adoptive families come in many forms and are composed for many different reasons. But whatever their story, these variegated ensembles, when presented for common scrutiny, brightly illuminate the limits, contradictions, and challenges of the ideal American family and clearly reveal the complex interplay between "family" and "nation." They offer, instead, a different global ideal, or hypothesis, and often (though not always) confirm preexisting racial hierarchies. This is especially true of the largest, most expansive families, held up as quasi-public properties, owned by an adoring fan base, and harbingers of the future of the nation, if not the world. To make sense of multiracial and transnational families, we endow them with a domestic mission. Adoptive families, the logic goes, are special; not just structurally different but cosmically unique and politically progressive. They are called into being to serve a higher purpose. They challenge racism without revealing the falseness of race. They show the gentleness of mankind. In their intense, well-meaning brightness, in their crazy, mixed-up arrangements, they show, their cre-

Detail from the promotional poster for *The Blindside* (2009). Movies like *The Blindside* offer themselves up as a test of the American commitment to color blindness, but they rely on brightly illuminated racial markers to make their political point, and they call our attention to racial divisions. In this case, the film rendered the black child—Michael—as a near-dumb mute, staging him as a hulk of flesh. This made Michael an object—a physical creature with unique gifts who performs for white men who talk about him but don't talk to him. The film forces our attention onto Michael's body, and to its contrast to the white world around him. From author's collection.

ators suggest, the hand of the God, or the triumph of enlightened reason over irrational prejudice.

It is tempting, of course, to view the initial establishment and ultimate acceptance of multiracial adoptive families as evidence of progress in race relations. One hundred years ago, such co-mingled families were unthinkable. When, at the dawn of the twentieth century, a trainload of Irish Catholic orphans from New York was placed with Mexican families in Arizona, the result was a riot. Local law enforcement and an accompanying posse removed the orphans from their new homes—devoutly Catholic but "brown"—and placed them instead with nearby white families, a forced march that the Supreme Court ultimately sanctioned.[1] To bring order to just this sort of chaos, new institutions were created to safeguard the interests of children, to scientifically guide child placement, and, ultimately, to displace racism and geographic prejudice in favor of the "best interests" of abandoned, orphaned, and refused offspring.[2] Today, just a century after that cargo of Irish orphans arrived in the desert Southwest, we stand in line to purchase a copy of *People* with news on the latest celebrity adoption and enthuse over their idealistic future tense, their creation of a *nuevo* world and what anthropologist Toby Alice Volkman has called "new geographies of kinship."[3]

If these adoptive families are of recent vintage, the general interest in the mixed ensemble is a long-standing, more durable feature of American culture. It stands as an object of intense fear and desire, of rejection and emulation. In marriage, in athletics, in military service, in neighborhoods, in the high school clique, and, again, in the family, the assemblage and juxtaposition of myriad "types," "stocks," and "bloods" is meant to highlight difference and construct it all at once, a "paradox" summarized by anthropologist Ann Anagnost as "absorbing difference into the intimate space of the familial while also reinscribing it."[4] This "absorption" and "inscription" can confirm that status of the United States as a "nation of immigrants," a "melting pot," or a "multicultural" country. It is no wonder, then, that the bigger, "famous" adoptive families—the Doss family, the DeBolt family, and the more recent Jolie-Pitt family—are built to be seen. They rely on this line of sight, this contrasting discriminating look, to make their most ambitious political points about the fate of the nation-state. And because they make race brighter and more visible, they simultaneously disrupt *and* sanctify our most certain conceptions of progress, change, and hope.[5]

In 1951, a *Life* magazine photojournalist visited the "One-Family U.N." of Helen and Carl Doss in Boonville, California. In the resulting photo essay, the lead image features the Doss's nine adopted children in a ring around their parents, suspended from a ship's ladder, which is hung from a mature, shady tree. "Ten years ago," the essay began, "like many childless couples, Carl and Helen Doss began their family by adopting a baby boy." Subsequent additions were largely "unadoptable" children, who, *Life* insisted, were of "mixed racial parentage." The conceptualization of the family as a "U.N."—or, perhaps, a gathering of refugees in a new safe harbor—is never broken down, except through a listing of the children's racial, ethnic, and national backgrounds. The presumption, perhaps, is that the function of the U.N. is primarily social, an arrangement of cast-offs with fair play ensured by American stewards. Stressing Carl's Methodist ministry, the magazine went on to describe the family as the epitome of American organization and thrift. "In the nightly ritual of bathing, the kids are dunked in an assembly line. Carl pops them into the soapy tub; they swish through the suds and emerge at the other end to be dried by Helen."[6]

A rich, black-and-white photo array takes up the following pages.

TOP Racial display and ethnic or national ornamentation in the multiracial adopted family. Young Jimmy Blake, newly adopted by a U.S. serviceman in Japan, c. 1955, in a kimono. Orlando-Stringer/Hulton Archives/Getty Images. BOTTOM Geoffrey Onuoha, adopted from Nigeria, clothed in the racially marked traditions of his homeland, surrounded by his white brothers, watching television, 1954. Don Cravens/Time & Life Pictures/Getty Images.

These iconic, if slightly banal portraits might have been staged by Norman Rockwell: Helen reads to two daughters on a big armchair; Carl plays with five children at the beach; the children, hands on their chest, reciting the Pledge of Allegiance at school; the girls, back-lit by a bright window, descend a staircase in their Sunday best and on the way to church. In a nod to the bathtub assembly line, one photo captures Helen, outside with laundry hanging behind her, confronted with a "haircut lineup." At the most basic level, these generic images establish the capacity of multiracial adoptive families to be fundamentally American—that is, to be churchgoing, patriotic, playful, and wholesomely familiar and normal.[7] The setting, content, and thematics are thus familiar for a reason: their proposed function is to establish national sameness, not difference.

These are not colorblind representations. At a deeper level, they seek to expand—but not necessarily to naturalize—this grand, more polychromatic conception of family. The very arrangement of the children suggests that the use of classically American backdrops is meant to highlight, not erase, the distinctions of race, ethnicity, and place, with a focus on heightened contrast. Helen holds her two daughters as she reads to them, but the light captures their coloring differently. Rita, in the foreground, is darkened by the whiteness of her immediate backdrop, and by her close proximity to Helen Doss, while Susan, set against a black headboard, is bleached. In another image, Carl holds aloft young Alex and looks into his eyes, but the camera purposefully hones in on their divergent profiles, tones, and textures, a juxtapositioning that attends to diversity within sameness, to the racial fractures within the "U.N. family."

True to the United Nations references, the entire montage is a loving representation of the utopia just around the corner. Thus, the resolution of sibling conflict is a metaphor for postwar harmony forged in the aftermath of war. In one subtle pairing, for instance, the Doss family provides a model of racial injury and subsequent repair—a child (Timmy) stands crying, and then "Standard Doss discipline . . . is invoked." Victim and villain must "sit together until willing to kiss and make up." The short storyline concludes with two grinning children locked in a tight, intimate embrace. The coupling of a different set of representations—the aforementioned quintet voicing the Pledge, and a shot of the "Home Grown Congregation," silhouetted by stained glass—shows the wider range of colonized peoples who might, if given the chance, be folded into American society. The multiracial assemblage in the pew stands attentively, with Mrs. Doss providing the center of gravity, while the open doors at the back of the small church suggest that the diverse ensemble is new to the scene. The world is now smaller, *Life*'s display of the Doss family suggested, and readers needed to adjust their way of thinking about "family" to meet the challenges of the future.[8]

Helen Doss, the conductor of this orchestral group, had wanted children for a very long time. For her, the absence of children in the house put an end to dreams of self-fulfillment. "No children," she wrote, "no sticky fingerprints on the woodwork, no childish tears and laughter, no small beds in other bedrooms. Just barren, empty years, stretching aimlessly into a lonely future." When a doctor informed Helen and Carl that they couldn't have children of their own, it seemed a crushing blow to her sense of womanhood. The mere sight of other mothers "strutting along the sidewalk behind a baby buggy" left Doss filled with "violent jealously, envy, and acute self-pity." Happily, as Helen Doss's memoir tells it, adoption proved to be an easy solution, and after some anxious waiting and searching, the Dosses brought home "a chubby little fellow with blue eyes, a perfect match."[9]

The Family Nobody Wanted—Helen's memoir—captures the postwar emphasis on color-blind love in such assembled families and the declining significance of racial matching. Seeking a companion for Donny, their first child, Helen is stymied by an adoption agent who refuses to place with her a "little Turkish-Portuguese boy" who is "mixed-blood." "If I get a child," Helen writes, "it's like getting a Christmas present. It's what's inside that counts. The color of the wrapping doesn't matter."[10] When the adoption agency suggests that the boy was "*very* dark-skinned, and you are both fair," Helen responds with principled emphasis on character, not color: "He could be brown or pink . . . red or yellow. We don't care." When she is asked by friends whether it would be possible to raise such a child without showing prejudice, Doss replies with a question: "How could we show something we didn't feel?" Famously, then, Helen and Carl reject racism, continue their search for more children, and set out to build a family and a home that will change everything. "We can't make the world better by just giving up," says Carl. To bookend this revolutionary family and spotlight its significance, Helen provides two conservative forces with which to struggle: Mrs. Pickles, a racist neighbor, and Little Beaver, an Indian boy too old, and too indoctrinated into his native identity, to become a part of the family.

Despite her explicit rejection of racism, Helen closely, even obsessively, attends to the supposedly fixed features that mark race on her children's bodies, and dwells on their hyphenate status as "mixed." She sees race in every detail but vehemently rejects racism. Each adoption, indeed, is presented an opportunity for a new racial assessment. Laura, described as English-French-Filipina-Chinese, was notable for her "exquisite ivory skin, her pink-cheeked, china-doll features." Teddy, who was "a Filipino-Malayan-Spanish boy," had "large brown, round eyes." Rita, a "Mexican-Indian" girl, "had a creamy-beige complexion, and sweeping black lashes that matched her patent-leather hair." Taro, who was "Japanese-Filipino," was a "chunky little boy with the round, Oriental face," with "the same stocky build, typically Japanese round face, and 'slanted' eyes as his father," Helen wrote. Alex, who was Japanese, Burmese, and Korean, had "mysterious, dark, 'slanted' eyes." "Look at those lovely Balinese eyes Elaine has," Helen remarked, anticipating another acquisition, "[a]nd Diane looks like a Hawaiian doll."[11]

This glorious variety wasn't meant for private enjoyment. It was better presented as a public "tableau." There was the *Life* magazine spread, of course, and an earlier essay written for *Reader's Digest*, along with the 1951 radio special on the "Christmas Family of the Year" and an NBC "Welcome Travelers" special. On the ground, the Christmas holiday offered a change for a regular display of the children. Carl's church would feature a nativity scene, with the older children dressed "as shepherds dressed in crude sandals . . . or Wise Men draped in discarded velveteen draperies. And with striped towels around their heads." Later, Carl would install another version of this mélange on the family front porch, complete with small animals, so that "our choir" could sing "Christmas carols which were amplified across the broad lawn to watchers beyond the curb."[12] The interplay between public and private, race and family, were critically important elements of these didactic displays. At home, in church, or anywhere, the "One-Family U.N." was a global lesson lying in wait.

Doss's assemblage lovingly reproduced stereotype and enduring caricature for broad consumption. In an epilogue to the 2001 new edition of *The Family Nobody Wanted*, Helen provided an update on the

A photograph of James Earle Fraser's *The End of the Trail.* From the American Sculpture Photograph Study Collection, Smithsonian American Art Museum.

children. Greg—once described as a Cheyenne-Blackfoot, "a brown-skinned boy, pink on the palms of his hands and the soles of his feet, with silky-straight hair and enormous brown eyes"—had become a renowned performance artist.[13] A proud mother, Helen recalled one of his pieces at the Laguna Beach Arts Festival. Serving as a "living tableau," Greg had embodied the sculptor James Earle Fraser's *The End of the Trail,* a turn-of-the-century nostalgic appreciation of the "vanishing Indian" that owed as much to the Beaux Arts movement as it did to Buffalo Bill's Wild West shows. Clutching a long spear tipped toward the ground, on horseback and bent over as if exhausted, the noble savage of Fraser's massive 1915 sculpture quickly became a popular and commemorative motif of the Old West, appearing in a thousand knockoffs, paintings, and souvenir trinkets. Placing himself in the flow of this history, Gregory Doss took up the spear, clad himself in costume, and mounted a horse, to become the cartoon his mother had always wanted. "Like the Indian he was," Helen recalled, Greg "sat perfectly still on his horse, and the audience was spellbound."[14]

Helen Doss is the white mother, a familiar representation. Dorothy DeBolt, another such archetype, may or may not have known that black women often wear their politics in their hair, but Lynn Thomas, the photo-journalist for *Ebony*, surely did. Every day, before her children left for school, Dorothy would comb her adopted African American daughter's hair. In 1974, *Ebony* magazine provided a picture of this commonplace event for its readers, which would not have been worthy of much notice, except that the photograph was featured in an essay about a black child named Karen who was adopted by a white family. The photo of Dorothy and the corresponding story on Karen's adoption was bookended by the usual array of advertisements for hair straighteners, relaxers, and beautifiers, juxtapositioning Karen's profile with dozens of stylized, perfect Afros. Dorothy wears a white sweater, and her light blond hair is perfectly swept back. She is slightly out of focus. Framed in this fashion, Dorothy becomes a part of the literal backdrop for Karen, who is dressed in darker colors and whose face is shadowed, emphasizing her blackness. Karen sits dutifully, with a small smile on her face, as her mother combs out her short hair. Damaged and remanded into the DeBolt family, her hair and her politics are now the province of her pristinely white mother.[15]

"When Karen came to our attention," Dorothy told *Ebony*, "we weren't particularly seeking a black child, but a handicapped child." The DeBolts' sixteenth child, Karen was the first African American addition to an adoptive family already full of international and special needs children. She was born without arms and legs—"she would never skip, run or play like a normal child," the *Ebony* profile confessed to its readers, "never hug a puppy or tear petals from a rose." And as the photo of Dorothy combing her hair suggested, Karen would never manage her own politics. She and Dorothy would always be engaged in a reversal of the master/servant dynamic, with the older white woman always at the service of the young black body.

If the DeBolts described Karen's adoption as proof of a color-blind American dream, *Ebony* had other ideas. Indeed, Karen's adaptation to the DeBolt family system—a philosophy of American bootstrapping deliberately developed for the wretched, the battered, and the forgotten—proved to be the second most important element of her biography. Readers turned the pages, Ebony hoped, in search of "that moment" when "race consciousness" was awoken in Karen's fragile psyche. If a small girl, without hope and cast aside by her birth mother and her doctors, raised in a multiracial family, could realize that black is beautiful, then she would stand as a powerful metaphor for the race question nationally.[16]

"It wouldn't have made any difference what color," Dorothy stressed. "We became aware of blacks needing homes. If you have a black child who, on top of not being adopted for his blackness, is also handicapped, obviously the need is going to be greater. Her blackness was a bonus so far as we were concerned, but our main reason was we just loved the whole idea of Karen herself." For Dorothy, Karen's blackness was a "bonus"—a detail missing from the original canvas. "Bob and I feel that the most important experience for any child—for anybody—is the human experience," Dorothy argued. Karen, Ebony reported, was convinced that her mother "don't got no color." And she confessed to Dorothy one night that "she didn't like black." Responsible for Karen's racial awakening, the DeBolts labored, as best as they could, to convince Karen that she was "magnificent" because she was black. "Black is like your skin," Bob told her, "and that's beautiful." "Black is all colors," Dorothy added, "and if you like a lot of colors then you almost have to like black." In an aside to the magazine, Dorothy noted that "[w]e ourselves have many black friends." Lynn Thomas, summing up for her Ebony readers, suggested that "[f]or now it is enough that Karen's environment and her parents' attitude keep her attention riveted on the positive." But it was entirely unclear whether that would be enough in the near future. In the DeBolt family, the simple act of combing a daughter's hair called dramatic attention to the interplay of the rhetoric of color blindness and the reality of racial sight.[17]

The DeBolts gained fame in the 1970s—a generation after the Doss family's adoptions—for their extraordinary adoption of children from around the world with severe physical and developmental handicaps. The story of the family's creation was profiled in most major magazines. A book by Joseph Blank—19 Steps Up the Mountain: The Story of the DeBolt Family—was published. And a 1977 documentary, Who Are The DeBolts?, directed by John Korty and hosted for television by Henry Winkler, won both an Emmy and an Oscar—an unprecedented feat.[18] In the wake of the film, the DeBolts were sanc-

The DeBolt family, partially assembled, 1972. Ralph Crane/Time & Life Pictures/Getty Images.

tified as human rights heroes; if the "recent outburst of adoption fervor" gave "rout to racism," one letter writer suggested, then the DeBolts deserve "much greater praise." "In this family," the *Washington Post* television critic summed, "'disability' is an unknown word, and 'handicapped' is virtually verboten."[19] Much like the Doss family, the DeBolts earned their celebrity through humanitarian assemblage, and broadcast their message through visual media.

Conceived in the midst of a serious national downturn marked by an energy crisis, blackouts, and race riots, *Who Are the DeBolts?* was a desperately needed "feel good" film, substituting a new national mythology for easy sympathy. It begins with an encouragement of a certain kind of forgetting. Dorothy DeBolt is telling a joke to an audience, in which she recalled an afternoon phone call from a child named Jennifer, asking for a bit more play time outside; after giving permission, Dorothy remembered that "[w]e don't have a child named Jennifer." "You're not going to be able to remember all the names or keep straight all the personal histories," the narrator disclaims, against a backdrop of sped-up family footage, rapidly cut and spliced in dizzying fashion, "but you're not going to forget the DeBolts." It is a bracing start, challenging the viewer to attend to the faces and bodies on display, to remember each name, each background story, each injury, prosthetic, or complication. It suggests, moreover, that no matter how compelling any of these details might be, the most significant object was the family—"the DeBolts"—once again, a metonym for the nation. Each child's melodrama, in the end, had to be sublimated to the story of the family.

The DeBolt "system" offered a better way of profitably organizing and orchestrating the wider array of bodies brought to America as a consequence of war and heartbreak. The end goal was the creation of independent citizens, responsible for their own well-being and progress, and not dependent on their parents, who stood in for the State. "There are," the *New York Times* reported, "no trips, no servants, few clothes, and, for food, 100-pound sacks of rice, gallon jars of peanut butter, and many, many chicken dinners."[20] The system valued austerity, not luxury, and productivity, not dependence. The older children, the *Times* continued, had to pay their own way through college. Everyone worked. Two boys, both on crutches, had a paper route. Another boy, once seriously wounded by shrapnel in Vietnam, repaired televisions. The comprehensive effect was a profound, if largely implicit critique of the idea of welfare entitlements, at least without a corresponding commitment to the perfectly American virtues of hard work, personal forbearance, and initiative.

Who Are the DeBolts? is, first and foremost, an advertisement for this system, chiefly administered by Bob, an engineer by profession, and Dorothy, a self-described "planner." Our first glimpse of it comes as the opening credits roll and the first-order question—"Who Are the DeBolts?"—has already been asked. The entire family is out for a jog along the Oakland waterfront. Because so many of the children are on crutches or in wheelchairs, the ragtag procession stretches out for about a hundred yards behind Bob, who runs in the lead at a brisk pace. Throughout, every child is personally responsible for his or her own fate. JR, blind and paralyzed below the waste, lifts weights to build upper body strength, and then learns, slowly and painstakingly, to make his way up a winding staircase to the second floor. Sunee and Karen, who are already veterans of the system, have nightly races to the top, a cheerful contest marked by the clatter of plastic, wood, and metal. The Vietnamese "boys" garden lying down, having set aside their braces. "Everyone has chores in the De-Bolt family," goes the narration, "and all the chores are necessary." Tran, a blind teenager recently arrived from Vietnam, sorts silverware and napkins for dinner. Sunee, her legs paralyzed by polio, ambles around the backyard to feed the dog, using her crutches to move the bowl into place. Even JR, so newly adopted, helps to mix cookie dough. The goal of the DeBolt family system, then, is to encourage the growth of an independent spirit, and to reject the idea that handicapped people need special treatment of any sort. But the documentary passively works against this goal, asking viewers to focus their attentions on the physical challenges of life in a "normal" house.

Throughout the presentation of the family to its public, the relation between race and empire is both obvious and unremarked. The great majority of the adopted children come from Vietnam, and many bear scars of the recent conflict there. Since the children were adopted at all ages, many speak Vietnamese, and some serve as translators between Dorothy and Bob and new arrivals. One notes, then, the presence of a foreign colony of sorts, as the camera repeatedly catches small pockets of Vietnamese children of all ages engaged in private conversations and intimate games, a pluralist future and postwar present sealed off by language from the Anglo-American past. Upstairs, as the *Times* put it, the children lay quietly, "all dreaming, thinking, or remembering in Korean, Vietnamese or English." The DeBolts' assemblage then was foreign policy reimagined as domestic policy, and their family was an NGO in the midst of a humanitarian assistance program. Their system could have been ripped from the pages of William Lederer and Eugene Burdick's Cold War classic, *The Ugly American*, with its enthusiasm for hardscrabble partnerships between American engineers and Asian entrepreneurs.

Karen—the African American congenital quadruple amputee—is at the heart of the racial dynamic in these public viewings. "The one with the hooks for hands," as Dorothy referred to her, was spotlighted in the *Times* story, engaged with Sunee and Wendy in horseplay at the dinner table. Her adoption—and Dorothy's careful maintenance of her hair, and her blackness—was the object of *Ebony*'s attentions. In *Who Are the DeBolts?*, she is a jubilant, laughing, comedic star, and the only black face. For a two-minute stretch of the documentary, the camera lingers on her after a swim in a pool (supported by an inner tube) while she carefully dresses herself. Clad, at first, only in underpants, she pulls on a pair of white cotton sleeves for her arms, and then pulls a white shirt over her head. Without music and nar-

A family meeting. From *Who Are the DeBolts?*, dir. John Korty (Charles M. Schultz Creative Associates, 1977).

rated in hushed, reverent tones, this protracted viewing of a small African American child ultimately confirms the dominant iconography of the day, full of dystopian cityscapes and angry, riotous dark faces. Karen, a "victim" of the failing war on poverty, struggles to get the sleeves on. Her shirt catches on her prosthetic arms. She very gently lowers herself into the "bucket" connected to her artificial legs. And then, mindful of the camera and the cameramen, she scoots away and toward Sunee and Wendy. These representations capture a family—and a nation—in the midst of repair; "wheelchairs, crutches, straps, braces, artificial arms, legs, and iron hands," the *Times* reported, "lie around the house as casually as forgotten mittens and old galoshes do in other houses." And Karen was another cast-off, the newspaper unsubtly confirmed, having been given up by her mother, who confessed at the moment of discard that "she didn't know what to do with such a child." Black failure, then, stood in contrast to the successful salvage of the child, of the family, and of the nation by the white father.

The point of such an assemblage was the display of variety in accord. And so, in the end, the documentary returns to the trio of Karen, Wendy, and Sunee, three small girls united in fictive sisterhood. As the film moves to a close, the entire DeBolt family has gathered around the grand piano. The room is filled with microphones, signs that the camera crew has wired the space to capture the voices of everyone. Dorothy plays the piano, and to her left, this trio sits, now clad—for the very first time—in matching, colorful housedresses. Together with their mother, their father, their brothers and sisters, they sing a gospel spiritual—"The Whole World in His Hands." Despite the presence of a vast ensemble, the scene centers on Karen, Wendy, and Sunee happily singing that song, and often unaccompanied by other voices. The other children are mere backdrop for their work. A shadow on the wall behind them—a trace of intent—reveals the presence of a spotlight, directed to illuminate their comforting vocalization of postcolonial piety, their healing racial harmonics.

The spectacular juxtapositions of the adoptive family continue to attract the attention of the public eye. Like Dorothy DeBolt and Helen Doss before her, Angelina Jolie, the actress, Hollywood royal, and United Nations Goodwill Ambassador for Refugees, has famously professed a strikingly similar interest in the adoption of poor, orphaned children from underdeveloped, subaltern countries, an interest that began with the adoption of a young Cambodian boy, delivered to her on a movie set in Africa.

Asked to account for her feelings as she stood poised to become "Hollywood's next Mia Farrow," Jolie replied, "Or Josephine Baker. I like that better." It is striking that Jolie, a nominally "white" actress, a child of Hollywood royalty, would style herself after a poor "plain ghetto girl" like Baker, another adoptive mother.[21] Still, this expression of similarity has since become a standard feature of Jolie's public image. *Vanity Fair*'s "Hollywood" issue, labeling her a "Tempest," includes a full-length nude of Jolie, lying chest down in a half-full bathtub, and notes that she possesses "the same all-encompassing mothering instincts and lack of inhibitions as 1920s diva Josephine Baker."[22] Jolie, much like Baker, has sought a home for her family in Europe, in London, in the French countryside, and in Paris, where she claims to feel more at home. When asked in 2005 at the first annual Worldwide Orphans Benefit where her "next" child might be procured, Jolie responded glibly, much as Josephine Baker might have, that "[t]here are so many wonderful places. There are so many

Josephine Baker, the iconic African American performer, with two of her adopted, hyper-racinated children, in France, 1950. Like the Jolie-Pitt family, Baker's assemblage—one of the first and easily the most famous of its day—was notable for its abridgement of celebrity and cosmopolitanism. Roger Viollet/Roger Viollet Collection/Getty Images.

parts of Asia, Africa, South America, so sooner or later I'll end up everywhere, I'm sure." As was the case with Baker, cynics have seen Jolie's interest in adoption as a kind of "retail therapy," through which famous Hollywood stars can "accessorize with brown, yellow, and black babies." Jolie, one *Village Voice* critic wrote, is "Our Lady of Humanitarian Narcissism."[23]

Romantics, in turn, have envisioned Jolie's adoptions as "rescue" and have hoped for a deeper, ensemble drama, full of innocent, heartfelt idealism and stories of salvation and triumph, all staged in the open air.[24] Because Jolie and Pitt were celebrities and accomplished actors before their establishment of the family, their day-to-day routines are not only featured in the occasional special issue photo spread in a monthly magazine. They are regularly profiled in mainstream magazines like *People*, obsessed over in the new media, and tracked by dozens of photographers to every family lunch, dinner date, or weekend holiday. "He's a two-time Sexiest Man Alive," one *People* piece noted. "She's the world's Most Beautiful woman. Together, they are building . . . the World's Most Beautiful Family."[25] Taking advantage of this attention to their finest detail, Jolie and Pitt have pushed back hard against the charge of faddishness, claiming the familiar mantle of a serious utopian, progressive politics. Mixing "biological" and "adoptive" children, they have proposed more than mere salvage. They offer instead a new ethics for the twenty-first century. Their rainbow tribe is not an American product but a global one. They choose world cities for their homes—New York, New Orleans, Paris—and refuse rootedness in any national context. They vacation as often in the Third World as in the First. They've chosen French as the family's "second language," an exquisitely cosmopolitan provocation.[26] And Shiloh, in a planned challenge to privilege, was born in Africa.

Along with the familiar internationalism, the family repeats the same emphasis on racial juxtaposition, display, and orchestration. In the special issue of *People* celebrating Shiloh's birth, Jolie is cradling Shiloh in her arms, with her back to the camera, and her trademark shoulder tattoos—the global latitudinal and longitudinal coordinates where her children were born—on display. Zahara stands behind her mother, back-to-back. Jolie wears white, while Zahara wears blue. Zahara's bare arms are against Jolie's bare back. The point of such an image is to capture the global aesthetic of the family, to naturalize the transnational family, and yet still create and subsequently attend to differences of shade and origin. The tattoos place Zahara in a complicated family geography. Jolie, an adoring smile on her face, is sainted, beloved, and heroic. She has, the image suggests, opened the door for a better world.[27]

In the wake of daughter Shiloh's birth, artist Kate Kretz produced a telling—and widely discussed—portrait of Jolie for the 2006 Art Miami exhibition. Titled *Blessed Art Thou*, the painting features Jolie as the Madonna, striding forward on a white cloud, with her famously adopted children, Zahara and Maddox, clinging to her form-fitting gown, and Shiloh, her newborn, in her arms (plate 5). Zahara and Maddox, salvaged from abroad, are cherubim; Shiloh, in turn, is messianic. At the bottom of the canvas—beneath the clouds, literally—there lies a version of purgatory, filled with corporate sym-

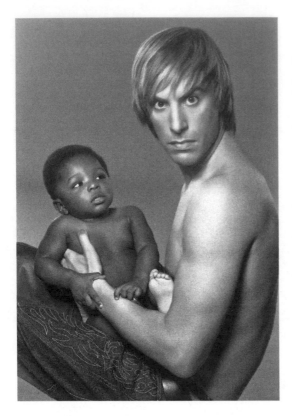

Sacha Baron Cohen as "Bruno," parodying the sanctimony of the celebrity adoption "craze." Bruno, the lead character in a 2009 mockumentary of the same name, is an insufferably self-centered Austrian fashion celebrity. In a fit of pique, he adopts a black child, names him David, and totes him along as an accessory to the runway. Shot in black and white, and marked by race and age, this image satirically overemphasizes the conventions of juxtaposition in the photography of adoptive families. The photograph was released to the media in 2009 as a part of the Universal Studios publicity campaign. From author's collection.

bolisms, bloated Midwestern stereotypes, and overflowing magazine racks. An American flag hangs in the lower, darker region, reflecting Jolie's apparent triumph over national chauvinism. *Blessed Art Thou*, the artist suggested, is commentary on "the celebrity worship cycle," and the focus on Jolie is important "because of her unavoidable presence in the media, the worldwide anticipation of her child, her 'unattainable' beauty and the good she is doing in the world through her example." "I think it's wonderful," wrote Llen, a visitor to the artist's blog. "It reminds me of murals I've seen in Central America."[28]

As was true with the families of Helen Doss and Dorothy DeBolt, it would be easy to script Jolie's trailblazing familial enterprise as a story for our postmodern time—a cosmopolitan drama, staged outside of the nation-state, full of innocent, heartfelt idealism, inflected with salvation, with the adoptions cast as "miracles." Named after powerful symbols—"Pax" for peace, "Shiloh" for the biblical messiah—the expanding Jolie-Pitt family seems to have been created to save us all. It is, though, nothing but an old masterpiece traced onto new paper. The basic premise is unchanged from 1951, when *Life* set out to capture the Doss family at play: the deeply symbolic establishment and orchestration of racial difference within the family, all of it premised on the stark juxtaposition of supposedly divergent types. "You're from Asia," Jolie says to Maddox, "you're from Cambodia. Asia is not Mommy's continent, it's your continent."[29] The distance—and the difference—is what matters. And seeing it is what matters most.

CHAPTER FIVE

Platoon Harmonics

L
ike the multiracial adoptive family, the mixed platoon draws the eye into the study of difference. A heterotopic ensemble, the platoon is a narrative device, always on the move, its movements always revealing the centrality of mixture to the nation's survival or failure. It creates a common structure—the army unit—even as it manufactures easy-to-recognize racial fractures within it.

At first blush, the 2011 film *Captain America* seems an unlikely example of the racial ensemble. Desperate to serve in World War II, young Steve Rogers has a good heart but a weak constitution, until a slightly mad German scientist, a refugee from the Nazis, compels a miraculous transformation. The costume and the shield follow, and so Steve Rogers becomes Captain America, clad in red, white, and blue, and still blessed with his good heart. The costumed hero at the heart of the story is, then, a singular man with a unique personal history and a chemically enhanced physique.

The promotional poster, in tacit agreement, features a lonely Steve Rogers, head bent, set against the wintry background of a war zone. But there, in the film itself, is "Cap," repeatedly teamed up with a wide-ranging group of soldiers, *his* men, all tough, all loyal to him as team leader. They are his literal backdrops. Despite the long and well-documented history of segregation within the military during World War II, the group is improbably mixed. At one end of the racial spectrum, there is the obligatory Asian face, "from Fresno," we are told, lest we think he is from China. An African American, generally mute during the movie, stands as a racial bookend. At the other end is an Irishman, his red handlebar moustache, his penchant for drinking and fighting, and his anachronistic bowler hat suggesting that he arrived in the European war zone by virtue of time travel from the mid-nineteenth century. In the middle there is a Frenchman, absorbed into the American military for some reason and providing the

The white-man-as-nation (top) and his mixed platoon backdrop. Promotional image from the campaign for *Captain America: The First Avenger*, dir. Joe Johnston (Paramount Pictures, 2011).

group with a little European flair. Rogers needs these men, and they need him. More importantly, America needs them all. So they work together, like a well-rehearsed circus act, blowing stuff up joyfully, cheering each other on, until the denouement, when Rogers finally must act alone, foiling the villain's plan for world domination and sacrificing himself in the process.

A platoon is, in many ways, bigger than the family—it extends outward into civil society, beyond the region, and sometimes even beyond the nation-state. Typically, these are imagined as small, racially and ethnically diverse, and organized according to a confusion of stereotype and skill, so that race becomes an instrument of the unit's success. They feature adults, not children, as further proof that radical change has already happened and that the future is already here. The common adult status erases or hides the great white father or mother. These, in short, are bands of brothers or friends, members of the same generation, ready for the serious combat of everyday life, ready to focus on what really matters. This imagining of the multiracial platoon as a diverse team, or set of bodies and faces, arranged in complementary racial sequence, is a sightline that encourages a focus on broader divisions, held together in immediate and productive relation. An enduringly popular sort of assemblage, it can be found in everything from to pop music to war films to science fiction.

Of course, the sanctioned story of the platoon is supposed to be devoid of racial content. We might see race, but it isn't, we are told, performed. In combat, the argument goes, all that matters is group survival, and so the platoon is officially stripped of all racial and ethnic animation once it is working on the ground. It is important to remember, though, that such an official narrative is an argument and not a truth. If it has power—in debates about the desegregation of the military, or the inclusion of women and GLBT soldiers in combat—that doesn't mean that it is the only transcript of the platoon in action. Indeed, for every testimonial, autobiography, and comprehensive survey that bolsters the notion of the color-blind (or, now, sex-orientation-blind) platoon, there are a hundred other dazzling examples that stress the dramatic importance of diversity on a military platoon, where every part has a racial "gift," plainly visible and routinely performed, and every gift contributes, in a very particular way, to the common good.

The definition of a "platoon" has a broad resonance and can be found well outside of the familiar contexts of war films and cowboy movies. More generally, it refers to a complex unit of citizens, usually men, engaged in the pursuit of a shared interest and utilizing their complementary skill sets to claim it. Platoons are everywhere. The album cover for the Village People's 1978 single "Macho Man" is, for instance, a typically detailed representation. Five male

Promotional poster for *The Losers* (2010), another ensemble in the service of the nation. Note the relationship between race, posture, wardrobe, and function. In the platoon, every racial part has a purpose. From author's collection.

bodies, each a perfect representation of some classic American type, face the viewer, their differences highlighted by a bright-red backdrop. Each wears a serious expression, emphasizing the importance of their collaboration and mature commitment to their interrelation. On the left, there is a cowboy, an "Indian" peeking around from behind him, like Tonto, a "Marlboro Man" type, complete with bolo tie, black hat, and leather chaps, and next to him there is a construction worker, wearing blue jeans, a flannel shirt, and a hard hat, his tool belt weighed down with a power drill. On the right, there is a brother from the streets, complete with Afro, and a leather-clad biker, dressed like Marlon Brando in *The Wild One*, and sporting a handlebar mustache, his jacket open, his hirsute chest revealed. Up front and center, sporting a sequined jumpsuit (he would later dress as a motorcycle cop), is Victor Willis, the putative leader of the group.

Singing in choral harmony and dancing in unison, the Village People were more than a 1970s concept group, another triumph of the entertainment industry's capacity to produce a financial success; they were also the embodiment of a national and global sightline. The promotional video for the single, shot in a dark, mirrored basement gym, stressed the same dynamic relationship between each performer's individuality and their increasingly composite physical aggregation. Toggling back and forth between shots of a single, faceless white male body in the midst of a workout and wider-angle appreciations of the full group, with Willis now dressed in shorts and a tank top, the video calls attention to the platoon in the process of formation, to the bodies moving to a single beat. The dialec-

The Village People. Michael Ochs/Getty Images.

tic between the single body, bending, lifting, and twisting in profit-able strain, and the assorted, costumed bodies, dancing and singing as one, suggests a relationship that is practical, or functional. The differences—the costumes, the makeup, the performances—are a source of strength, not weakness.

As *Captain America* reminds us, the mixed platoon is not just a way of seeing race through contrast; it is also a way of seeing race in narration. Other ensembles may emphasize distinctions and grada-tions within a group, but they aren't inevitably drawn into a nation-alist storyline. The platoon, in contrast, is an instrument, largely as-sembled to accomplish a specific goal, indicating our cohesion as a nation in moments of extraordinary stress. We are drawn to watch it in combat precisely because we wish to see whether the unstable partnership of so many diverse bodies can be a productive thing, or if each component of the platoon is equally willing to sacrifice himself for the good of the nation, and for the protection of presumably innocent citizens far from war. As the platoon goes, so goes the nation.

To say this, and to see this, one has to recognize the lengthy political history and visual work of the sightline. The representation of the platoon is merely the latest iteration of a long-standing commentary on equality and democracy in a heterogeneous republic. In 1915, the philosopher Horace M. Kallen worried about the drift toward U.S. involvement in the ongoing Great War and suggested that there was a profound choice to be made between "Democracy" and "the Melting Pot." Entry into the war, Kallen supposed, raised related domestic questions—questions about the very meaning of America— that were perhaps bigger than the distant concerns of European fratricide. In "the Melting Pot" ideal, Kallen found an unwelcome "like-mindedness," and an enthusiasm for compulsory adherence to old-stock, conservative ideals. In the short term, this enforced superpatriotism served the interests of the Anglophile warmongers, silencing dissent and encouraging support for entry on Britain's side. In the long term, though, the effect would be chilling, transforming the majestic variation of America's cultural landscape into a flat, plain plateau. As a consequence, Kallen predicted, the nation would have to continue to "cut-off" the "ancestral memories of our populations," to prescribe English as a national language, and to force-feed narrow-minded patriotism in public education. These actions would do "violence" to the "fundamental law and spirit of our institutions," he stressed, and would weaken "the qualities of our men."[1]

The alluring alternative to the melting pot, he thought, was "harmony," which he supposed was both less wasteful and more attuned to the "spirit" of American political institutions. "Starting with our existing ethnic and cultural groups," he offered, the focus on harmony "would seek to provide conditions under which each may attain the perfection that is proper to its kind." Harmony, for Kallen, revolved around an ideal of racial and ethnic complementarity, "a multiplicity in a unity, an orchestration of mankind." "As in an orchestra," he noted succinctly:

> every type of instrument has its specific timbre and tonality, founded in its substance and form; as every type has its appro-

priate theme and melody in the whole symphony, so in society each ethnic group is the natural instrument, its spirit and culture are its theme and melody, and the harmony and dissonances and discords of them all make the symphony of civilization, with this difference: a musical symphony is written before it is played; in the symphony of civilization the playing is the writing, so that there is nothing so fixed and inevitable about its progressions as in music, so that within the limits set by nature they may vary at will, and the range and variety of the harmonies may become wider and richer and more beautiful.[2]

Such a thing, he admitted, wouldn't merely spring into full flower without a little help. State resources would have to be committed, and aggressive public policies enacted. Mass culture would need to celebrate it, too. The end result would be something new, something radical, and something that looked genuinely different. Choosing democracy over the melting pot, then, meant choosing a pluralist aesthetic for the United States, and committing the nation to what amounted to the strategic deployment of racial and ethnic resources in the midst of a new kind of global war.

As Kallen defined them, the harmonics of the racially pluralist state are at once both utopian and backward. Various bodies and histories, brought together for an open viewing and performance, and willfully arranged out of disciplined sequence, establish difference and positively associate it, too. They firm up a commitment to racial distinction and turn it into the foundation of human society. They provide (or pretend to provide) a true North for a future *with* race and *without* hierarchy. They build and maintain a new cosmopolitan aesthetic, appropriate for a heterogeneous settler society at the center of the world's flows of people, goods, and culture, and entirely consistent with the belief in a clean array of types, bloods, and stocks. Thus, they push in at least two different directions—weighing their randomness against order, against discipline and power, and against the exceptional nation-state, even as they commit, with little hesitancy, to racial difference. But perhaps most significantly, they make a claim for the nation-state as a particular kind of immediately accessible utopia, parallel to the adoptive family, but also quite distinctive from it.

Kallen proposed a well-orchestrated racial and ethnic symphony, progressing toward a common end point, a mixed platoon born of authority and rooted in tactical necessity. An instrumental fantasy woken to real life by the state, or by authority, the symphonic platoon has an aim and a goal. And its success in achieving those aims and goals is utterly dependent on the inner harmonics of the group, on the capacity of all the parts to labor together effectively under great strain, and to achieve spectacular results. And race, not talent, establishes each role.

The significance of harmony in the mixed platoon is clearer when that construct is compared with other racialized group portraits—the random, chaotic assemblage or the well-ordered racial hierarchy. "Hall's Vegetable Sicilian Hair Renewer" was, according to its own early-twentieth-century advertisements, a marvelous product, capable of purging even the most stubborn gray hair, restoring a lush and thick mane where once there was only thin scarcity, and eliminating a host of other embarrassing social maladies. To broadcast this claim, the company produced a bookmark-sized image of five women from around the world, their profiles joined by the branches of delicate flowering trees. America—whose consumer attentions were the desired object of the advertising campaign—sat at the center of the array, surrounded by Japan and Holland on one side and Persia and Spain on the other. Though each woman is dressed in local costume, we are meant to see them as women first and then as women of the same age and social position, sharing a concern with the perpetuation of their fragile beauty. Alone among this group, "dear America" wears no racially, ethnically, or nationally marked clothing or headdress. Her hair—abundant, with slight curls and a reddish-brown color—is unbound. Her costume is a blur. She is a luminous everywoman, presented as white but framed by her beautiful, racially differentiated sisters from around the world. Even within the logic of advertisement, the grouping seems haphazard enough to require explanation. "Of these five attractive faces," reads the seductive doggerel that scrolls along the top and the bottom, "differing widely in their graces—It is needed that we properly explain." "They are grouped," the ad explains, "that you may scan pleasing pictures." Except for the instrumental centering of America, the five faces aren't arranged hierarchically, commonsensically, or in any orderly fashion. Their sequence doesn't correspond to an evolutionary spectrum, and they don't range, as was common, from

A late-nineteenth-century advertisement for Hall's Vegetable Sicilian Hair Renewer, a random, disorderly array, without racial hierarchy but still confirming and establishing race. Warshaw Collection of Business Americana, Series: Hair, Archives Center, National Museum of American History, Smithsonian Institution.

dark to light. They represent a truly diverse, pretty random quintet of nation-states and peoples—their only shared attribute, and the only source of their commonality, is their femininity and their presumed beauty. Randomness, here, is an important detail. It allows the grouping to be read as something both like and unlike a platoon, focusing the eye on commonality and distinction, but it offers no narration of nation or national mission.

Racial orderliness, in contrast, required simplicity and strict hierarchy in all things. When, for instance, Heppenheimer's Lithographers and Printers laid out five faces on a Chinese fan, the surface intent was to show off their skills and recruit new business. It might well have been a disorderly array, except that the sample image—labeled "Professor Darwin"—made this pitch for new business by relying on a prevailing thesis about race and evolution to order the profiles. At the far left edge of the fan, a smiling simian gazes outward, matching the far right edge, where one finds a comely, well-dressed, and impeccably coiffed white man. In between these two presumed extremes, one finds representations of "the Negro," "John Chinaman," and the "Noble Savage." Like the English language, the ensemble is to be read left to right, with the troublesome black visage pressed close to the ape, and the noblest "type" proximate to the white ideal. The overall effect is to reproduce—in five profiles, assembled in a particular sequence—the ascending racial hierarchy supposedly predicted by "Professor Darwin," and opposed by the

A contemporaneous and contrary portrait of race and racism, now in perfect lockstep. Warshaw Collection of Business Americana, Series TT & I, Archives Center, National Museum of American History, Smithsonian Institution.

seemingly chaotic and disorderly comparatively value-free aesthetic of "Ladies of All Nations." An obvious orderliness, in this case, was an expression of a fully conscious white supremacy. Here, too, the emphasis is quite different from that of the platoon, where, at the very least, every member brings respected skills and a commitment to common cause.

Though narratives about disparate, deadly men, brought together as unlikely comrades-in-arms by the needs of the state can be traced back to the romance of Arthurian legend, or even Thucydides, the multiracial platoon's prominence in American cultural life is, like the multiracial adoptive family, also a unique product of the mid-twentieth century imagination. Faced with a multifront war in Europe, Africa, and Asia, and concerned about the ethnic and racial tensions that have often accompanied the expansion of military commitments, the United States sought proactively to make an argument about the role of difference in securing American greatness for the future. It sought, in short, to turn technicolor into a strategic domestic asset.

During the so-called American Century, the bleak portrayal of

The *Magnificent Seven* (1960), all of America, bound together by mission, and determined to protect less fortunate neighbors, their hats and horses and wardrobes capturing their ethnic variety. Reproduction of a promotional lobby card, in author's collection.

the violent territories beyond the pale provided ample justification for the deployment of dangerous types abroad. For the Hollywood studios, though, the platoon was also offered up as proof of idealistic concept, revealing an American ensemble that was productively, even healthily fractured along racial lines. In John Sturges's *The Magnificent Seven* (1960), a besieged Mexican peasant town appeals to a ragtag group of American mercenaries, including a Mexican Irish "half breed" and a young hothead named "Chico," who come together and accept paternal responsibility for their brown-skinned, indigenous charges. In *The Dirty Dozen* (1967), a strange collection of military misfits, most of them destined for the gallows, are drawn together by the army in pursuit of a single strategic objective. "The Hollywood platoon," Richard Slotkin reminds us, was a "utopian projection," a fantasy of an achievable ideal nation, "that we should and could become through the testing and transformation of war."[3] Like the bildungsroman, this postwar platoon was a narrative device meant to be seen in progress, moving toward the realization of an ideal.

Such films, Slotkin continues, made "the realization of the 'melting pot' values at home the symbolic equivalent of a war aim."[4] But the point, generally, wasn't *melting* at all. Instead, these narratives were meant to call attention to race's fixed surface qualities and link them to skills and behaviors, not to dismiss or destabilize race, and to ask the viewer to "see" such differences as both enduring and instrumental. Indeed, as studio productions, novels and comic books and movies and television shows had to make race visible in order for the formula to work. So if these artifacts of the Cold War provide a vision of "mythic" foreign policy imperatives—stressing the values of modernization, liberty, and even diversity—they are also, on a much deeper level, a guide to quite literally envisioning a more polyglot nation and world.

Along these lines, the 1987 Cold War film *Predator* quite consciously mixes an imperial landscape with a pluralist sightline. Set exclusively in a nameless Central American jungle and during a particularly long, hot summer, the storyline revolves around a small group of special forces men who have been sent on a mission by the U.S. government but who end up engaging a sojourning alien hunter who stalks them for sport and who takes skulls for trophies. Overmatched, the members of the platoon are slowly and dramatically picked off by the alien, until one man (played by Arnold Schwarzenegger) remains. It is left to him to kill the alien in one-on-one combat, which he does—in a protracted battle that flattens the jungle. The film was generally derided as a formulaic action piece, loud and booming, and without character development or plot. It seemed like a campy derivative of other high-minded films with similar subjects—for instance, Ridley Scott's 1979 classic, *Alien*. And it was politically backward, stressing the importance of men—and of men-being-men—to the national interest. Dismissing its cinematic contributions but noting its historical weight, one could list it as one of the most thoroughly sexist works of American filmmaking, a remarkable feat for a forgettable film produced in an age renowned for its macho action heroes—and the backlash against feminism—and its dumb blockbuster movies.[5]

The predictability of *Predator* makes it easier for us to understand the way that race works in the film. Because the film so heavily underlines the diversity of the platoon and boldfaces their group harmonics, we are afforded an opportunity to see the racial array at work in different contexts, with different results. Despite its meaty formulaic qualities, *Predator* isn't, I believe, just another ham-fisted, clichéd celebration of the masculine platoon; indeed, it is the capstone of the platoon genre, and the very best expression of an oft-idealized way to see race in American culture.

Dutch and his men. From *Predator*, dir. John McTiernan (Amerecent, 1987).

There are seven men in this extraordinary team. Hawkins is a geeky, bespectacled, communications man, eager to make jokes and to laugh. Blain is a serious, drawling, tobacco-juice-spitting hulk who carries an M134 minigun (nicknamed "Old Painless") and wears a cowboy hat ringed with snakeskin. The former is quick-witted and street smart, and the latter is a barroom brawler—familiar regional and ethnic archetypes, sitting at opposite ends of whiteness. Ramirez, lean and tanned, speaks Spanish and slickly handles a grenade launcher. Mac, very dark skinned and southern, repeatedly shaves with a dry razor as if were a nervous habit and seems too tightly wound, speaking in half whispers and staring into the middle space with sunken eyes. Dillon, a contrasting figure, is the smooth-talking government man, a light-skinned African American, higher up the chain of command, and capable of complexity, contradiction, and cover-ups. We know from his headband, his long, dark hair, and his medicine bag that Billy, a conglomeration of stereotype, is an Indian ripped right from *The Lone Ranger*, but in the context of this cohort of overdrawn racial representations, we need an even stronger set of clues. And so he is also an expert tracker who prefers to fight with a knife and is thick-witted and unable to grasp American humor. Finally, to lead them all, there is Dutch, with his bronzed and bulging biceps, his cigar, and his incomparably thick Eastern European accent, marking him as an immigrant through and through. As the opening credits roll, we see each man arrive at his point of departure in street clothes and in his own vehicle, before suiting up in military garb, a stylized introduction that serves not merely to elaborate their racial identities but also to show, without exposition, the coming together of the platoon.

The narrative of the film moves this mixed and matched septet—loudly echoing Akira Kurosawa's 1954 classic *Seven Samurai* and Sturges's *Magnificent Seven*—through the dense canopy of some troublesome banana republic in a three-act melodrama. In the first act, the team's precisely tuned harmonics are perfectly displayed and, indeed, utterly dominating. Having been brought in under the cover of night, we watch as they glide through the jungle in search of a paramilitary camp where hostages are rumored to have been held. Swiftly and silently, they crawl, creep, hustle to the depot, a near-silent passage that is meant to impress, and to convey both their familiarity with each other and their capacity to work symphonically. Once they find their Central American counterparts, that same familiarity and capacity is spotlighted once again. In the ensuing battle, the polyglot American unit, relying on the clockwork synchronization of their ethnic and racial differences, easily massacres their mestizo opposition. When the battle is done, the depot is a smoldering ruin and Dutch's platoon files out triumphantly, with every part having done his bit.

As they leave, though, the second act begins. High up in the trees, something has decided to hunt them. We see through its eyes and watch them from up above. Only Billy, the native uniquely attuned to the ways of nature, senses that something is amiss. For a long while, he stands in the midst of swirling smoke and stares upward. Then, uncertain, he turns and rejoins his comrades.

While the creature systematically tracks and kills off the team, there are moments where the complementarity of the men is presented with astonishing clarity. When Blain is killed, Mac charges up and retrieves the minigun and the men form a single line—a literal array, in this instance—and empty their tailored weaponry into the verdant background. Blain and Hawkins are taken, Dutch decides to set a trap, and the men work together using the materials provided by the jungle. In one shot, notable for its simultaneous emphasis on unity, difference, and harmony, all five remaining soldiers stand close, their long arms extended as they attempt to draw down the top of a tree for a spring-loaded trap. In a reversal of Joe Rosenthal's

Pulitzer Prize–winning photograph of the raising of the American flag on Iwo Jima during World War II, the viewer is close enough—and the men are stripped down enough and in color—so that the eye can focus on tone and shade, and find race on display.

Their collective efforts to catch and kill the alien fail dramatically, though, and within minutes what remains of the platoon is racing in retreat, attempting to make it to a pick-up zone. Mac and Dillon, antagonistic to each other and representing diverging notions of blackness, set aside their dislike for each other to attempt a kill, but fail. Billy, appointed the noble savage drawing up the rear of the retreat, chooses to wait in the middle of a fallen tree trunk spanning a vast chasm, hoping to stall the creature and ensure the escape of Dutch, a severely wounded Ramirez, and a local woman, captured earlier in the film. Stripping away his vest, Billy clutches his medicine bag in his hand, discards his rifle, and draws a long knife. Always the white man's Indian, he uses the tip of his knife to draw blood from his chest in a long arc, a tribal ritual, we are meant to presume. Before he dies in hand-to-hand combat with the "predator" of the film's title, we see Billy through the alien's eyes, the rainbow silhouette of a grown man crouched like a young brave. His deep, manful death cry can be heard across the landscape, signaling the end of the platoon.

Billy and Mac and Dillon are critically important racial referents, defining the complicated representational landscape for the viewer. Mac's homosocial loyalty to Blain and his blind obedience to Dutch make him a variant of the "faithful slave," dutifully attending to the needs of his white charges. Billy, like Mac, adds an old Western feel to the film, echoing the Lone Ranger's monosyllabic sidekick, Tonto, always there to help his white friend. These defiantly old-school portraits of black and Indian characters would be seen as more troublesome if the platoon in question wasn't military, and if the racial structure of the unit wasn't so thoroughly subsumed by its organizational structure. In the logic of the film, Dutch isn't in charge because he is white; he is in charge because he is the biggest bad-ass in the group, and the purportedly color-blind military rewards bad-asses with leadership positions. Likewise, because Dutch and Dillon are equals—and, as brothers-in-arms, have shared the field of combat once before—we are presented with the possibility that, had circumstances been different, it might be Dillon leading the platoon and Dutch playing the role of CIA spook. When the two men clasp

Dutch and Dillon, skin on skin. From *Predator*, dir. John McTiernan (Amerecent, 1987).

hands early in the film, their sweaty biceps taut, their handshake prolonged so that the camera might linger over it, we are meant to see black and white as equally in charge and manly to the exact same degree, though not to the same effect. Dillon's addition to the platoon thus further destabilizes any strict racial hierarchy (plate 6).

Dutch's challenge to the creature (in a short third act) builds on the film's gradual rejection of modern weapons and the embrace of primal manhood. The platoon is gone. It is clear that machine guns have failed, as have the sorts of primitive traps once set by the Viet-cong. Even Billy's native mysticism—lower on this bizarre evolutionary scale, it seems, than the punji stakes of Southeast Asia—hasn't stopped the predator. To win and to live, Dutch breaks down all of his weapons, strips away most of his clothing, and fashions a crude set of booby traps, along with spears and bows and arrows. Smearing himself with mud so that he will be invisible to the creature, Dutch's low-tech assault works. He wins, and, as a consequence, he lives.

Like Captain America, Dutch's inherent superiority emerges only when he is released from the platoon. When he is a part of a team, every part works together harmonically. But when the platoon is in ruins, or left behind, the last component is typically the strongest. If we needed further confirmation of the dynamic tension between white supremacy and the multiracial platoon, we can find it, then, in Dutch's survival, deep in the jungle, after the loss of his mates. The white guy lives, again. But in this case, the film's lesson about the value of whiteness is hidden, literally, by the light-brown mud that Dutch applies to his skin to stay invisible.

In movies like *Predator*, the nation holds the platoon together, gives it gravity and density. These men are there, in the steamy jungle, to protect the national interest. Sequels to the original feature a different polyglot band of protagonists, but they fail to hang together. *Predator 2*, released to much fanfare in 1987, transports the story to the crumbling, gang-riddled urban jungle of Los Angeles and offers up the standard mix of heroic bodies. We get a grizzled black veteran, his two flashy Latino partners, and the young white hotshot desperate to join the group. But we also have the lumbering, deeply politicized bureaucracy of the LAPD, as well as an unwanted federal intrusion—a team of military scientists hoping to catch the alien. These disparate groups of people are scattered across the vast, deteriorating city, divided by interest and motive, and generally disunited. The core group of police detectives rarely shares the screen. The film, quite simply, fails to keep the platoon in focus, refusing to let us see their dissimilar bodies in close proximity. As a consequence, the central function of the film is lost, and the narrative feels incoherent.

Sometimes, though, visual diversity can be confirmed, even as the platoon plotline is challenged. In the 2010 sequel, *Predators*, a random assortment of dangerous types are cherry-picked by the aliens for a hunting game and removed to a foreign planet. But, here, too, their randomness pits them against each other, making the ensemble less coherent, less unified. Diversity is merely cosmetic, and it can't be seen through the same nationalist or imperialist sightline. We aren't presented with anything quite like the first act of *Predator*, where the multicultural team reveals its well-grooved synchronicity against a larger squad of racially homogenous foes. Instead, the film literally begins with their descent, via parachute, from the sky. Admittedly, they are quite an international crew, composed of yakuza enforcers, Russian military muscle, African paramilitary men, prisoners, serial killers, a woman sharpshooter from the Israeli Defense Force, and one well-traveled mercenary. But, lacking a common raison d'être, they fight and bicker ceaselessly, keep secrets, and scheme for their individual fortune. They share no tactics and strategy. They have no history together. And no destiny, either. They share only their racial and national markings, rendered in brighter relief by the color-saturated jungle backdrop and the bright alien sky.

The variegated platoon redux: the 2010 film *Predators* repeats the plot of the first film and the racially diverse ensemble, but without any link to the nation, the platoon falls apart. From author's collection.

Despite the lesson of *Predators*—that without the nation-state, the platoons of the future may fall apart—there is still ample reason to believe that the platoon sightline will endure. Platoon narratives are enormously popular, if only because of their explicit optimism. It was, for instance, in the context of the 1970s, a politically interesting move to assemble a crew of Russians, Scots, African Americans, and Asians and set them peaceably adrift in space, and to imagine a utopian future where the old divisions had been successfully bridged. Viewers of the original television show *Star Trek* could tune in each week to see a hopeful conception of the future, where the blood and fire of riots and war had been reconceived as old history, replaced by teamwork in the service of the common good. Like many, the platoon aboard the starship *Enterprise*—a name that suggests a direct link to American military might—is united by a power larger than itself, namely an interplanetary federation that seems deliberately modeled on the United Nations. In the show, and the many subsequent spin-offs and movies, life aboard the *Enterprise* is presented as an expanded version of life in the military, set on the "new" frontier, with little concern for wages, no real emphasis on party politics, silence about class struggle, and a lot of drama about dangerous adventures and military engagements. In this future, race seems a mere aftereffect of old, long-forgotten divisions.

There is no discussion of race in the Star Trek universe, though at times speciation—or the distinction between different populations of aliens and humans—is a futuristic metaphor for the problems of the late twentieth and early twenty-first centuries. The ship's crew, though, is a fabulously diverse construct of the American Century, reflecting the desire of the producers to make a statement about the long-term legacies of the civil rights movement and the peace movement on civil society. Centuries may have passed, but the ship's lone Scotsman, nicknamed "Scotty," still sounds like he hails from Linthlingow. Lieutenant Uhuru, encountering another "black" crew member—black, that is, by the standards of 1968, not 2266—begins a conversation with him in Swahili; her name, in that language, means "freedom." Helmsman Pavel Chekov speaks with a deliciously and unmistakably thick Russian accent. The dashing Hikaru Sulu was meant, George Takai once recalled, to stand for all of Asia, but, to judge from fan commentary, most assume he is Japanese. And the captain of the *Enterprise*, James T. Kirk, an Iowa-born symbol of all that was presumed to be good and right with white America, is perhaps one of the most self-possessed and supremely confident white authority figures ever created for television or the silver screen. Every member of the crew corresponds to the pluralist ideal, in which racial and ethnic differences are both discrete and solid, and useful if deployed in just the right manner. Despite the postracial premise of the franchise, race is still offered up as an object for visual scrutiny. And every sequel, prequel, and alternative timeline in the *Star Trek* chronology has featured a version of this racially and ethnically diverse platoon.

The comfort drawn from the racially familiar, and repeated over and over again, is precisely the point of the platoon. With a hypnotic ability to draw attention and generate enthusiasm, platoons make it possible to see other things. Or more precisely, they make it possible to see the thing that matters. In highlighting the social function of the happily united and seemingly random spectrum of colors, they call attention to those moments when such unprescribed diversity isn't

The crew of the starship *Enterprise*, offering a vision of the platoon of the future, now in the service of a larger "Federation."

present. By limiting the social context for these platoons to military expeditions, real or metaphorical, they suggest that extraordinary measures are needed to create a more level racial playing field. By offering a white authority figure within a chain of command that is never questioned, they not only reproduce a racial hierarchy but also deracinate his authority, offering it up as mere happenstance, having his comrades celebrate it, and justifying it, in the end, through the ennobling narrative of success in combat. If the white mother is the logical leader of the adoptive family, the white man is the anointed head of the platoon. And in offering the platoon and other such ensembles as an ideal expression of the national family, of brotherhood in national service, they inflect all other such expressions as slightly perverse, or wrong. The best of all possibilities, they explicitly argue through their arrangement, is for the diverse peoples of the nation to come together in harmony and with purpose. When seen in contrast to the mixed platoon, other assemblages seem retrograde, or naive, or less heroic, and that is exactly the point. Looming in the background as a mythic representation of the broad and sundry peoples that make up the nation of immigrants, such ensembles also make it possible to see any unmixed pairings, black or white bodies standing alone and without complement, as backward and even racist. We learn, in short, to look for platoons, to note their absence, and to wonder, or hope, for their return.

PART III

Multiple Exposures
The Evidence of Things Not Easily Seen

> Elaine: "Well, what do you think?"
> Jerry: "What? About you dating a black guy?
>   What's the big deal?"
> Elaine: "What black guy?"
> Jerry: "Darryl. He's black, isn't he?"
> Elaine: "He is?"
> George: "No, he isn't."
> Jerry: "Isn't he, Elaine?"
> Elaine: "You think?"
> George: "I thought he looked Irish."
> Jerry: "What's his last name?"
> Elaine: "Nelson."
> George: "That's not Irish."
> Jerry: "I think he's black."
> George: "Should we be talking about this?"
>
> FROM "THE WIZARD," EPISODE 15, SEASON 9, *SEINFELD* (1996)

Sometimes, race can be very difficult to see. In "The Wizard," an episode of *Seinfeld*, and a subtle send-up of white discomfort around racial ambiguity, Elaine Benes and her new boyfriend, Darryl, both suspect that the other person is nonwhite, and they script their relationship around this presumption, but they refuse to discuss it out loud. Elaine suspects—but cannot confirm, despite her efforts to divine the truth—that Darryl is black; and Darryl suspects—but dares not ask her to verify—that Elaine is Hispanic. Independently, each is titillated by the idea of an interracial relationship. And that titillation is only enhanced by the mystery of the racial body. In the end, though, when they realize that they are "just a couple of white people," they decide to go to the Gap, a signifier in their time and place for the all-absorbing banality of whiteness.

Sometimes, when it is hard to see, race is assumed to be more complicated than a single category, or more complicated still than a mere binary or the dyad of "black" and "white." The assumption is that what is hidden, or masked, is complex, richer than a single category. There are sightlines through which to visualize the racially complicated body, but they work differently than the others described in this book. They still labor to produce racial sight, but they provide little, if any, simple clarity about what is being seen. They train the eye to focus on things not easily seen.

These unique sightlines are not merely a feature of the recent past. In the 1920s, novelist Jean Toomer, the product of a light-skinned, "mulatto" elite, once described himself as the "first self-conscious member of the American race." Tracing his lineage back to a wide range of racial "stocks" and "bloods," he labored to create a space outside of the white/black dyad, the reigning conception of race, that sifted and sorted the great bulk of Americans into one of these two antipodal categories. In this new space, his complex racial history would go unchallenged, his myriad bloods and histories allowed to come together in productive, even complementary tension.

But in *Cane*, his first novel, Toomer had "featured" the "Negro," part of himself, adding an emphasis that subsequently led the press to name him a "New Negro" author. An emergent civil rights initiative, hoping to beat back racial prejudice with artistic achievement, seized upon his success as evidence of progress, offered him up as the very first "Negro" novelist. And Toomer's metaphorically dense prose and his cryptic interviews made it easy for people to misread, misunderstand, or willfully disregard his self-conception, in which it was possible to be white, black, and much more. He was unable to get anyone to understand that he was not *just* a "Negro," and that his prose drew strength, situationally, not from the "one drop" of black blood but from the racial complexity that flowed within his veins. He

Winold Reiss's portrait of Jean Toomer, c. 1925. National Portrait Gallery, Smithsonian Institution/Art Resource, N.Y.

spent years trying to explain his position, and struggling to be heard by readers and publicists and fellow artists, and failing to write a second novel, before eventually giving up, moving away, and leaving his past behind.

In his contemporary portrait of the man, Winold Reiss set out to capture Jean Toomer in all of his ambiguity and complexity. A German immigrant and portraitist, Reiss had been commissioned by Alain Locke to capture the essence of the New Negro for the special issue of the *Survey Graphic*, and then to expand on his survey of "representative" men and women for Locke's canon-defining collection, *The New Negro*, first published in 1925. In an age renowned for racial caricature, on the one hand, and for sentimental portraits of the mulatto elite, on the other, Reiss's portrait is jarring, largely because it strives to closely correspond to Toomer's self-description. In a work that is rather unlike any of the other images he produced, Reiss gave Toomer wavy hair, a prominent high forehead, and a serious "English" nose. His head is tilted down, and he is slyly smiling, as if he were a man with a secret. He is framed by a faint aura, suggesting a kind of dynamism and electricity, hinting at the hybrid racial qualities of the portrait's subject, at his capacity for change and composition.

Some have noted that Reiss's paintings reflected a shift away from "types" of "the Negro" and toward a "representative" sampling. But his representation of Jean Toomer is uniquely confusing; it is entirely unclear what, exactly, Toomer "represented" to Reiss. For this reason, this famous image of the brooding, mystical author is often deployed as silent visual testimony, as if the brushstrokes laid down by Reiss all those years ago can reveal the details of Jean Toomer's racial complex self, and as if the author's later intent to "pass," can be found in the illustration of the physical.

In this last section of the book, I bring into the light a series of sightlines that challenge the eye. Some things, like the instrumentality of Jean Toomer's interior mixture, are hard to see, but knowledge of them persists, and evidence is produced for anyone to see. We can't easily discern the proper outlines or details. But we know, like Elaine Benes, that there is something to see, if only we bear down and focus as best we can on the blurry, or often multiply exposed, outlines. Indeed, the eye craves verification. So the more elusive the object, the more interesting it becomes.

CHAPTER SIX

Hybridity

The hybrid body, as Jean Toomer imagined it, is a racial ensemble, or platoon, in miniature, not easily categorized as a "mulatto" or "mestizo." With its component features easily viewable, discrete, and engaged productively, this body is an anachronism, out of sync with national time and space, but a useful one, serving as a vehicle for conversations about the new world that is, in these representations, on the verge. It focuses our attention on the steely body—typically but not exclusively male—capable of toggling back and forth between one racial position and another. Born of a disharmonious blending, the racial expressions of this complicated figure sharpen the color lines within the body, allowing for parallel readings.

In our conceptions of these supposedly heroic mixed peoples, we historically set aside the white/black dyad, shaped by the one-drop rule and theories of hypodescent, in favor of mixture with the native, the indigenous, and the Asian. Hybridity and blackness are not easily related in racial sight. As a consequence, these figures are often understood positively, as fetishized attractions and not merely as objects of fear. These oversized archetypes of masculinity and mixture beg us to attend to the swirling, minute details on the surface, details that suggest the dynamic tension between the unmixed bloods beneath the skin. Overwhelmingly featured in visual media and often staged heroically, these hypermasculine bodies are, in the end, just as often suffused with a powerful melancholy and loneliness. As living indicators of some great and immediate transformation, they are offered as evidence of the simultaneity of racial problems *and* proof of racial solutions.

In his classic exposé of whiteness in visual culture, *White*, Richard Dyer suggests that "muscle heroes are not indigenous." Tarzan, he continues, is "not of the jungle."[1] John Rambo, though of mixed parentage, is an "ideal"—one of several a "tanned white male bodies" from Reagan-era muscle movies, "set in colonialist relation" and geared toward the construction of "the white man as physically superior . . . built to do the job of colonial world improvement."[2] For Dyer, the "tanned" white body is not a marker of hybridity but a sign of "everyman" status or class position. "The muscle hero is an everyman: his tan bespeaks his right to intervene anywhere."[3]

Dyer lumps when he could also split, for some of these figures are intentionally conceived as indigenous, while others are not. In some cases, that tawny skin stands not as a physical "tell" of the everyman but as a feature of the supposed native—either out of place or in place, either whole or hybrid. In Rambo, Tarzan, and others, we see an interest in the external and internal character of the racially mixed body, and of the white body relocated to racially foreign territory, and transformed as a consequence. Reimagined in this way, the racially hybrid hero is a fixture of the modern American landscape. He is self-consciously "hybrid," a consequence of one generation's simple mixture of two different "strains." We know him by a single name: Hawkeye, Tarzan, Rambo. Capable of extraordinary violence— which is to say, more violence than his unadulterated match—he is a creature of borderlands, of foreign territories, and of peripheries. His partial whiteness is what allows him to serve as an object of romantic desire and public fascination. His status as an indigene is the wellspring of his violent tendencies. His survival—and success, by his measure—in territories that would otherwise be inhospitable to the ordinary and the pure is balanced with his inability to exist within the pale. His role and location are determined by a variety of possibilities, from adoption to birth to tragic circumstance. In the visual economy of race, the hybrid hero does not merely mark the limits of whiteness or the cutting edge of domination. Having "gone native," he is an uneasy, incomplete metaphor—his body's racial components working together—best seen against the backdrop of empire's cutting edge.

European settlers and their descendants have long adored Indian blood in small amounts, routinely claiming an Indian grandparent or great-grandparent. Laws governing racially mixed marriages famously included exceptions for those who were distantly related to Pocahontas—exceptions that were entirely absent from the emerging "one-drop rule" governing white/black relations. As significantly,

PLATE 1 Artist Winold Reiss's 1925 portrait of a young Langston Hughes, National Portrait Gallery, Smithsonian Institution/Art Resource, N.Y.

PLATE 2 A pedestrian walks in front of an Apple billboard featuring a diverse range of silhouettes. The contrasting colored backdrops call attention to the racial details of the stark black profiles. Justin Sullivan/Getty Images.

PLATE 3 Benetton's racial checkerboard, with every face meant to be a distinctive type. From the "Beige and White" catalog, c. 1990, in author's collection.

PLATE 4 Juxtapositions, either in a larger ensemble or in a simple pairing, are a common means of establishing racial difference. Here, in a Fairy Soap advertisement, white and black scrutinize each other, searching for racial details, even as we are meant to see them as a pair. Warshaw Collection of Business Americana, Series: Soap, Archives Center, National Museum of American History, Smithsonian Institution.

PLATE 5 Kate Kretz, *Blessed Art Thou* (2006), 88x60 inches, oil and acrylic on linen. Used here with the permission of the artist.

PLATE 6 Here, in a scene from *Predator*, Dutch and Billy, the white leader and his mystic Indian sidekick, stand together like the Lone Ranger and Tonto removed to a Central American jungle. The costuming, makeup, and hair all accentuate the discriminating details. From *Predator*, dir. John Mc-Tiernan (Amerecent, 1987).

PLATE 7 "Two performers in blackface, facing each other, one in tuxedo, other in suit," c. 1899. Two stock minstrel characters, offering a slight contrast of class while reinforcing racial sameness. Courier Lithography Company, Buffalo, N.Y., Library of Congress, Prints and Photographs Division.

PLATE 8 "Take a good look at this woman," the scrawl reads, encouraging a close reading of her face; "she was created by a computer." In truth, though, she wasn't. With brown eyes and light-brown skin, she was imagined by renowned graphic artist Milton Glaser, conceived through software created by engineer Kim Wah Lam, a composite of hundreds of photographs taken by Ted Thai. A chorus line of willing employees in the Time Life building provided the visual DNA. The design team selected a handful of idealized "types," borrowed features from them, and assembled the image by cutting the features out and stitching them together. The near future in digital flesh, "she" stood without clothes, with a slight smile and a direct gaze, and looked right into the eyes of the present tense. The "New Face of America," from *Time*, November 18, 1993, © 1993, Time Inc. Used under license.

PLATE 9 A racially hybrid subject—a descendant of the mutineers of the H.M.S. *Bounty* still living on Pitcairn Island—marked for the viewer's gaze. "One of many islanders," the *National Geographic* noted, "is Ailsa Young. At 15 years she wears the flower and soft good looks of her Tahitian ancestors. Few Pitcairners look so strongly Polynesian; most resemble their English forefathers. They speak an accented English, mixed with some Tahitian words and phrases. The younger generation, having a New Zealand schoolmaster, is losing the island way of speech" ("I Found the Bones of the *Bounty,*" *National Geographic*, December 1957). Luis Marden/National Geographic/Getty Images.

PLATE 10 From the promotional poster and DVD cover of *The Human Stain*. With the racially "mixed" Wentworth Miller absent from the image, the visage of Anthony Hopkins was noticeably darkened, blackened up to stand in contrast to the pale skin of Nicole Kidman. From author's collection.

Hawkeye, or Natty Bumpo, his head bowed in solidarity with his Mohican comrade. From James Fenimore Cooper, *The Last of the Mohicans*, illustrated by Frank T. Merrill (New York: Thomas N. Crowell and Co., 1896), p. 420.

these hybrid figures—estranged from their reservations or from their tribe—are allowed an unusual degree of psychological complexity. Billy Jack, the self-appointed guardian for a peace-loving, multicultural freedom school, is capable of awesome, violent outrage. Ray Levoi, played by Val Kilmer in *Thunderheart* (1992), rediscovers his partial Indianness only after suffering through a traumatic series of visions. Frank T. Hopkins in *Hidalgo* (2005), played by Viggo Mortensen, affirms his commitment to his tribe after being stranded in the desert, where he has visions of the Ghost Dance in the midst of an Arabian horse race.

Like Hopkins, John Rambo hears voices and has visions, though his are proof of trauma, not evidence of spirit. As portrayed by

Promotional poster for *Thunderheart*. From author's collection.

Sylvester Stallone in four films released between 1982 and 2008 John Rambo is a Vietnam War veteran with some form of post-traumatic stress disorder, a consequence, in part, of his military service. His origin story, abstracted, is that of a tragic man without a place, a soulful wanderer with an extraordinary collection of skills, who is routinely placed in situations where he must stand up for "the little guy." The Indian "side" of John Rambo contributes spiritualism and overwhelming physicality, while the "white" side provides intellect and strategy. Only Rambo's divinely perfect, tawny body, then, holds everything together. Rambo is not autochthonous (at least, not in Washington, Vietnam, Afghanistan, and Burma), but he is still an indigene (or, rather, the glib representation of one), a Native American, at least by blood quantum, and a running stereotype, filled with sadness and estrangement, one with the earth and nature, and, it often seems, destined for wandering. He is routinely relocated by the nation-state, his nominal parent, making him a metaphor for the soldier's life and for Indian removal. Each film makes use of color and background texture to emphasize Rambo's racially complicated physiognomy.

In *First Blood* (1982) and the two sequels that quickly followed, Rambo has been generally understood as an expression of the long-standing obsession with white male heroes. This is Dyer's point, too. Such an interpretation relies on the idea that tanned skin is the only marker that matters, and that it can often stand in for working-class status. Far fewer scholars have taken the "Navaho" side of Rambo's

Rambo in flight, the cowboys in chase. From *First Blood*, dir. Ted Kotcheff (Ababasis N.V., 1982).

character as a subject of serious scrutiny, though his character conforms, to a striking degree, to very common and familiar ideas about "the noble savage." This elision makes little sense. As Susan Jeffords once explained it, John Rambo is the nation-state famously condensed into a single, irrepressible "hard body." Setting this national ideal within the context of Ronald Reagan's ascendancy, Jeffords was able to illuminate the role of Hollywood in the re-masculinization of American political culture after Vietnam. In *First Blood*, she reminds us, Rambo was a wandering relic of a bygone age of American military might: a battle-scarred Vietnam veteran.

And yet Rambo is also a distinctive, unique racial character. The prevailing representations of the war veteran in the late 1970s and early 1980s surely stressed the psychic impact of the conflict, including the notion of a durable trauma that persisted even after the return to the home front. But they also emphasized the broken and battered bodies of former servicemen, their addiction to pain-killing drugs and hallucinogens, and their general status as unwanted, dangerous, and deteriorating ex-soldiers. Steven in the 1978 film *The Deer Hunter* has lost both of his legs in the war. The same is true of Lieutenant Dan in *Forrest Gump* (both the 1986 novel by Winston Groom and the 1994 film). Both men are shattered, inside and out. John Rambo shares some of these traits—he has nightmarish dreams, and he wanders—but his physical body is immaculate, without flaw of any kind. Indeed, it is superhuman. His dreams and his wanderlust can be partly tracked to his Indian blood, even if it seems certain his experience in Vietnam was hellish. And so, too, can his vigor and strength. Rambo, a recognizably hybrid body, is not your typical veteran.

It is worth returning to *First Blood* again. Entering idyllic Hope, Washington, a small town filled with soft, pasty white men, he is first turned away and then beaten by local cops before fighting back and then fleeing into the wilderness, where his jungle training supposedly gives him an advantage over his growing army of pursuers. Then, confusing the dense evergreen of the Pacific Northwest with the tropical Southeast Asian canopy of Vietnam, Rambo systematically kills or grievously wounds everyone who tracks him, turning the forest canopy into a weapon. *First Blood*, Jeffords argues, is a narrative of "national deterioration," a narrative that critiques the failure of the nation-state "to produce more bodies" like that of John Rambo.[4] Viewed in this way, *First Blood* laid the groundwork for the later Rambo movies, with their far more explicit sanction of Reagan-era machismo, and their enthusiasm for the durability and global utility of these rare, dangerous hard bodies.

Sight and misrecognition are important parts of *First Blood*. From the very start of the film, Rambo's body cannot be read properly. When he first enters the town, his long, dark hair, casual duffel bag, and unshaven appearance mark him as different. The men in this small town—representatives of the post-Vietnam malaise—have not seen "hard bodies," and thus cannot fathom their purpose or origin. His physical form is an object of study, an ancient text not easily deciphered. But when he flees into the wilderness, his body becomes invisible, fading into the mottled dark brown and green of the woods. Those who hunt Rambo, Jeffords concludes, "cannot recognize his body when they see it because . . . they are not used to seeing men like him anymore." Viewers were supposed to leave the theater wanting more indecipherable, hard bodies. "The true success

Rambo and the sheriff, or, the primitive man and his Western opposite. From *First Blood*, dir. Ted Kotcheff (Ababasis N.V., 1982).

of *First Blood*," Jeffords continues, "is to have created the desire in citizens/audiences to see more bodies like Rambo's."[5]

For Jeffords, this is a problem of gender: Rambo looks odd, or distinctive, because he represents an older conception of manliness, long lost but newly returned. But one could also say that his look—his racial profile, if you will—is too enigmatic at the start of the movie. Rambo's nature is entirely unclear at first. Only after breaking out of jail, and after his cowboys-and-Indians chase through downtown Hope, is Rambo's supposedly natural self revealed. After recklessly making his way toward a mist-shrouded mountain on the back of a motorcycle, he completes his ascent on foot. Along the way, he stops to create a canvas poncho, tied around the waist with a piece of twine, and to tear off a piece of it for a headband. Armed with his knife, and scaling a granite cliff-face alongside a waterfall, he is a meme for a thousand Westerns, resembling nothing so much as the proverbial buckskin brave, chased, of course, by white men wearing cowboy hats. While they march stolidly along, Rambo runs and leaps, seeming balletic and almost joyful in the woods. As they stalk him for the rest of the day, he fades into the scenery, his body indistinguishable from the natural tapestry. And he gets darker, too. And at one critical moment, he erupts from the bush, blackened with earth, and holds his knife against the pale throat of the sheriff, played by Brian Dennehy, whose whiteness is illuminated by a flash of lightning. These scenes are less an expression of otherworldly manliness, as Jeffords contends, than they are a classic fantasy of the savage Indian. Stallone's body—the faux buckskin and headband, the use of primitive weapons, the limbs now tawny with dirt and blood, eyes dark and mysterious, his mouth closed, his jaw set—is a signpost for viewers. In the mountains, John Rambo is an Indian. And Stallone, the actor, is in temporary, or situational, redface. "There's something about nature as part of him," Stallone notes, "something about the primitive man, he's almost an Indian."[6] We should linger, when watching these films, on that word "almost."

As a half-breed, John Rambo is capable of willfully toggling back and forth across the color line, a practice marked by carefully placed visual cues. When he descends the mountain to seek revenge, for instance, he re-appropriates his whiteness. One moment, he is dirty and savage, huddling over a fire and cooking a wild animal on a homemade spit, and the next he is cleaned up, relatively fresh-faced, has discarded buckskin for an olive-green army tank top, and is driving a stolen vehicle into Hope. He emerges from the truck carrying a massive machine gun and wearing a gleaming bandolier of brass bullets, having set aside his rudimentary bow and arrow. In short, he has been repackaged as the whitened master of the technologies created by the military-industrial complex. In these latter scenes, delivering devastation on a massive, "civilized" scale, Rambo is a much clearer example of the critique envisioned by Jeffords. Here he is a cinematic justification for the Reagan-era buildup, and for the replacement of old, soft bodies.

The various sequels play up this same racialized back and forth. One minute, John Rambo is buried in the mud, armed with nothing but his knife. And the next minute, he is dispatching an armed helicopter with a surface-to-air missile. Often shirtless and always with his headband, his bow and arrow, his chosen weapons, are ubiquitous, no matter who or where he fights. "Of Indian-German combination," as a narrator reminds us in *Rambo II* (1985). "That's a hell of a combination."

Building on these earlier films, the most recent *Rambo* is, in many ways, a return to the classic captivity narrative, in which the civilized settler or missionary was held captive by savage natives. Now removed to the edge of Burma, and no longer haunted by dreams of the war, John Rambo makes his living as a snake-handler and guide on the river. Enlisted to shuttle a handful of earnest white missionaries upriver into Burma, he must later rescue them from their own folly when they are captured by a cruel paramilitary army and imprisoned in a bamboo fortress deep within the jungle. At first, Rambo merely serves as the faithful, stone-faced Indian tracker in the service of the polyglot platoon of mercenaries sent out on a rescue mission. As the quintessential noble savage, he offers cryptic moral instruction and speaks very rarely.

From the very first scene of the movie, though, John Rambo is wound tight, waiting for action. When the missionaries arrive, he debates their purpose, challenging their notion of how to fight evil. Unconvinced, Sara, the white missionary draped in ivory, bestows upon him a wooden cross, which he wraps around his hand. When he learns of her capture, Rambo takes the time to make a knife: specifically, he works a piece of steel and beats it, over an anvil, into an enormous, brutal-looking machete, very much like Billy's knife in *Predator*. He seems to know, intuitively, that there will be a single man responsible for the abduction, and that this man should die a terrible death. During his rescue, his pursuit of the Burmese militia is relentless, and the death toll is extraordinary. At each step, Rambo inhabits nearly every known visual stereotype about the Indian: the bow and arrow, the acute sensitivity to and oneness with nature, and the constant running. The headband is still in place, and the hair is still jet black.

In the end, unsurprisingly, he does not win the girl's affection. She is too fearful of him and too afraid of his darkness, his vast capacity for violence. The "noble savage," of course, is always walled off from the white woman at the end, even if he is a hybrid. But his distinctive contribution to the rescue mission—and his supplanting of the multiracial platoon of mercenaries—remind us that he is a "hell of a combination" and that his mixture allows him to both be a skillful tracker and commit violence on an apocalyptic, "Western scale."

Rambo's capacity for violence—his central "Indian" skill—is wrapped in millennial symbolism. The penultimate scene in *Rambo* (2008) takes place on a hillside along a river in Southeast Asia. At the bottom of a steep rise, a small, bloodied band of white Christian missionaries and their would-be rescue platoon kneel, hands behind their heads, before their captors and tormentors, a literal swarm of smallish, swarthy, sexually predacious Burmese soldiers. At the top of the knoll, a grim angel, John Rambo, a onetime veteran of the conflict in Vietnam and a much-abused soldier in America's dirty wars, stands up in the back of a Burmese armored vehicle, his visage filthy, a generic, patterned native headband keeping the blood and sweat out of his eyes. Angrily looking down on the scene at the water's edge, his thick body cannot much longer contain the coming release. His corded arms and gnarled fingers hastily swing the half-tank's massive machine gun down into the valley.

When the violence comes, it is overpowering and disproportionate. The Asian demons do not just die; they evaporate into clouds of dark red mist, broken down into smaller, messier chunks by the wave of bullets. As Rambo's massive, redemptive machine gun pounds relentlessly, one pacifist missionary is transformed by the staccato rhythm, taking up a stone to beat his tormentor to death. And when the drumbeat stops and the tattered remains of the Burmese finally fall to the ground, the legions of the saved look around, gazing upon a terrain drenched in blood and cleansed of evil, amazed at the power of God's wrath. The missionary, still on his knees and mumbling a prayer, looks up at the hilltop at the distant figure of the dark-clad Rambo and raises his right hand in obeisance.

This "new," post–Cold War Rambo is, just like the old, a revolutionary Jesus figure, his messianic qualities flowing from his status as a half-breed. Critics have noted the emergence of a "Warrior Jesus" figure in hard-right evangelical culture, a "darker, more martial, macho concept of the Messiah."[7] "These days," Martin Marty writes, "because our opponents have an Allah, seen by our Christian militants only as a warrior God who inspires jihad, we evidently need a warrior Jesus." The Christ figure in the apocalyptic *Left Behind* series, like John Rambo on the hillside, is a "fearsome Jesus," dispensing pain, fire, and torture, heralding the End of Days with his grim pyrotechnics. In one recent novel in this series, the forces of evil, authors Tim LaHaye and Jerry B. Jenkins write, "seemed to explode where they stood" when confronted with the "Warrior Jesus": "their flesh dissolved, their eyes melted, and their tongues disintegrated." "Rambo Jesus," Marty concludes, prefers "personal disembowelment and mass evisceration" to pacifism. A war against Islam, or terrorism, or some combination of the two, requires a messianic figure capable of just warfare and cruel retribution.[8] Sizing up Rambo in Vietnam, where he has come to rescue POWs in the sequel to *First Blood*, one man asks, "You're the chosen one, huh?"

In the "wilderness" scenes, Rambo's appearance and performance echoes—and contradicts—other somewhat parallel, equally hybrid

Tarzan, seen in profile and in silhouette in the frontispiece to the 1914 edition of Burrough's *Tarzan of the Apes*.

figures in American mass culture. In his 1914 classic, *Tarzan of the Apes*, for instance, Edgar Rice Burroughs refined an enduring archetype of American whiteness and masculinity. Orphaned and alone in the jungle, Tarzan climbs the social ladder quickly, relying on his internal racial "gifts"—superior intellect and a vast learning capacity—and his Darwinian context. He survives, in large part, because he is a part of the community of great gray apes, and because his Anglo-Saxon "gifts" are perfectly partnered with his intense and dangerous African landscape. Indeed, he thrives in subaltern soil. When savagery is needed, he can summon it up—becoming, as Gail Bederman once put it, a "one man lynch mob," using a knife, a bow and arrow, or just brute strength. But his whiteness is never called into question.[9] Burroughs had created Tarzan after the closing of the frontier and during a pronounced moment of fear, when it seemed that American men would no longer be able to test and refine themselves through exploration, conquest, and violence. He set Tarzan within the uni-

The medallion on the cover of Madison Grant's *Passing of the Great Race* (1916).

verse of James Fenimore Cooper, where it was possible for a white child adopted by "savages" to stand "straight as a young Indian," to seek, with stout heart, to rescue the captive civilized woman from the hands of his darker fellows, and to be, in a very real way, "native." Through it all, Tarzan remains "godlike," marked by "the graceful majesty of his carriage, the perfect symmetry of his magnificent figure, and the poise of his well-shaped head upon his broad shoulders."[10] Like Rambo, he draws his messianic power from his observable physical character and his demonstrated capacity for both savagery and civilization.

Burroughs had Tarzan captured in silhouette in the frontispiece of the original book. Seated on a branch, his long limbs and lean naked figure blend into the architecture of the forest. A diamond pendant—featured in the novel—drapes around his neck. A quiver of arrows, their shafts and fletchings providing the only straight lines in the scene, dangles from his back. His facial features—captured in profile at the very center of the silhouette—suggest a man of what would then have been called Nordic type, with a "high, narrow, and straight nose . . . great stature, and a long skull."[11] Here, Burroughs and his publisher repeated the common ethnological practice of making racial commentary through simple facial profiling, a practice I discussed in greater detail earlier. The cover of Madison Grant's contemporaneous blockbuster, *The Passing of the Great Race*, an apotheosis of scientific racism published in 1916, featured the profiles of a Civil War veteran, an Athenian, and a Viking on its cover, emphasizing the long-standing superior physicality—all captured in the nose

Cora, Hawkeye, and Chingachgook, in profile. From *Last of the Mohicans*, dir. Michael Mann (Morgan Creek Productions, 1992).

and the shape of the brow—of the Nordic type. Tarzan's profile could easily have been added to this lineup, but his loose-limbed slouch and his longish hair trouble the viewer's certainties. The same could be said of John Rambo—always with a patterned headband, always with a bow and a knife—at least as embodied by Stallone, an actor known for his stoic, implacable visage.

Tarzan, of course, is a twentieth-century elaboration of Cooper's Hawkeye, who—like Tarzan—was orphaned and adopted by "the savage." Repeating the tropes on Rambo and Tarzan's backstories, Hawkeye is able to triumph in the wilderness precisely because of his learned capacity for the hybrid performance. He can think like an Indian. He can track like an Indian. But he is only "almost" an Indian. As brought to life by Daniel Day Lewis in Michael Mann's *Last of the Mohicans* (1992), Hawkeye is neither white nor Indian, but both. Like Rambo and Tarzan, he is long-haired, lean, and strong. His dress is as distinct from the Mohicans as it is from the settlers and British soldiers. Mann plays with set design, color, and sight through the film but nowhere more so than in one of the final scenes, where Cora (Madeline Stowe), Hawkeye (Lewis), and Chingachgook (Russell Means) stand in a row and we catch them in staggered profile, their faces lit by the sun. Lewis, through this juxtaposition, is framed by lighter and darker shades and tones, even as the camera angle draws the viewer's attention to his symbolically freighted high brow and his prominent, "noble" nose.

The most interesting thing about these hybrid figures is not their whiteness but their variegated racial profiles, their capacity for situational performance, their utter lack of a disguise or costume, and their refusal of any deliberate racial masquerade. These are not a minstrel figures. Rambo is not in redface. Tarzan has not adopted a "savage" dress to score a political point. Nor has Hawkeye donned a disguise to make a joke. They are not, in short, "playing Indian," to borrow from Philip Deloria, who tracks a very different tradition in American culture. Starting with the apocryphal Boston Tea Party, Deloria's work has focused on the role of "the Indian" in the national imaginary, and on the deliberate attempts to act, or perform, as Indian, and in so doing to shore up the whiteness of the self and define the racial nation. But Rambo's performance, in contrast, is that of the half-breed, and we are also led to believe that it is honest or genuine. He is *both* white and Indian. John Rambo, the half-Navajo Vietnam veteran, instinctively and unconsciously retreats to the wilderness when threatened, and he thrives as a consequence. Rambo, trained by the nation-state, toggles to the indigenous weapons of the violent frontier—the stereotype of the bow, the arrow, and the knife—even when confronting modern Soviet weaponry. So, in his own way, does Hawkeye.

Kwai Chang Caine is another half-breed hybrid. The chief character in the early-1970s television series *Kung Fu* (1973–75), Caine is the son of an American man and a Chinese woman, orphaned in China and adopted by Shaolin priests in the mid-nineteenth century. As the "made-for-television" movie and series pilot reveals, he is the first mixed person admitted into the priesthood's enclave. Thoughtful and serious, Caine thrives as a young initiate and quickly becomes the favorite student of Master Kam, the head of the priesthood, and Master Po, the laughing, blind philosopher of Buddhism. The series pilot goes to great lengths to establish that Caine is an ideal priest, until he reveals a frightening and focused capacity for retaliatory violence. When he accompanies Master Po on a visit to the Forbidden City, the younger priest is thunderstruck when his mentor is inexplicably shot by a nephew of the emperor. Quickly retaliating, Caine kills the royal offspring. As a consequence, a price is placed on his head, and he escapes—with the deathbed blessing of Master Po and the support of Master Kam—to the American West. Still a committed Shaolin priest, he wanders on foot in the desert, from town to town, offering Buddhist piety and kung fu strength in the service of what might be called a nascent civil rights agenda. He is a borderlands hero of the downtrodden—children, women, the Chinese, all railroad workers, and old folks—and a critic of the worst abuses of frontier justice. At every step, he is stalked and challenged by agents of the Chinese government, local opportunists, and hired assassins, all of whom hope to bring him back "dead or alive" and thus collect a considerable reward.

By casting David Carradine as Kwai Chang Caine, the producers of *Kung Fu* confirmed that only "white" actors could play hybrid figures. The role of Caine was originally intended for Bruce Lee, then a rising star on television and in the theaters, and already a legend in martial arts circles. Indeed, Lee would later claim that Warner Brothers executives had stolen the idea for a Western featuring an Asian actor. He had even interviewed for the role, but the producers and the studio preferred a native speaker of English. As a consequence of the studio's choice of Carradine, however, every effort was made to employ more Asian American actors, many of them veterans of the Hollywood machine. Behind the camera, the producers employed Asian American martial arts experts and production teams. The presence of so many confirmed Asian faces on the set of *Kung Fu*, and the "biracial" status of the main character, helped, in the end, to sanction Carradine's racial performance, categorizing it as something more than mere yellowface.[12]

Carradine/Caine's status as a half-Asian man is, for instance, routinely confirmed by surface assessment. To capture the prevailing conception of the contemplative, civilized quality of the upper echelons of Chinese society, Carradine deployed a blank, serene mask, largely devoid of emotion. Caine has two tattoos, legacies of his Shaolin initiation, which, when revealed, leave local Chinese railroad workers gasping, as Shaolin priests are rare in the Old West. Fight scenes are invariably in slow motion, further emphasizing grace over brute force. When another Asian enters the scene as a combat opponent, Caine dons what is presented as a traditional costume, gearing up, so to speak, for the ritual fight. On a normal day, his clothing is a mixed bag—he wears buckskin and a hat, but the cut is pan-Asian; his shirt is improbably unbuttoned to the waist, and he carries the small leather satchel given to him by Master Po, a treasure trove of secret medicines and powders. Often, he is barefoot. His

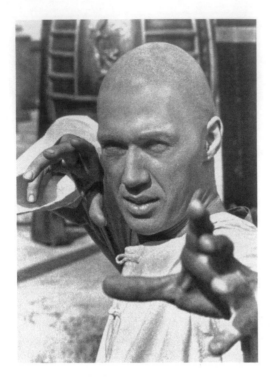

The Carradine squint, offered as proof of Chang's hybridity. ABC File/Associated Press.

voice is incomparably soft, with a singsong locution that confirms a Hollywood imagining of Chinese speech. Most importantly, Carradine incessantly squints in a very specific way, raising his bottom eyelids, keeping his expression slack, and mimicking the "slant eye" presumed to mark the Asian subject.

It is a central conceit of the show that Caine is repeatedly acknowledged as Asian in every episode and that sight is critical to this acknowledgment. In the pilot, Caine's arrival in a small town precedes his racial recognition. He walks in from the desert and heads straight for a saloon, open only to white people. An elderly Chinese man in a ceremonial blue silk outfit sitting in a wagon across the street immediately marks Caine as a fellow countryman, a marking that is captured by the camera as a distinct double take followed by a close-up. (The astonishment, we are led to presume, comes from the sight of a Chinese man entering a racially segregated tavern.) As Caine orders water and then adds a mysterious red power to it, a nearby white gambler says that he "smells a little yellow" and tells him to leave. The ensuing rumble is—perhaps not surprisingly, given the title of the series—resolved by kung fu's triumph over the clichéd six-shooter and upraised chair. His supremacy assured, Caine's subsequent calm departure from the now broken-up saloon introduces him to the older Chinese man, who is a local stand-in for Master Po and a railroad worker at a nearby camp. Through the show's three seasons, the presence of so many Asian actors in the show helped the viewer to locate Caine racially. They see Caine, and the camera comes to a halt, narrowing in on their eyes, switching back to Carradine's famous squint, and sometimes back and forth several times. The camera's focus on the Chinese gaze—on brightly lit scenes of racial recognition and discovery—established the shape of the eye as one primary site of the Chinese racial physiognomy. But it also reminded viewers of the role of the eye in seeing race.

Kwai Chang Caine's status as outsider—not all white, nor American, but certainly half-Chinese—is determined by the diverse group of people chasing and confronting him. In addition to white bandits and entrepreneurs, a global team of hard bodies, all wildly costumed, arrives in the Old West to chase him down, including Japanese and Brazilian martial artists, witches, Ninjas, Chinese immigrant gangs, and dozens of Chinese martial artists. When actor Carl Weathers (who later played Dillon in *Predator*) was cast as an assassin in one episode, he wore a Fu Manchu moustache, a fedora trimmed with palm fronds, and a silk scarf in the Garveyite red, black, and green; he spoke, as well, of having magical powers drawn, we are led to believe, from voodoo. There are dozens of "Indians"—some with loincloths, some with bandanas, but all with feathers and turquoise— who regularly challenge Caine—not for bounty, though; only for the spatial transgression. With silent disdain, Caine chops their streaking arrows out of the sky. The influx of "bad guys"—white frontier toughs, savage Indians, and exotic mercenaries—establishes Caine's hybrid position in the overlapping racial geographies of the imagined Old West and 1970s America. And the escalating internationalism of the cast of characters gives the show a "mash-up" quality that still resonates.

Kung Fu labors—and sometimes strains—to establish the halfbreed's white bona fides. In the show's first season, upon finding his grandfather, Caine is summarily rejected as "tainted." The scene begins with a look—with the blue eyes of the grandfather scrutinizing Caine, who refers to the elder as "venerable sir." "What did she look like, your mother?" the grandfather asks; "Slanty eyes? Yellow skin?" "I should have died before I saw you," he continues. "Let me be dead before I see you again." Caine's father, we learn, had been sent away with his Chinese wife, their interracial union disavowed. Sitting down on his grandmother's grave in silent protest, Caine is asked by a housekeeper to state his intentions and to clarify his desires. He wants what is "rightfully his": "Roots. My heritage." Caine waits quietly, patiently for ten days without food and water until his friend, a blind preacher named "Serenity," intervenes and forces the grandfather to acknowledge Caine and to bestow upon him the rootedness he so desires, which comes in the form of heirloom timepieces and news of a half brother named Danny. The hamfisted staging of the racially charged family reunion relies on sight and sightlessness: the grandfather, whose discriminating eye sees Caine as "tainted" Chinese, and the blind preacher, who is capable of a more abstract, color-blind humanism. It also demands, however, that viewers see Carradine—squint still in place—as visibly mixed.[13]

As the show neared its conclusion, Kwai Chang Caine finally meets his half brother. Danny Caine is a wanted man with a price on his head. Holed up in an old mine, he has been told—by that aforementioned Afro–West Indian assassin—that a bounty hunter has come to collect him: a "special killer," who is half-Chinese, deceiving, and all-powerful. He is predisposed, then, to see Kwai Chang Caine as foreign and threatening. After the West Indian man has been dispatched in a ritual fight by Kwai Chang, the two Caines stand and face each other, with Danny holding a gun. "Can you not see in me your brother?" Kwai Chang asks in his stilted, faux pidgin English. Ornamental Asian music plays in the background, and a gong sounds. For a long while, Danny Caine stares at Kwai Chang, stripping away the "yellow skin" and "slant eyes." And then, with family resemblance confirmed, Danny slowly lowers his gun. The show's relentless focus on racism in the mythic Old West has set the stage for this moment, for the chance of this reconciliation of half brothers born thousands of miles away from each other, each shaped by dramatically different racial circumstances. Danny, logic dictates, needs to step away from the alluring simplicity of the sightline, to see Caine from a different angle, in order to see him as family.[14]

Seeing the hybrid body is thus a parallel to seeing the single racial body alone. It relies on the same technologies of assessment, the same focus on details, and often the very same specifics. But it also requires the performance of hybridity. For John Rambo, this was merely a matter of establishing a working familiarity with the full range of modern weaponry, from handmade knives to rocket-propelled grenades. For Kwai Chang Caine, half whiteness is demonstrated not only in repeated triumphs over the gunslingers of the Old West but also by the man's politely stubborn refusal to be like every other Chinese person he encounters. In the frame of the Gold Rush and westward settlement, they are all sojourners, while Caine, the questing paladin, is not. To buttress these performances, and to make it easier for the audience to see racial hybridity, the studios cast familiar white actors in these two roles, a decision that freed them to emphasize, in wardrobe and makeup and plotlines, the most useful features of the Indian and the Oriental.

CHAPTER SEVEN

Masquerade

T he squint of David Carradine, playing Kwai Chang Caine, is sort of akin to yellowface. The same is true, of course, of Stallone's patterned headband, his bow and arrows, and his long knife. Both parallel—very obliquely, given that their subjects are hybrid— the long-standing tradition of blackface minstrelsy. The oblique part of this is important because Carradine and Stallone were cast as biracial characters, with squints and stoic, thousand-yard stares that are meant to be sincere, and the eye isn't meant to see their performances as minstrelsy, or to look at their embodiments with the same strategy as a viewing of the blackened-up face. The half whiteness of the role assures that the sightline guides us to a very different conclusion.

To gaze upon a body in blackface or yellowface or whiteface is, however, to see race twice, to note the very obvious exterior façade and the supposedly just as obvious subterranean real. There is no subtlety, no obliqueness, in such masquerades. To lead the eye to this perverse second sight, such a masquerade requires significantly more than a simple color change: it demands an attention to the wretched detail on two levels at once.

The men face each other. Both wear blackface. Their skin tone is identical, but nothing else is. One stands erect, with pitch-perfect posture, and stares manfully at his partner. The first figure has a mouth set in a tight grimace, a burning cigar tucked in the corner. There is something slightly off in his comportment. His hat is one size too small, his vest and pants are just slightly too colorful, and his corsage seems three times too large. He grips a dandy's cane in his right hand. The other man is taller, rounder, and stooped. His features are ethnologically disordered, his teeth are crooked, and he is bald. His clothes are oversized, but his hat is only as big as a teacup. Like a clown, his shoes are elongated cartoonishly. Both men have a hint of red around the lips, a faint gesture to the minstrel's more typical bright-red gloss. They stand, in this brilliantly colored turn-of-the-twentieth-century poster, as partnered representations, asking viewers to attend not merely to their common blackface but also to the detailed costumes and significant physical specifics that suggest the importance of diversity within caricature (plate 7).

The most obvious point of blackface, as many have already noted, is the replacement of one set of features with another, so that the performer's individuality is greatly, if incompletely, obscured.[1] The skin becomes jet-black and glistening, uniformly incapable of conveying more than one tone. The outline of the lips is transformed—broadened, clownish, and reddened. The eyes are self-consciously widened, suggesting perpetual surprise and excitement and expressing the emotional maturity of a small child. A blackface character, those eyes suggest, is capable of guile, but—like a child—he cannot successfully deceive. A set of deeper, physical transformations often accompanies blackface—a stooping shuffle, a tall strut, all taking the body out of the normal range of motion and into the realm of caricature. And there is, inevitably, a rich and perverse costuming, from hand-stitched rags to formal dress with gloves and top hat. The end result is a racial cartoon brought to life.

The cartoon is not, however, simple. It invites close attention. It encourages an attention to detail. Vaudeville performers would use very particular wigs and costuming for each character they created on stage, whether their role was a blackface minstrel performance, a parodic dramatization of *Arabian Nights*, or a public performance of Shakespeare. A poster for William West's Big Minstrel Jubilee, for instance, juxtaposes the white face of the "artistic comedian" Carroll Johnson with his blackface persona, but a dozen things have changed for the viewer—from skin color to eye color, from the slope of the nose to the shape of the mouth and the ear, from the texture, arrangement, and color of his hair to the color and style of his shirt.

Wigmaker's catalogs—composed for minstrel performers from this same era—emphasized this exact particularity. A handful of unique "Coolie" wigs were different than "Chinese" wigs, and there were also three different variants of the latter. There were Japanese wigs and wigs for female Chinese, young and old; a half-dozen wigs for distinctive versions of "Sambo"; myriad variants of "Rastus"; and multiple "Jewish," "Arab," and "Irish" wigs. In each case, the differ-

ABOVE Promotional poster for William H. West's Big Minstrel Jubilee. Prints and Photographs Division, Library of Congress. BELOW Al. G. Field Minstrels. Library of Congress, Prints and Photographs Division.

ence was a matter not of price but of style and shape—of the various meanings attached to each peak, bevel, weft, and flair. A specific racial joke or dramatic point required a specific set of details. A blackface or yellowface performer did not, therefore, simply pick up whatever wig was at hand. He or she chose carefully and deliberately, employing a common visual practice, aspiring to use the features of the costume to better communicate with the audience, to more "accurately" capture an archetype of American racial fantasy, and to provide the signposting for those who needed to see the body twice over, so that the genius of the performer could be recognized alongside the effacing "truth" of what passed for racial comedy.

This catalog was published almost a century ago, in roughly the middle of a long fascination with minstrelsy. After World War II, and especially after the civil rights movement, such performances slipped off the silver screen and became relics, some might argue, of a different age. Still, blackface—and racial masquerade generally—continue to serve as a racial sightline, as a means of visualizing racial difference. And the variations within blackface—those dozens of wigs, makeup shades, and costuming details—still make sense to the American eye.

In January of 2009, Robert Downey Jr. was nominated for a best supporting actor Oscar for his role as Kirk Lazarus in *Tropic Thunder*, a role that required the actor to wear blackface for the great bulk of his screen time. "Look, I get it—I'm no bluenose prude," wrote *Los Angeles Times* film critic Scott Feinberg. Downey's role, Feinberg continued, was "so absurd and over-the-top that it's not meant to be taken seriously. Still, I can't help but feel a certain degree of shock and dismay that the Academy [would] . . . nominate this type of performance, regardless of its intentions, in the 21st century, and just two days after Barack Obama is sworn into office and becomes our nation's first black president." At the time, Obama's election was imagined to be a repudiation of American racism. Giving an Academy Award to Downey for his performance in *Tropic Thunder*, Feinberg complained, made it seem like the nation had "magically entered a post-racial period in which the wounds of the past have been forgiven or should be forgotten" when, in truth, there was abundant evidence that those wounds were still raw and bleeding.[2]

The history of blackface confirms Feinberg's outrage. Long before the nineteenth century, it was not uncommon to see white actors

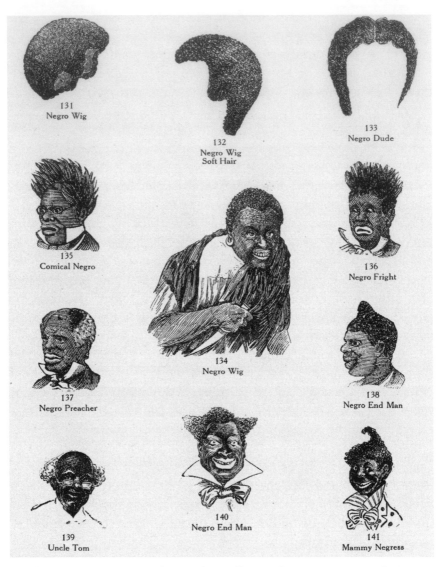

131
Negro Wig

132
Negro Wig
Soft Hair

133
Negro Dude

135
Comical Negro

136
Negro Fright

134
Negro Wig

137
Negro Preacher

138
Negro End Man

139
Uncle Tom

140
Negro End Man

141
Mammy Negress

Detail from Ostermayer wig catalog. Warshaw Collection of Business Americana, Series: Hair, Archives Center, National Museum of American History, Smithsonian Institution.

in dark stage makeup, playing the role of Africans, Moors, or slaves, but the staging of a troupe of comedic actors in blackface truly became popular during the 1830s and 1840s, as the sectional crisis foregrounded the place of racial slavery in the republic, and as immigrants flooded the northern states. Faced with wretched social conditions and a seemingly permanent future as a wage-dependent underclass, these new arrivals and their poor white fellows clamored for blackface spectacles as restorative escape, as a means of tilting the social landscape to their imprecise advantage. On stage, a diverse review of characters—Topsy, Rastus, and others—tripped, danced, schemed, sang, and romanced each night. Acting troupes toured on a circuit or assembled at fairs and amusement parks. Thus established as a cornerstone of the national popular, blackface prospered for well over a century, confirming—for those who sought such confirmation—the righteous inferiority of African Americans and making a joke of their claims to citizenship. Relying on a stock set of caricatures, this early form of the musical review eased through laughter and stereotype the assimilation of new immigrants from all over Europe into whiteness. It made the idea of a socioeconomically capacious and welcoming America possible, but it also sharply, perversely limited that possibility, walling off the hopes and dreams of nonwhites.[3]

Tropic Thunder drew deeply from this dark, troubling well. Ostensibly a send-up of the seriousness of the tragic war genre—and especially Oliver Stone's *Platoon*—the movie nevertheless features a heavy racial coding. The single most prominent example is Lazarus's "scientific" blackface, the primary object of the movie's humorous attention. Lazarus's blackface is also a deliberate distraction from other, decidedly less self-reflexive performances, including a lengthy parody of severe mental retardation, instances of covert blackface and yellowface, and the projection of what the critic Manohla Dargis has called "Jewface." To call attention to the racial dynamic on the screen, director Ben Stiller saturates the film with greens and browns. The lush tones of the film do far more than establish the authenticity of the tropical landscape. They also force us to focus on color generally, to see it as a feature of the film, and thus to concentrate, willingly or not, on the shoe-polish-brown shade given to Kirk Lazarus (plate 8).

The film revolves around a troupe of superstar actors that, we learn, has been assembled in the jungles of Southeast Asia to shoot a platoon film. This dazzling ensemble includes Kirk Lazarus, a serious Academy Award–winning actor; Tugg Speedman, a fading action movie star; Jeff Portnoy, a drug-addicted physical humorist; and Alpa Chino, a globally famous hip-hop performer hoping for crossover success in black popular culture (his stage name is a clever reference to the popularity of the 1983 gangster film *Scarface*, starring the actor Al Pacino). This unlikely cast is there to make a film based on a grim memoir of the Vietnam War, also titled "Tropic Thunder" and written by John "Four Leaf" Tayback, a grizzled, battle-scarred veteran who has hooks for hands and growls his commentary from the shadows. Not surprisingly, the cast—with its array of method devotees, wooden performers, and improvisational comics—struggles to act (as Horace Kallen might say) symphonically. After one particularly wasteful day, the exasperated director, Damien Cockburn, leads the group off into the dense canopy, hoping that a more naturalistic setting and some survivalist experiences will generate a better group ethos and truer expressions on film. When the director is accidently blown up, the faux unit must make its way back to the movie set, treking through literal and metaphorical minefields.

To frame the film-within-the-film for viewers, Stiller begins by offering parodic references for the viewers through a series of fake film previews and accompanying commercials. Alpa China offers a hip-hop advertisement for his soft drink, "Booty Sweat," and his candy bar, "Bust-A-Nut," while wearing a hoody and dark sunglasses, his face framed by the jiggling bottoms of two dancing black women clad in silver bathing suits that have rhinestone dollar signs stitched to the back. Previews for upcoming films from the central actors— Speedman's tired action sequel, "Scorcher VI," Portnoy's vulgar "The Fatties: Fart 2," and Lazarus's critically acclaimed "Satan's Alley"— establish decidedly different career trajectories for the three principals. Then, with character arcs established, the screen fades to black.

As his words appear in typescript on the screen, Tayback (played by Nick Nolte) gruffly tells the story of his rescue in the winter of 1969 from a prison camp. "Of the 10 men sent" on the rescue mission, Tayback sums, "4 returned. Of those 4, 3 wrote books about what happened. Of those 3, 2 were published. Of those 2, just 1 got a movie deal. This is the story of the men who attempted to make that movie." Because all of the narratives share the same name—the film, the film-within-the-film, and the book are all titled "Tropic Thunder"—there is a deliberately layered, confused quality to the story. The film-within-the-film is eventually renamed "Tropic Blunder: The True Story Behind the Making of the Most Expensive Fake True War Story Ever" and rearranged as a documentary, suffused with verisimilitude. The new title may still be a charade, but it has the quality that comic Stephen Colbert once named "truthiness."

Lincoln Osiris. Image from the promotional campaign for *Tropic Thunder*. From author's collection.

The exposure of artifice is central to *Tropic Thunder*. As the film progresses, and everything unravels, the disguises and deceptions fall away. Alpa Chino, the parading embodiment of gangster masculinity, comes out of the closet and confesses his love for another man, later revealed to be Lance Bass of 'N Sync. Lazarus, the confident, accomplished actor, is shown to be insecure and distant. Tayback—the author of the all-important urtext—is revealed to be a sham, wearing false prosthetics and, as a Coast Guard "sanitation expert," having never been to Vietnam. His story—the source of the original memoir and the faux film—is a convenient fiction; "you are," the film's demolitions expert angrily jokes, invoking the patron saints of fakery, "the Milli Vanilli of patriots."

Blackface and racial masquerade play an outsized role in the film. Lazarus—played by Robert Downey Jr.—underwent a "pigmentation alteration procedure" prior to his arrival on set, a process that darkened his skin and enabled his portrayal of the Sergeant Lincoln Osiris. A lead-in television clip shows the blond-haired, blue-eyed Lazarus on the operating table and then laughingly smoking a cigarette in celebration. On set, he wears a short wig of tight curls, sideburns, and brown contact lenses. His helmet—a billboard authenticating his blackness—is decorated with the words "Black Power," a panther, and an upraised, clenched fist. He portrays Osiris as a comforting black figure—deeply southern in manner and outlook, his gruff, drawling speech laced with bright colloquialisms that illu-

Alpa Chino. A detail of an image from the promotional campaign for *Tropic Thunder*. From author's collection.

minate, we are left to presume, the outlook and backstory of an older black man. Lazarus never leaves character, even after the accidental death of the director, and thus remains in blackface until the final scenes, bridging the gap between the faux film and Stiller's production. We are always meant to watch the interplay of his layers, his buried Australian-ness, hidden beneath his false blackness.

He is matched, in both the film and the film-within-the-film, by Alpa Chino's black portrayal of Motown—a character added to the film by Stiller as a political prophylactic. Wearing a do-rag and sporting tattoos, drinking Booty-Sweat and speaking in a contemporary patter, Chino routinely slips in and out of his familiar, "ghetto" character. In addition to his comic relief, he is the movie's internal critic of perpetual blackface. "What to you mean, 'you people'?" Lazarus/Osiris asks Speedman during an argument, assuming that there is racism hidden in that expression. "What do *you* mean, 'you people'?" Chino, standing ten feet behind, asks incredulously. "Ya'll might be in for a treat," Lazarus/Osiris purrs when the group stops to make camp and looks forward to dinner. "I was a saucier in San Anton'. I bet I could collar' up some of those greens, yeah, get us some crawfish out of the paddy, yo!" "That's how we all talk?" Chino responds with disgust, parodying the minstrel undertones of the Osiris character. "You're Australian," he pleads. "Be Australian!" Later, when Lazarus/Osiris belittles Alpa Chino's contributions to the film, the younger celebrity cites the need for someone from "the community" to more accurately "represent" blackness. "I'm sick of this koala-hunting nigger," Chino angrily complains, earning a slap in the face. "For four hundred years," Lazarus/Osiris whispers in Chino's ears during the forgiving embrace that follows, "that word has kept us down." Then, with a smile on his face, the older man offers up the familiar, gospel-tainted lyrics to *The Jeffersons*; in the face of racism, he has only nostalgic artifice to give.

This dialectic between "real" and "covert" blackface calls our attention to differences of kind, not degree. Spike Lee's *Bamboozled*—a masterpiece of blackface as social critique and a parallel, in many ways, to *Tropic Thunder*—is played with this same dialectic, creating a self-contained minstrel show for television, "Mantan: the New Millennium Minstrel Show," sponsored by "the Bomb" malt liquor and "Timmy Hillnigger" fashion. Within *Bamboozled*, the show is savagely, murderously critiqued by a self-styled revolutionary rap group, the Mau Maus, fronted by Big Black Afrika, who kidnap the lead character, force him to dance at gunpoint, and shoot him on live television. Lee's point—which is notably harsher and more cynical than Stiller's—is that every black person is a complicit performer, dancing for a white audience, and devoid of control over his or her fate. The Mau Maus are minstrels of a different sort, but they are minstrels in blackface nonetheless. The twinned "black" faces in *Tropic Thunder* have the same function in the film, forcing a closer, analytical focus on the performance of blackface, real or covert, and the entertainment of an assumed white audience.

Still, when compared to Spike Lee's devastating send-up of the entertainment industry, *Tropic Thunder* has a substantially softer edge. The charged repartee between Lazarus and Chino is, for example, consistently played as comedy, not as satire, and it loses some of its bite once the audience learns that Chino himself is in the closet. Moreover, the two films have radically different arguments about race in general. The tragic, ironic tone of *Bamboozled* is a consequence, in many ways, of racial certainty. Blackface is exploitation, pure and simple. On and beneath the surface, everything is clearly marked, unwavering. We know this after watching Lee's epic because the performance is psychologically ruinous for all of the African American characters; most, by the end of the film, are dead or damaged. We know this, too, because the main white characters laughingly profit, directly and indirectly, from the death and destruction wrought from the use of blackface. And we know this, finally, because many of the African American characters say it, nakedly and plainly, within the context of the film.

There is no parallel moral simplicity in *Tropic Thunder*. Everyone within the film plays with identity. Everyone screws around with race, molds it and adapts it. Nothing is certain. And not everyone engaged in such charades is damaged, or wounded. Indeed, blackface—

and racially masquerade generally—is a method of deliverance for Lazarus in particular. He is, improbably, a better man at the end of the film for having worn blackface. If, in the twenty-first century, American culture struggles to reconcile irony with sincerity, it is a struggle reflected in these two films. One could watch *Tropic Thunder* in the age of Obama and feel, sincerely, that race was both easy to see and impossible to pin down.

Tropic Thunder's dogged and intense focus on blackface unfolds to reveal other, complementary cover-ups. Attempting to make his way back to the movie set, Speedman gets separated from the platoon and is captured by a gang of small, brown, squinty men, drug-dealing Asians of indeterminate national origin, led by a young, heavily tattooed boy. As a part of an elaborate plan to free Speedman, Lazarus/Osiris dons an Asian costume over his blackface, complete with an additional layer of yellowface makeup and heavy mascara. His brow furrowed in some approximation of supposed Chinese seriousness, he wears a rice farmer's conical hat covered in tropical leaves. His body is stooped, and he speaks a strangely halting, pidgin Mandarin, weighed down with mixed metaphors and unwitting double entendres, and colored with his stagey "black dialect." When the time comes to strip away this top layer, Lincoln Osiris (and not Lazarus) stands revealed as the hero of the film, claiming access to the hypermasculine representation of what Michelle Wallace once called "black macho."[4] Clutching an M16 in each hand, Osiris proclaims himself "a lead farmer, motherfucker," and—after a brief firefight—he stands manfully over the prone, cowering bodies of his pan-Asian conquests. This revelatory image of Osiris as a black superhero is, to borrow from Wallace and Donald Bogle, not merely an homage to blaxploitation; it is also a reference to "Buck," the only aspect of the nineteenth-century minstrel iconography to be deemed dangerous to white folks. Within the logic of the film, though, Stiller's use of yellowface on top of blackface, followed by a dramatic reveal of "the real," muddies the racial politics of the film and allows it to claim a certain "postracial" quality.

In the end, though, the film is a decidedly, unapologetically, overly sincere racial thing. As the credits roll, we witness the return of Tom Cruise's characterization of the studio head, Les Grossman. Wearing a massive prosthetic-flesh suit, including thick, hairy forearms, beefy forearms, and a broad, bald head, Cruise's Grossman is ob-

Les Grossman, or Tom Cruise, wearing "Jewface," his visage contrasting with that of his accompanying "yes man." *Tropic Thunder*, dir. Ben Stiller (Dreamworks, SKG, 2008).

sessed with money and power, he wears thick, steel-frame glasses and a diamond-encrusted dollar sign necklace and curses liberally, if not excessively. He is brutally honest and vulgar, too. Repeatedly, in a nod to the film's racial trickery, Grossman has a habit of playing Flo Rida's song "Low," and dancing "gangster-style," in slow motion, as if he were standing behind a woman who he'd bent over, clutching her hair in one fist and spanking her behind with the other hand. It is another version of this perverse mimicry of sex that graces the screen as the film closes, with a soundscape that once again references the urbanity of hip-hop, with all that it purportedly signifies. But it is Cruise, not Grossman, who is in costume. It is his costume to which we are meant to attend. And, like all such physical performances, even those aimed at parody, the joke buried within Cruise's masquerade only works if people can see it, only if they can see the famous body within the prosthetic "Jew" suit. Unlike many of the traveling minstrels of the past, Cruise is a global celebrity.

Cruise's adoption of Jewface, like Lazarus's donning of yellowface on top of blackface, reminds us that if each of these masquerades has a very different political valence, they all rely on the same practice of racial sight, the same sightline, so to speak. Whiteface, for instance, is, James Hannaham once suggested, "funnier than blackface." It is funnier, he continued, in part because it is decoupled from the long history of racism and segregation, and in part because it contains a modest amount of subversive material.[5] Still, I think that whiteface relies on the same visual practices that empower the comedic mimicry of blackface, and must be seen in the same manner.

Shawn and Marlon Wayans as Kevin and Marcus Copeland as Brittany and Tiffany Wilson. From author's collection.

Hannaham singles out the Wayans brothers film *White Chicks* as an example of the supposed innocence of whiteface. The slapstick plot of *White Chicks* clings to the lanky forms of two brothers, Kevin and Marcus Copeland, both FBI agents. In the doghouse for a recently freelanced and failed sting operation, the Copelands are assigned to convey two wealthy young white women—Brittany and Tiffany Wilson—to the Hamptons for a long weekend of dinner parties and fashion shows. The Wilson sisters, embodying the white, blond, blue-eyed ideal, have been the subjects of kidnapping threats. Along the way to the Hamptons, a minor car accident leaves Brittany and Tiffany, both vain to a fault, with minor facial cuts, and they are self-confined to a hotel. The Copeland brothers, aspiring for redemption, then don whiteface and assume the identities of Brittany and Tiffany, once again without informing their FBI superiors. As they search for the mysterious potential kidnapper, the Copelands encounter rivals, Megan and Heather Vandergeld. They also pursue (or are pursued by) new love interests, fend off the anger of Marcus's wife, and create new friendships with a comely trio of young white women who cling desperately to the edges of the Hampton's social scene as near-outsiders.

White Chicks is—like *Tropic Thunder*—a playful upending of the traditions of racial masquerade. The Copeland brothers first appear in deep disguise, acting as Afro-Cuban immigrants running a convenience store. Their looser, finer black hair, coarser skin texture, dangling gold crosses, and guayaberas mark them as older foreign subjects who have relocated to the United States but are still deeply rooted elsewhere. And their outrageous, clichéd physical performances—including the use of a loudly singsong and repetitive Spanish, and a stooped-over, loose-limbed shuffle—confirms the collateral physical props. Despite the association with latinidad, though, these bodies are still marked as black. The scene relies on hackneyed minstrel caricature to simultaneously confirm the blackness of the Copelands and reveal their mastery of national disguise.

Once the costumes are stripped away, the brothers no longer need their Caribbean stoop and shuffle, but their powerful embodiment of the black masculine is merely a different form of blackface. Playing the comedic Marcus, for instance, Marlon Wayans repeatedly offers up a bug-eyed expression of surprise that could have been ripped from any early-twentieth-century blackface performance. And Lamont, played by Shawn Wayans, is, in turn, an easy lover, a gentle lothario in the Jean le Nègre/Billy Dee Williams mold, whose professional duties and responsibilities are consistently set aside in favor of his dogged pursuit of a comely African American newswoman. To bookend these twinned representations, White Chicks also offers two equally familiar archetypes of blackness: Marcus's shrewish, suspicious, and physically tough wife, and Latrell Spencer, a basketball star and rippling stereotype of black male perversion, who is referred to as "Mandingo" or "King Kong," and whose sexual tastes and rituals of courtship are presented as disturbing, primitive, and weird. To dispense with any remaining subtlety, Spencer appears shirtless, sweaty or oiled-up, exhibiting little, if any, self-control, or is dressed in white, to call greater attention to his darkness.

Within the logic of the film, the Copeland brothers, once disguised, are practically indistinguishable from Brittany and Tiffany Wilson. The transformation of two black men into two white women is accomplished by a team of white scientists with lab coats, computers, and thick-framed glasses, who descend on the hotel and labor to transform Kevin and Marcus into perfect replicas of the Wilson sisters. Their ruse is entirely successful. Friends, family, and professional associates are hoodwinked, with very little effort, by the mere application (by spray can) of skin color, facial prosthetics, new contacts, and haute couture. Despite their size, their physicality, their grotesque and unladylike behavior, and their occasional use of a barking, masculine voice, men—white and black and rich—are drawn to them sexually, and women seek friendly intimacy with them. When they arrive at their resort in the Hamptons and first stand revealed in whiteface, the brothers are subjected to a series of lusty wolf whistles. At the front desk, when asked to provide their identification and a credit card to access their reservation, they claim their right as "white women in America" and are promptly shown to their rooms. And when they meet three close friends, the greetings are immediate, sincere, and unqualified—fuller lips, though, are dismissed as evidence of collagen treatments.

At the same time, the viewing audience is consistently provided with an overabundance of obvious cues alerting the eye to the unmistakable act of racial and gender subterfuge, and thus revealing the satirical foundations of the film. There is never really any doubt that the Copelands are black men dressed up as white women. They fight men—and they fight, as one is meant to see it, like men. They are routinely noted for their height and size. They often speak like men, forcing out a baritone when sexually approached by other men. They even walk like men. The doubled sight here is important, for whiteface allows, in many different ways, the performer to lay a stronger claim—stronger, perhaps, than could be made in traditional blackface—to his or her individuality beneath the makeup, and it thus tightens our focus on those aspects of the performance at the deeper level. So one sees in White Chicks the deeper blackface routine beneath the whiteface, recognizing the covert minstrelsy of the Copelands and the over-the-top style of the blindingly white Wilsons at the same time. The brothers are disguised not just as white but as profoundly white, with eyes that are sapphire blue and skin that is almost the color of copy paper.

At this deeper level, the physical and performative details confirm for the viewer the all-too-obvious, just-barely-under-the-surface blackness and the maleness of the Copelands. Lamont repeatedly signals his interest in other women while he is in whiteface drag. At a pajama party, Marcus braids the hair of one of his girlfriends into cornrows, prompting her to suggest that he "must have been black in another life." When the disguised Copelands, attending a dance party, are confronted by Megan and Heather Vandergeld, archenemies and heiresses who are cut from the same general cloth, they defeat them in a dance-off of sorts by break-dancing to Run-D.M.C. Now a part of a platoon of white women, Marcus and Lamont act as the group's defenders, regularly fighting, threatening, and chasing away other men, and in the process making their "real" selves manifest in nearly every scene.

As a whiteface satire, *White Chicks* is related to what Marvin McAllister has described as a performative critique of racial privilege, a critique that is perfectly expressed in Eddie Murphy's brilliant 1980s *Saturday Night Live* skit "Undercover."[6] In this documentary-style investigation of whiteness, Murphy—disguised as "Mr. White"—endeavors to experience the "truth" of white privilege. At every step, whenever Murphy is alone with other white people, he is treated differently—showered in very public spaces with stacks of cash, free newspapers, scantily clad women, and luxurious service. The mere presence of a black person, however, changes the dynamic completely, with everything returning to "normal." The "disguise" that enables this charade is not just "flesh-colored" makeup but also a "Harry Rheems" mustache, large, wire-rimmed classes, a three-piece suit, a host of discomforting postures and gestures learned from watching *Dynasty*, and a larger collection of unassuming aphorisms stolen from the insides of Hallmark greeting cards. What makes the skit such a brilliant critique is Murphy's over-the-top physical mimicry, his too-perfect embodiment of whiteness. The entire joke relies on our recognition of those subtler elements of his performance, even if we only remember it as Eddie Murphy in "whiteface." For Murphy, the donning of whiteface is conceived as an act of deliberate subversion, in which the joke is on white folks. Thus, for Murphy, the creation of "Mr. White" is racial espionage, serving the interests of black people everywhere with the intent of redistributing the spoils of white privilege. The skit ends, then, with a panorama of black men donning whiteface, smiling and waving to the camera, and preparing to continue the mission.

Likewise, in Whoopi Goldberg's 1996 film *The Associate*, the assumption of a progressive, antiracist politics runs through the film. Denied promotion on account of her status as a black woman, Goldberg's character conjures up the idea of a shadowy white male backer, a sort of silent partner, never to be seen but always to be trusted. Eventually, of course, she is forced to embody her fantastical creation, the tycoon Robert S. Cutty. Aided by her feminist-friendly

Mr. White, Eddie Murphy's whiteface performance, an amalgam of Hallmark greeting card aphorisms, the physicality of the 1980s telenovela *Dynasty*, and the mustache of porn star Harry Reems.

allies, she dons whiteface—and becomes a stocky, grey-haired white man. At the end of the film, speaking to a group of potential investors, Goldberg removes her costume, and, with her white genius now revealed as black female savvy, racism and sexism are vanquished. The point of whiteface, here and in Murphy's "documentary," is to parody the foolishness of white racism and to challenge privilege.

But *White Chicks* has no similar politics. The Copeland brothers work for a black man, have a diverse cast of coworkers, and make no effort to attribute their job performance issues to race. They are, themselves, a mix of old and new—strong black men who also happen to be unlucky, capable of speaking in falsetto, and comedic in (and out of) costume. They are surrounded by various archetypes of blackness, all of whom behave boorishly and in accordance with racial convention and none of whom suffer for their skin color. The companionate friendship forged between the Copelands and their trio of white girlfriends is genuine, heartfelt, and, the closing sequence assures us, enduring, even after the disguise has been stripped away. To hammer home the depoliticization of whiteface, the girls and the Copelands bond, in one scene, by gaily singing a hip-hop tune with lyrics featuring the "n-word." In all of this, *White Chicks* is much closer to *Tropic Thunder*—with its playful meditation on race as both easy to see and impossible to define—than to the grim plotlines of *Bamboozled*.

Hannaham once suggested that *White Chicks* has a single radical beat—"imitation as revenge"—but this is a too generous reading of the film, and it assumes that *White Chicks* shares much with Murphy's documentary and Goldberg's *The Associate*.[7] But by excising the critique of racism from whiteface, *White Chicks* seems driven, at a deeper level, to call our attention to the overlapping, orchestrated racial boilerplating of black bodies in the film, to focus attention not on the performance of whiteness but on the subterranean minstrelsy of the rather familiar black male figures at the heart of the film. One is asked, in short, not to suspend disbelief but to embrace it, and to see the truth of blackness in the depths. The whiteface helps the eye to see the black body better, clearer, in sharper focus.

Bold masquerades, then, constitute a very distinctive way of seeing race. On the surface, they shock and provoke an attention to familiar racial representations that are supremely easy to see— linking them, for instance, in the case of *Tropic Thunder*, to "bro-ing" explicitly. But then, on several barely submerged levels, they direct the eye to other racial truths, and from there to the recognition of multiple exposures, to the simultaneous envisioning of a set of overlapping racial features, each superimposed on top of the other. What looks, then, like an easily marked body is actually seriously, too obviously complex.

CHAPTER EIGHT

Passing

U nlike the boldfaced racial masquerade, racial passing—historically, the dark body blending, without any remark or notice,
into whiteness—offers nothing on the surface to see. Where
the masquerade exposes its layers—spotlighting the gap between
the false surface and the deeper real—racial passing refuses such
attention, and substitutes the surface for reality, a sleight-of-hand
substitution that makes it difficult to see the passing body up close.
In order for the passing body to be visualized, then, it must reveal
itself, either through testimony or through the discovery of interior
biological "proof." The body is never marked clearly; if it were, the
attempt at passing would fail. A racial masquerade clamors for our
attention, while, hidden in plain sight, masked by a perfect subterfuge, the passing figure leaves little trace, ethnologically or otherwise, of the passing.

George Schuyler's richly satirical, 1931 classic, *Black No More*, focused on a New Negro scientist who, through some magical formula,
could turn jet-black skin into fairest white. Once the process was
complete, there would be no physical sign whatsoever of a person's
blackness. In Schuyler's tale, the chance for anyone in Harlem, no
matter their hue or shade or class, to permanently and fearlessly
cross the color line prompted many African Americans to become
"pork-colored." The resulting chaos—as troubling for the light-
skinned New Negro elite as it was for the architects of Jim Crow—
encouraged white supremacists to begin a forensic accounting of the
slaveholding past to determine—now that skin color was no longer
a reliable metric of race—who rightly deserved privilege. The much-
anticipated results of that investigation, which showed surprising
mixture even in older white families, led some to flee to Mexico,
where such mixed heritage would presumably be no impediment to
social progress. Throughout the novel, one gets the sense of racial

orchestration and social commitment, as if the passage into white-ness through scientific alchemy was deliberately intended to desta-bilize the order of things, and as if those who had recently departed blackness were still dedicated to maintaining their previous friend-ships and solidarities.[1]

Schuyler's novel was a satirical entry into a rich debate about how, precisely, to determine who was black in an age of deception, move-ment, and mixture. But it was also a challenge of sorts to the conven-tional wisdom. It was a clever attempt, for instance, to offer a pass-ing narrative that refused racial ambiguity as the sole access point to some supposedly different, and discrete, white experience. It repre-sented a cheeky rebuke of the mulatto elite, and especially of W. E. B. Du Bois, who, rendered in fiction, was given the extraordinary name Dr. Shakespeare Agamemnon Beard. And it was a critique of the idea that racial passing was the logical extension of "the genteel perfor-mance" of this African American elite, and that only the very best and very lightest, or the luckiest, should be granted the chance to become, performatively, white.

Passing, as Schuyler and others defined it, is an act of artifice and illusion, a trompe l'oeil performance that foregrounds one set of racial figurations and displaces another. In one form or another, racial passing has been an object of academic attention for decades, first as a biological problem in need of social scientific study, and then as a genre form in African American literature. When framed in racial terms, to pass is to deceive. It is to shield the supposed racial truth, to take advantage of presumed misperception, and to present a carefully constructed racial illusion. In any given moment, not everyone can perform such artifice. Passing is a possibility only for those imagined to be visually liminal, physically ambiguous, and guileful. The passing body, in turn, is a problem precisely because its racial markers cannot, by available measures, be tracked, and its dif-ference cannot be calculated with surface facts. The details are hid-den—either masked by clothing, shrouded by the performance, or inscribed on the bones. In the history of racial sight, passing is the thing not seen. A national fixation for well over a century, passing is a consequence of generations of debate about racial mixture that have produced new bodies outside of old categories, and that have fostered the very idea of the body that can cut, like the shamefully hidden consequence of some unforgiveable crime, straight across the color line. We like to think that slavery and mixture make passing, but it is really the debate that makes difference.

Popular culture has often dwelled on passing, and offers—in the absence of scant autobiographical testimony and very little historical work—our best chance to understand this visual and social phenomenon.[2] But it has been most attentive to those visually marginal figures, to those marked as lighter, or whiter, or with European hair and Caucasian features. Such a focus misses out on the way that racial passing has always functioned, metaphorically, as class passing. No one in the educated "high yellow" upper crust, Schuyler might have said, passes into whiteness to become a plain stevedore. To plot the sightlines of racial passing we need to follow Schuyler's lead, and to imagine racial passing and class passing as closely and strangely related practices. We need, in other words, to think hard about what it means to see class *and* race, together *and* apart.

In the 1983 film *Trading Places*, two men—one black and one white, one poor and one rich, one played by Eddie Murphy the other by Dan Aykroyd—are forced, obviously, to exchange social positions. Based loosely on Mark Twain's *The Prince and the Pauper*, the film is a comical critique of greed and Old Money featuring two silver-haired commodities brokers, the brothers Randolph and Mortimer Duke. Whimsically inspired by a *Scientific American* article on the "nature versus nurture" debate, the Dukes make a bet for a single dollar. Randolph hopes that, with a slight push, the proverbial beggar on the corner could be transformed into a refined gentleman, and, conversely, that the well-groomed aristocrat can be reduced to the status of a desperate drug fiend. Aloof and beyond humanity, the Dukes choose as their test subjects their prospective grandson-in-law, the *petit blanc* Louis Winthorpe III, and a conveniently available con man, Billy Ray Valentine, born of the blackest ghetto. As fickle as the Greek gods, they frame Winthorpe as a drug dealer, ruin him, and then secretly appoint Valentine as his replacement and school him in the fine art of acting rich. They also keep his beggar's raiment in storage, since they fully intend to return him to the streets once the gambit is over.

The experiment goes smashingly well until Valentine learns of the bet and seeks out Winthorpe, now a shadow of a man, to exact revenge on the Dukes. Working with the bricks and mortar of the service economy, the two men forge an unlikely alliance with a friendly prostitute and a quietly subversive butler and attempt to impoverish

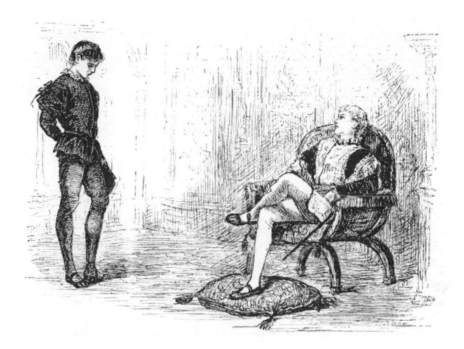

TOP From the 1881 edition of Mark Twain's *The Prince and the Pauper*. But for their wardrobe and their status, the prince and the pauper are indistinguishable. Their racial sameness makes it possible for them to switch roles, a trade that is hard to see. BOTTOM Detail from the promotional poster for *Trading Places*. From author's collection.

the Duke brothers. Masquerading and passing are critical aspects of their plan. On a train, hoping to capture a secret commodities report the Dukes desperately want, the new compañeros embody the interconnected global South, with Valentine, wearing a fez and kente cloth, carrying a cattle switch, introducing himself as "from Cameroon," and Winthorpe, in blackface and with dreadlocks, gamboling about the cabin in some imagining of a Rastafarian costume. Jocularly bound together by their faux blackness, the two men attempt to distract the Duke's agent by recounting their chance meeting, several years prior, in the Haile Selassie Pavilion at the African Education Conference. Later, with the report now in hand and their plot against the Dukes ready, they enter the commodities exchange in Philadelphia, now dressed as respectable bankers, pretending to be willing agents of the First World but truthfully allied by their newly realized common class interest. We are all brothers under the thumb of the overlords, the film suggests, seeking and deserving more than we presently have.

Like any story of racial passing, *Trading Places* dwelled on the authenticity of its subjects. Once the switch is made and the new man has been dressed in a tailored suit, Valentine is brought to the Dukes and given a lecture on the function of a commodities broker. Pork bellies, he is told, by way of introduction, become bacon. And grain becomes bread. The day-to-day value of these things, the Dukes assure Valentine, is determined by the market—and more specifically by commodities brokers, who game the system to line their pockets—and not by some intrinsic worth. That is, nothing is worth anything, unless the Dukes and their market gatekeepers assign it some greater value. And, by the same logic, anything can be worth something. Indeed, the central commodity in the room is Valentine—alternately a "nigger" or a "terrible awful negro" in the film—who has been repackaged and glossed up to satisfy the whimsical ambitions of the Dukes. His glance at the camera during the discussion of commodities conveys a wry incredulity, as if he can hardly believe that two old white guys are attempting to educate him—and the history of racial commodification he presumably represents—on the meaning of intrinsic and surplus value. His gloss is thin, however, and his new value is only as durable as that whimsy.

Trading Places was an unusual class passing narrative, snapping race and class into sharp synchronicity. As the film opens, we survey the full range of Philadelphia, from the tree-lined streets of the wealthiest neighborhoods to the desolate, postapocalypse cityscape of the lost. Slowly, this kaleidoscopic view incorporates features from Winthorpe's daily life, following his tailored English butler through the creation of breakfast, the ascent up a wood-paneled staircase, and the ritual delivery of the serving tray, with an accompanying copy of the *Wall Street Journal* perfectly folded in a side pocket. When we meet Valentine, he is homeless and pretending to be both blind and war-wounded. The two men meet, by chance, outside of the gentlemanly "Heritage Club," in an accidental physical encounter—a bump—that can only be understood, in the logic of the Reagan era, as a crime. In the moment of this brief, remarkable collision, we are meant to see these two men as representatives of the full socioeconomic spectrum, with Winthorpe's conspicuously maintained whiteness shockingly opposed to Valentine's unlucky, hardscrabble blackness. For the film to do its work, these extremities need to be defined in both racial and economic terms, with race and class as nearly perfect synonyms, so that a story about the injustice of the robber barons can be transformed, through the usual Hollywood magic, into a capitalist parable in which a platoon of stereotypes—the uptight white guy, the footloose black guy, the stiff butler, and even the hooker with the heart of gold—get righteously and riotously rich. When we see them all one last time, this unlikely quartet is on a beach, their yacht parked offshore, eating cracked crab and lobster, attended by a Spanish-speaking, brown-skinned servant.

This happy ending marks *Trading Places* as a popular studio film produced by mainstream director, perhaps not intentionally meant as a critical commentary on the shifting economic tectonics of the early 1980s. Like other movies from this era—for instance, *Working Girl* (1988)—its concerns with the machinations of power brokers, and the perpetuating "reality" of racial and socioeconomic disparity, reflect not the avant-garde but the popular, and the concerns of ordinary people unhappily caught up in the maelstrom of recession and the new policies of fiscal austerity.

Most passing narratives, of course, don't end with a plush seafood feast. Indeed, narratives of racial passing are typically suffused with tragedy, not farce. For James Weldon Johnson's unnamed protagonist in *The Autobiography of an Ex-Colored Man* (1912), passing required the refusal of a precious "birthright" and then the subsequent confession that little had been gained from the sacrifice of so much. After a lifetime's illusion is stripped away, Nella Larsen's "Claire," a mixed-race woman pretending to be white in the novel, *Passing* (1929), tumbles to her death, either by choice or against her will, and a fitting end in either case, we are meant to believe, for a "tragic mulatta." Sarah Jane, the petulant older daughter in the 1959 *Imitation of Life*, played by Lana Turner, rejects her dark-skinned mother and lives to regret that melodramatic turning away. And yet, as critic Gayle Wald notes, the story of the passing figure was less a cautionary tale than it was a challenge to the very concept of race.[3] Indeed, through their emphasis on careful negotiation and deliberate strategy, passing narratives expose the unpredictable, historically contingent qualities of race, even as they demonstrate the power of socioeconomic structures to shape human possibilities. Racial passing, in short, was a matter of desperate advancement up the social ladder, progress that came (many authors and filmmakers thought) at too great a cost.

Blackness and whiteness have determined popular notions of passing, but there are other modes here worth exploring, if only because they reveal something more broadly of the intent that can lie behind passing. Rarely, racial passing is framed as a matter of immediate, desperate survival. On May 30, 1942, Fred Korematsu, the twenty-three-year-old son of Japanese immigrants in Oakland, was captured and confined by federal authorities at a local racetrack. The western United States, frightened by Pearl Harbor, had become deeply suspicious of its "yellow" immigrants. Military officials had hastily created a series of internment camps and subsequently ordered the Japanese—long rumored to be spies for Tokyo—evacuated from the coast and imprisoned far from their lives as fishermen and businessmen, shopkeepers and farmers, mothers and fathers. Korematsu ran from all of this surveillance. He ran from Fort Topaz, one such internment site, in the dry, desolate Utah desert, to stay with his girlfriend, Ida Boitano, an Italian American woman. And, to stay hidden, he had plastic surgery, hoping for a permanent "Caucasian" crease in his eyelid, which would give him wider, brighter, whiter-looking eyes. He had the surgeon change his nose, too, "building it up." When he was told that the "facial operation" wouldn't make him look "American," Korematsu changed his named to Clyde Sarah, hoping to "pass as a Spanish-Hawaiian."[4] In short, to elide

Fred Korematsu, c. 1940. National Portrait Gallery, Smithsonian Institution/Art Resource, N.Y.

his previous identity and escape imprisonment, Korematsu changed the way he looked not by altering the color of his skin but through elective, if illicit, plastic surgery.[5] But Korematsu's desperate, fugitive flight from racial profiling, incarceration, and removal doesn't contain the hallmarks of the classic passing narrative: the emphasis on psychic turmoil, the permanent flight from family, and the determination to escape the political economy of racism as defined by the imagined crispness of the white/black dyad. Instead, it emphasizes racial sight as an instrument of personal liberation, as if details shape access to privilege.

Class passing has its own set of distinctive narrative conventions. Like its racial cousin, it, too, assumes that if difference is born, not made, the markers of social position still cannot be reliably found on the surface. At the extremes, perhaps, the visual economy of class continues to maintain that an English nose, or a high brow, a strong jawline, and an erect posture are representative of the very best of the aristocracy, just as the profile of an Irish rogue can still stand as the representative of some lower sort. Class profiling, in this sense, is about focusing on the clear ends of visual representation, and not the muddy middle. In one scene in Trading Places, when he is pressed to verify his privileged background, Winthorpe presents his "soft hands" as proof. And Ophelia, the comely call girl, accepts them as a sort of gold specie. But, for most others, there are no genuinely reliable physical indicators on the body—only countless performative distinctions. If the very idea of class passing assumes—against the grain of American culture—that social difference is structurally, culturally, even biologically real, then our study of it requires an attention to the performance itself, to the secretive acts, the hidden truths, and the myriad anxieties.

To call Trading Places a story of class passing is, I think, to focus on those moments where Billy Ray Valentine publicly maintains—or secretly disrupts—the illusion: his quiet pocketing of a marijuana joint, later to be smoked in a bathroom stall; or his breathless and forthright return of a money clip, dropped on the floor of his new office as a test of his manners. It is also to foreground deeper anxieties about queerness, and to suggest that the loss of socioeconomic certainty—and the performance of a dramatically different class identity—demands a heightened supervision of one's own sexuality. Billy Ray, led to a Jacuzzi by his new butler, is convinced that the Dukes and their servant were lusting after him and that his entry into the Jacuzzi will signal his interest in sex with men. Louis, confined to a jail cell and stripped of his fine clothing, shudders at his metaphorical—and nearly literal—encounter with jailhouse rape. Such concerns are a leitmotif of the film, and they mark moments of profound socioeconomic ascent or descent.

Typically, from Shakespeare's Henry V, to Audrey Hepburn's Princess Ann in the 1953 film Roman Holiday, to Barbara Ehrenreich's empathetic 2001 exposé of the challenge of life after welfare reform, Nickel and Dimed, class passing is framed as a story of downward-facing obligation where a missing figure of royal blood and noble countenance slips into the world of commoners, seeking to better understand their plight. This is the point of Secret Millionaire, a late-2000s "reality television" show, featuring the wealthy in costume, pretending to be poor, and concluding with the bestowal of gifts on the deserving. It is the story of Disney's 1992 *Aladdin* and of Twain's *Prince and the Pauper*. When racially coded, this sort of class passing resembles the story recently told by Martha Sandweiss in her chronicle of a wealthy white man's daily sojourn across the color line and into blackness, all for the woman he loved.[6]

But there is an alternate, upward-focused story of class passing— often, but not always, fictional—that more closely parallels the plot points of racial subterfuge. A country rube seeks a place in the big city, adopts an urbane manner, seeks a step up on the social ladder, and thus Lula Mae Barnes of Texas becomes Holly Golightly in *Breakfast at Tiffany's* and Dick Whitman becomes Don Draper in *Mad Men*. An innocent case of mistaken identity gives someone unexpected access to power and privilege, and the intoxicating attempts to keep that access point open lead to costumed melodramas, fears of discovery, and increasingly convoluted theatrics, and so Patricia Highsmith's literary creation, Tom Ripley, falls in love with, and then becomes, Dickie Greenleaf. A new immigrant wants to adopt a meaningful last name and accelerate his social climbing, and so a German draft-dodger, Christian Gerhartsreiter, becomes a New England aristocrat, Clark Rockefeller. Often, these narratives are presented as public tests of the American dream. When a construction worker pretends to be a millionaire, aided and abetted by a major television network, and seeks a bride from an eager harem, the audience is meant to watch for the moment when he strips away his disguise, reveals his blue-collar nature, and to look closely for her discomforting grimace. When Jack Dawson, the peasant waif from steerage and the hero of the 1997 film *Titanic*, joins the Astors and their crowd for dinner aboard the luxury ocean liner, we are meant to applaud his rapid mastery of manners, his gentlemanly honesty, and his polite conversation.[7] Likewise, when Tess McGill, the secretarial character in *Working Girl*, the 1988 feel-good comedy about one ordinary woman's triumph in the business world, takes on the persona of her convalescent and entirely unlikeable boss, the audience is supposed to cheer her on, to see in her bottle-blond hair and hear in her Irish-sounding name the heroic ambitions of a working-class girl kept down for no good reason.

These are enduringly popular narratives. In the recent past, they

Clark Rockefeller
2008 Photo

**Christian Karl
Gerhartsreiter**
1978 INS Photo

Photographs of Christian Karl Gerhartsreiter, also known as Clark Rockefeller, on display during a news conference, Friday, August 15, 2008, at a FBI office in Boston. Lisa Poole/Associated Press.

have acted to blur the widening gap—here and abroad—between the rich and the rest. Class passing seems, in its most popular form, to be merely ambition squared. It seems excusable, less a problem then a phenomenon. And these narratives are less of an interest to the state, partly because the relation between class and blood and inheritance is so undertheorized and disenfranchised in the United States, but also because the concern with mixture, with hypodescent, and with the dangerous deception of passing is so consistently racialized. In a country that professes to have no bar to advancement, where society is understood as a ladder on which family fates ascend or descend regularly, class passing is benign, even playful, a threat only to those who have quasi-royalist pretensions. As such, it stands in stark contrast to the paranoid fantasies of infiltration and unwitting miscegenation routinely sheltered by the conservative right wing of American political culture.

Billy Ray Valentine is meant to be the hero of *Trading Places*, for his success—if it is sometimes inflected with race—happily troubles the supposed permanence of class. His passage into the world of wealth, which relies on the Duke brothers' backroom support, is the triumph of the little guy against undeserving snobbery. But Louis, once described by film critic Janet Maslin as "a rich twit of peer-less pomposity," gets the comeuppance he deserves.[8] It is Valentine who passes, presenting himself as "one of the boys" at the Heritage Club, quickly appropriating the material atmospherics of a wealthy banker, and comfortably presenting himself as man of means—rather than a homeless man wearing a suit he didn't buy, living in a home he didn't purchase, being driven in someone else's car by a butler he didn't hire. And it is his blackness, in turn, that helps us to "see" his passing, to highlight his performance as a black-man-in-a-white-man's-world, and as a homeless beggar living, for the moment, like a rich man.

The film's production of blackness is richly pinpointed. The stock assortment of black character actors surface briefly, as you might expect, as chauffeurs, prisoners, or partygoers. The usual jokes—about musically gifted "negroes," or about the black propensity for theft—are offered up hollowly. The film is set against the winter holidays, and the white actors are presented as excessively pale, even blanched, calling attention to Murphy's darkness, which is further intensified by his light-gray suits. Most significantly, the filmmaker, John Landis, relies heavily on Murphy's sprezzatura, a courtier's penchant for the performance of profound disinterest, and his comfortable physical relations with the literal sea of white folks around him. His passage into another class is so flawless, so unremarkable, so rapid, that his blackness often stands as the only reminder of his previously downtrodden existence. His always accented skin tone is, in short, a reminder of his true social position.

Despite this reading, Trading Places wasn't meant to be a damning social critique. The alignment of race and class in the film confirms and contrasts with Murphy's more provocative 1985 skit, the aforementioned "Undercover." There, you may recall, Murphy—disguised in whiteface as "Mr. White"—sought to experience the "truth" of racism, and then plotted to take advantage of what he'd learned, and to give black Americans, collectively, a new edge in their struggle to get ahead. Unlike "Mr. White," Billy Ray Valentine of Trading Places isn't a folk hero for African Americans but an opportunist who is undercover by—and for—himself. On the promotion poster for the film, Valentine and Winthrop are smiling and laughing together, in close embrace, with their fists filled with cash. Standing in the shadows of the stock exchange, and positioned on top of a mountain of

Billy Ray Valentine. From *Trading Places*, dir. John Landis (Cinema Group Ventures, 1983).

$100 bills, they are hardly a subversive pair, preparing to rend the American social fabric. Such a representation serves as the beguiling paratext for the film, softening the harshness of the opening montage and giving the audience a sense of anticipation, or hope that, in the end, the bright and clear divisions defined by the city of Philadelphia will be trumped by the shared acquisition of all that money.

As the hero, Valentine establishes that the performance of wealth is not merely about the display of expense or the manifestation of nonchalance in the face of luxury but also about the production of the cosmopolitan and global. This, too, is fairly commonplace. Holly Golightly, the timid star of *Breakfast at Tiffany's*, is a creature of the world city of New York; chameleon Tom Ripley's engagements in the Patricia Highsmith novel that bears his name are set against an Italian backdrop, featuring Mediterranean blues and whitewashed stucco; *Joe Millionaire*'s demonstration of the link between desire and social status is enabled by Evan Marriot's faux home, a comely chateau in the Loire Valley, and his well-worn Australian butler. "Motherfucker?

Moi?" asks Billy Ray, in what seems a throwaway line but is really a work of *décalage*, joining blackness with cosmopolitan pretension. And then, of course, there is that Caribbean ending for *Trading Places*, defining our four protagonists outside of Philadelphia, and outside of the nation-state, as representatives of what Christopher Lasch once derided as "the new elite . . . at home only in transit."[9] One subtle point of this class passing narrative isn't, then, merely to highlight real socioeconomic cleavage and to dramatize its individual human consequence, but to suggest that the gaps between the rich and the poor can also be measured by the distance between the cosmopolitan and the provincial.

Measuring this distance is, admittedly, a different thing than manifesting it. Louis, for instance, refuses to accept his financial diminishment and proclaims his once-upon-a-time wealth to just about everyone he meets. Once his bank accounts are frozen and his reputation is stained, Louis appears at the Heritage Club to ask his friends for help. Wearing a rabbit fur coat, and a garish, mismatched ensemble—a sort of perverse parody of what he once wore—he reintroduces himself with a gesture toward his clothing. "This looks completely awful," he says. And then, rejected by his fiancé and hoping to regain his class position, when Louis decides to pawn his wristwatch, he is confronted with the same cognitive dissonance between the global rich and the local poor. "This burns my fingers," says the pawnbroker, played by Bo Didley. "It's so hot, it's smoking." Louis, incredulous that he should be mistaken for a thief, offers up the watch as evidence of who and what he is, truly. "This is a Rochefoucauld," he says, "the thinnest, water-resistant watch in the world, singularly unique, sculptured in design, hand-crafted in Switzerland, and water-resistant to three atmospheres. This is the sports watch of the 1980s. $6955 retail." "Do you have a receipt?" Didley asks, wanting to verify not just legal ownership but also the claim to class affiliation. "It tells time simultaneously in Monte Carlo, Beverly Hills, London, Paris, Rome, and Schtad," Louis argues, hopefully. "In Philadelphia," Didley replies, "its worth $50."

To consider class passing, then, is to trouble the relationship between cosmopolitanism and humanitarianism. The positive image of cosmopolitanism as the welcome antithesis of small-mindedness is transformed, in these stories, into the use of the global south as a meaningful adornment, draped on or around the bodies of the world's wealthiest peoples. When Valentine and Winthorpe perform their comedic blackface routines on the train, their invocation of Cameroon and Jamaica—relatively obscure geopolitical reference points, given that they are attempting merely to distract someone—is a part of their subterranean performance of wealth. It is an expression of their professed cosmopolitanism, as access to the global and the unusual is presumed, in the universe of Lasch's new elites, to be limited to members only.

And this performance of imperial cosmopolitanism, of course, is the kind of class passing we don't generally notice because it is presently available to anyone with credit. It enables us to fill our homes with markers of ambition, squared, but also to think of these markers as reflections of our open-mindedness. At the higher end, furniture makers like Dedon from Germany, selling to an English-language clientele, appropriate Third World necessity and repackage it as First World lawn furniture. Their catalog features white models lounging on reproductions of hanging pods and hammocks, often surrounded by natives in local dress. In the middle of the market, we can see the same thing in the bamboo aesthetic offered at Pier 1 Imports, or the faded paint and faux mahogany of World Market, or in the pan-tropical furnishings that appear, every once in a while, in Target's version of the global marketplace. "Hand-crafted" benches, weather-beaten spice racks, colorful "Asian" fabrics—none of them genuinely antique, but all of them presented as old-looking and authentically Third World–ish—are a visual adornment for private displays of class. These things make nearly poor people look rich by making them look worldly. They resurrect deeply archived memories of old empires, and they reproduce, in the homes and private lives of relatively ordinary people, a new family history linked, through the display of goods that can be traced, metaphorically, to conquest and empire, to the ancient rule of the white race. Like Louis Winthorpe's Rochefoucauld watch, these displays are useful only in certain company.

Perhaps, then, it is important that the final scene of *Trading Places* is staged on an unnamed island, somewhere in the polyglot tropics, far from the bounds of nation. Such a liminal, ungoverned space is needed if Louis and Billy Ray and Ophelia and Coleman are to be joined as equals. They can feast on lobster and cracked crab, but they can't do it in Philadelphia, where they will always be distinguished from each other, their everyday lives outside of the club, or the trading floor, or the parlor always determined by the relation of race and class. Through the narrative of the film, we've already surveyed the nuclear fallout of the global recession, already seen what it means, in the cold winter that followed, to be black and poor in the city. To continue his performance of class passing, Billy Ray has to leave the city limits and go where he can't be seen, or profiled. And if the film wants us to feel good about this leaving, everyone else has to join him, and do so happily. The scene on the promotional poster—the image of Louis and Billy Ray, laughing and hugging atop a giant pile of money—can't be staged in America. Fortunately for our quartet, this departure doesn't involve a retreat to some ascetic hermitage or dusty retreat. Instead, they can merely slip down to the tropics, the playground of the truly rich, where unlikely contrasts have a different meaning, and sip champagne in broad daylight, without fear of any police action, any surveillance, or any discrimination.

It is astonishing, though, to think about just how impossible it would be to frame a similarly happy ending to a racial passing narrative. Emphasizing that it is only about class subterfuge, *Trading Places* offers up a very dark skinned black man and a very light skinned white man and keeps them well-illuminated throughout, providing clear visual evidence, right from the start, that there will be no racial passing within its storyline. If Billy Ray Valentine had been very light skinned, and if his assumption of Louis's work had required a racial elision, it would have been a very different film. Such a film, though, would have required very different lead actors, and a different range of surface details, to remind viewers of the truth behind the incredible subterfuge. It would demand, in other words, that a more ethnically and racially ambiguous body be substituted for Murphy's famous, unambiguous blackness.

CHAPTER NINE

Ambiguity

I n the late 1990s, a new category of actor, performer, and model, described by fashion writer Ruth La Ferla as "ethnically ambiguous," appeared, seemingly overnight. "Ambiguity is chic," La Ferla noted, "especially among the under-25 members of Generation Y, the most racially diverse population in the nation's history." Describing a fascination with this "melting pot aesthetic," she called attention to the efforts of H & M, the "cheap chic clothing chain," which had "increasingly highlight[ed] models with racially indeterminate features," and the continental clothier, Benetton, whose newer ads "play[ed] up the multiracial theme," foregrounding bodies that offered a confusing hodgepodge of racial details. Advertisers, La Ferla concluded, were intensely interested in "neutral" bodies, capable of appealing to multiple constituencies, and capable of being read in different ways by different groups of people.

The multiracial backgrounds in play weren't subject to any specificity—all that mattered was the "fact" of racial mixture itself, which allowed for one body to stand in for a dozen presumably parallel combinations and mixtures. Likewise, the physical details were imprecise. Leo Jimenez, a commercial actor with a geopolitically complex background, chalked up his recent success to a sudden, even unexpected "demand for my kind of face."[1] Jimenez, La Ferla described him, was "a model, has appeared in ads for Levi's, DKNY and Aldo, but he is anything but a conventional pretty face. His steeply raked cheekbones, dreadlocks and jet-colored eyes, suggest a background that might be Mongolian, American Indian or Chinese." In fact," she concludes, "he is Colombian by birth, a product of that country's mixed racial heritage." "I've heard casting agents say I'm ethnically ambiguous," offered actress Moon Bloodgood in *People*, who presented herself as "half Korean, half Irish-Dutch." "That means," she continued, "I get the parts when they want a little

The "melting pot aesthetic":
Leo Jimenez, by Joseph Blue
Photography. Courtesy of the artist.

edge and not a cookie-cutter white girl." Bloodgood went on to describe how she played with her look to take advantage of this interest: "If I want to look more Asian, I go darker with my hair, or I can go blonde and look more Latin-white."[2] The confusion of categories here—all thoughtlessly mixed up by scale and concept—reflects a prescribed focus on confusion itself, as if a sense of difference and a corresponding lack of definition were the hallmark of this "Generation E.A." What mattered, in the case of Jimenez and Bloodgood, was that there was something—something easy to see but hard to pin down—physically distinctive about their skin, their hair, and their facial features (plate 9).

Generation E.A., of course, has a specific national pedigree. A cohort of seemingly similar bodies, all of them difficult to place, it makes sense only within the confines of the national popular. Jimenez, for instance, might not be seen as ambiguous—and certainly wouldn't be imaginable as tantalizingly untraceable in exactly the same way—within his native Colombia. He just as surely wouldn't have been understood as "like" Bloodgood, born on the other side of the hemisphere. The categorization of racially and ethnically ambiguous bodies, then, is a consequence not of genetic mixture in the body

LEFT "Peruvian mulatto," c. 1868. The documentary effort to capture the enigma of mixture in an image is long-standing and hemispheric. From the album *Recuerdos del Peru*, vol. 1, Library of Congress, Prints and Photographs Division. RIGHT Marion Post Wolcott, "Child of mixed-breed Indian, white and Negro, near Pembroke Farms, North Carolina." During the Depression, documentary photographers in the South attempted to capture the relationship between mixture and impoverishment. U.S. Farm Security Administration/Office of War Information Photographs Collection, Library of Congress, Prints and Photographs Division.

but of a way of looking, of a sightline that produces the same result in the mind's eye, no matter the body's origins.

This obsession with producing and proffering the "ethnically ambiguous" body stands in gentle contrast with the long-standing use of "Latin" and "Mediterranean" actors and actresses as liminal bodies, capable of playing the lighter range of the color spectrum and, sometimes, the darker range as well. One thinks, immediately, of Greek immigrant George Chakiris playing the Puerto Rican antihero "Rocco" in *West Side Story*, or of Italian immigrant Rudolph Valentino, inventing the "Latin lover" and playing Sheik Ahmed Ben Hassan in *The Sheik*, or of Jennifer Lopez, the child of immigrants from Ponce, Puerto Rico, playing Mary Fiori, the quintessential Italian American, in *The Wedding Planner*. "The map of Italy is not on Lopez's face," one critic barked. "Her brown eyes, wide jaw and coloring declare Puerto Rico."[3] In this tradition, the geographical specificity of the body's origin—all hail from the old world and new world

ABOVE Marion Post Wolcott, "Mulatto servant on John Henry cotton plantation." A photo taken near Melrose, Natchitoches Parish, Louisiana. U.S. Farm Security Administration/ Office of War Information Photograph Collection, Library of Congress, Prints and Photographs Division. RIGHT Rudolph Valentino as the Sheik. Hulton Archive/Getty Images.

Mediterraneans, long reputed to be sites of physical and cultural exchange—matters as much as the simplicity and certainty of the actor's identification. In public discourse, Chakiris, Valentino, and Lopez are defined as "Greek," "Italian," and "Puerto Rican," as if those were solid categories, lacking any uncertainty or complexity of their own. Within the American national popular, they come to embody race outside of pristine whiteness and outside of their origin, but this crisscrossing embodiment is noted and acknowledged.

The racially or ethnically ambiguous body, however, is different. It contains a multiplicity within, an apparently random combination of carefully managed racial components. It isn't the platoon or ensemble in miniature, because the representative men and women embedded in those concepts are immediately recognizable, or sequenced in a particular manner. In the ethnically ambiguous body, though, it is the "melting," not merely the mixture, that matters. "Half Korean," as Moon Bloodgood put it, "and Half Irish-Dutch." Or, in the case of Jimenez, a body from "mixed" Colombia, and seen as, alternatively, "Mongolian, American Indian or Chinese." This public randomness, which functions like a descriptive label underneath an illustration, is critically important, not merely because it allows these performers to play many different roles, to be ethnic impersonators without the damaging political fallout that comes with donning blackface, but also because it asks us to look across the face, and to find evidence of the various racial bits and pieces in the corporeal truth laid out before us.

Above all other things, the ethnically ambiguous body, like many other racialized bodies, is useful. The passing narrative, for instance, is one of the most durable features of the American cultural landscape. But producing it on stage or on screen or capturing it in print is tricky. By nature, we think, passing is unmarked on the surface. Its drama is a matter of interior life, of the agony of loss, and of secrets that want to be known. And so, for the discriminating audience, seeing the passing body requires a little help, so that we can be distant spectators to someone else's fiction, and can access by virtue of that distance the single detail that no one within the closer frame can see. In recent years, this help often comes in the form of a sort of physical substitution, in which a supposedly racially ambiguous body is offered up as the unmarked passing figure, sharpening our sight.

The ambiguous body and the passing body, though, can get tangled up, even if they are distinct. The plot of Philip Roth's *The Human Stain*, for example, draws deeply from the traditional passing narrative. In the shadow of the unfolding hearings on the Clinton-Lewinsky scandal, Coleman Silk, a renowned professor at an elite New England liberal arts college, refers to two perennially absent black students as "spooks." When accused of racism, Silk adamantly proclaims that he knew only the primary meaning of the term, which related to phantasms and spirits, and no meaning of more recent vintage. Still, the charge of racism lingers and grows heavy, especially with old enemies at hand, and Silk resigns in outrage after a dramatic meeting with attorneys and faculty. His ultimately unsuccessful defense revolves around the image of the classicist, deep in his books, too focused on his close readings and antiquated histories to care one wit about politically correct speech. But his insistence that he is ignorant of racist language, it turns out, is a lie. For Coleman Silk, raised in East Orange, New Jersey, is, beneath the surface, a very light skinned

African American and has been passing for Jewish since he was eighteen. He claimed his new racial persona to join the navy, to go to a better school than Howard University, to date and then marry white women. He severed all ties with his family. He chose the whitest field of study and settled himself as an overwhelmingly white institution. But deep inside, where his faith in the "one-drop rule" remained unshaken, he knew full well the meaning of the word "spook."

Silk, his neighbor and confidant Nathan Zuckerman notes early in the novel, before he has learned of the older man's burdensome secret, was a "small-nosed Jewish type, with facial heft in the jaw, one of those crimped-haired Jews of a light yellowish skin pigmentation who possessed something of the ambiguous aura of the pale blacks who are sometimes taken for white."[4] Still, despite Zuckerman's initial racial assessment, Silk's lifelong commitment to the art of concealment is unwavering.

A series of flashbacks frame his subterranean storyline. Unwilling to be a "nigger" or a "negro," young Coleman Silk, having completed a degree at Howard, removes himself to NYU and allows the sea of local Jewish students to implicitly whitewash him. Dating a young white girl, he worries that her knowledge of his body might have revealed some black feature on or under the skin, but he is conflicted enough to bring her home to introduce her to his mother and to reveal his blackness, a revelation that ends the relationship. And, more actively committed to passing, he marries a Jewish woman, and decides to walk away from his family, content to perform a very particular kind of midcentury, powerfully intellectualized Jewishness. "You're as white as snow," his mother says derisively, in their final meeting, "and you think like a slave."[5] Imagining himself as a "heretofore unknown amalgam of America's historic undesirables," Silk keeps his racial sleight of hand from his wife, from their four children, from his friends and colleagues, and from everyone else.[6]

Silk's passing body remains undetected—and undetectable—until he dies suddenly and violently. Presiding over the service, Herb Keble, a recently estranged African American colleague from Athena, stands up at the chapel service, and offers a heartfelt defense, putting to rest the "spook" affair. And Zuckerman, attending the funeral, introduces himself to a woman in the audience, thinking that she is Keble's wife. "I could tell she wasn't white," he remembers, "only by the thrust of her jaw and the cast of her mouth—

by something suggestively protrusive shaping the lower half of her jaw—and, too, by the stiff texture of her hairdo. Her complexion was no darker than a Greek's or a Moroccan's."[7] When Zuckerman looks at her, his vision clears, and the truth long hidden by Coleman Silk is revealed. "It wasn't a resemblance to Coleman that registered," he confesses, "and registered quickly, in rapid increments, as with a distant star seen through a lens that you've steadily magnified to the correct intensity." "What I saw," he continues, "when, at long last, I did see, see all the way, clear to Coleman's secret," was "the facial resemblance to Lisa," Silk's daughter. In the end, Coleman Silk's race was not revealed by his living body, nor by his autopsied corpse, but by the physiognomy of his daughter, who had been conceived as white and Jewish, had lived her life according to that certainty, and knew nothing of her father's lifelong deceptions.

The Human Stain was a portrait of a sympathetic liar, passing to escape racism. It dwelled, in the end, on the entanglements of race, and on the refusal of one man to be defined by categories with limits and downsides. This is a familiar story. Indeed, Coleman Silk is a classic expression of the long literature on passing. From a middle-class, upwardly striving home, he is exceptionally light skinned but also well versed in the "genteel performance," certifiably cultured and well-raised, and thus able to circulate in polite, "white" society with relative ease. His body is, in general, unmarred by any corporeal manifestation of blackness. His falsified life cannot be challenged. No one suspects anything, even when his façade begins to fall apart. But his inner psychology, in contrast, is obsessed with a jumble of haunting representations—captured in words like "spook," "Negro," "nigger," and even "lily-white."

When *The Human Stain* was first published, reviewers invariably linked the arc of its protagonist to the deceptions of Anatole Broyard, the famously demanding *New York Times* book critic (and admiring fan of Philip Roth), who had followed the same narrowing path. Though Roth denies the influence, the parallels are worth noting.[8] Broyard, a creole product of New Orleans, had passed over into whiteness, much like the young Coleman Silk, in the 1940s, after service in World War II. Like Silk, he could be a cruel champion of standards and quality. Like Silk, he was known to offer a racial slur as proof of his successful passage, as if the utterance of a word like "spook" could firm up the performance at a critical moment. And, as

Anatole Broyard, *New Yorker* critic and racial fugitive. Broyard's passing was a subject of great speculation, especially in the African American community, but the "truth" of it was not generally known until after his death. Fred W. McDarrah/Getty Images.

was true in *The Human Stain*, Broyard's passing—a "euphemism for death," as Brent Staples reminds us—was a secret only to white folks and a feature of hushed conversation in African American circles. "Broyard was born black and became white," Henry Louis Gates Jr. writes in a critical portrait, also stressing that "rumor surrounded Broyard like a gentle murmur, and sometimes it became a din." Broyard's physical presentation, as Gates tells it, became an object of dispute, dissected in Harlem, shrouded by his famous eloquence and charm in the Village. "He became a virtuoso of ambiguity and equivocation," Gates continues, "shed[ding] a past and an identity to become a writer—a writer who wrote endlessly about the act of shedding a past and an identity."[9] Like Coleman Silk, who spent his forced retirement endlessly plotting and drafting a book about his reference to the word "spook," Anatole Broyard's passage was an act without end, only fully revealed after his death.

In Roth's novel, Coleman Silk's subterfuge was unremarked upon while he lived. Through the medium of Coleman Silk, Roth's meditative genre piece brilliantly captured the complexities typically associated with racial passing and creatively coupled it with the author's long-standing fascination with Jewishness. Coleman Silk's indignant resignation and his subsequent, and often explosive, actions fit the standard passing narrative, in which a light-skinned African American abandons racial communion for white privilege and, as a consequence, lives a troubled life in the psychological margins. Breaking down, losing his capacity to keep his secret, and struggling to keep a lid on his emotions, the passing Coleman Silk is at war with himself, eager to strip away his impenetrable disguise. And yet, at the end, he is so convincing in his performance of Jewishness that he is murdered by an anti-Semite, a disturbed Vietnam veteran who is envious of Silk's affair with his ex-wife. "Roth gives Silk a Jew's life," critic Lorrie Moore writes, "but also a Jew's death."[10] In the end, despite his concern, Silk's secret was perfectly kept.

When *The Human Stain* was translated into a film, the author's focus on the invisibility of Coleman Silk's blackness was necessarily displaced. A visual medium, after all, requires a minimally legible racial body. The challenge for the filmmakers, then, was to make Silk's deeply buried blackness available for public viewing without contradicting the central premise of the novel: that his passing was a complete and flawless abnegation of his racial past. Addressing this challenge required more than just shaded makeup and a creative hair stylist, especially after Welsh actor Anthony Hopkins was cast as the elder Silk. It demanded the complementary use of a supposedly new kind of body, one conceived as racially ambiguous, or unspecified, but still, for the American eye, certifiably, if just slightly, off-white, an ambiguous body that attracts attention but defies classification, that simultaneously raises and elides race. And some measure of that ambiguity had to rub off onto the famous Hopkins, a "white" man playing the passing figure, or else the audience might fail to accept the premise of his casting.

The man cast to play the younger, more liminal Coleman Silk was Wentworth Miller, a relatively unknown young actor blessed, as "Generation E.A." might see it, with a racially complex family tree. "Miller's origins," Nick Paumgarten, a writer for the *New Yorker*, began, "are mixed. His father is black; his mother is white. To be precise, his father is African-American-Jamaican-German-English; his mother is Russian-Dutch-French-Syrian-Lebanese; and, like most people, he has a Jewish great-grandmother, on his father's side. Miller doesn't look black either, whatever that means." Paumgarten's

Wentworth Miller, the man who
would be Coleman Silk. Fotos
International/Getty Images
Entertainment.

use of the nation-state as a more "precise" marker of "origins" is fas-
cinating, as each of these locations cited in this genealogy as themselves "mixed," and full of demographic tumult and complexity. So,
too, is his final remark—that Miller "doesn't look black"—and the immediate caveat that follows—"whatever that means." Miller's body
can't confirm for Paumgarten the actor's blackness, but the film critic
himself seems unwilling to think too long or too hard about what,
precisely, is missing from the surface. Other critics likewise offered
up Miller's ambiguity as evidence of a perfect match between actor
and role, noting that he shared "a similar racial background" with
the younger Silk and that his "intelligence and ambiguity" gave the
film a naturalistic feel.[11]

Beyond the gestures to physical ambiguity and genealogical multiplicity, Miller also publicly presented himself as someone who shared
a great deal with the enigmatic Coleman Silk. After a first reading for
the role, he informed the casting director that the script "resonated"

with him "as a minority," and he suggested that he "knew a lot of the subtext of what was going on with the character." Unable to discern his minority features, the casting director, Deb Aquila, seemed "surprised," and so Miller revealed the history of his family, as well as a telling anecdote from his college days.

As a junior at Princeton, the story went, Miller had published a cartoon critical of African American professor Cornel West, featuring a white girl named "Muffy" preparing for a lecture, delivered by the popular West, titled "Rhythm—Why None of You Have it, and How You Can Get It." In a tongue-in-cheek manner, the comic made gentle fun of the mythic Princeton student, seeking knowledge of black culture from an erudite and established academic, who was then poised to leave for Harvard. But in the context of the culture wars, Miller's critique was misunderstood, and it provoked a surprising backlash on campus against the young cartoonist. "Passing," Miller told Paumgarten over breakfast years later, "is something that never crossed my mind." But, he added, "instead of stepping forward and explaining what I'd meant by the cartoon and positing my own racial background as evidence that I'd really meant no harm, I chose to remain silent." Pilloried by West and his admirers, and admonished by Princeton faculty member Toni Morrison, Miller let the local community read him as they saw fit, and, he admitted, "They probably assumed I was white." By raising—and then dismissing—the subject of passing, Miller did in real life what Silk did on Roth's pages: he let a distracted gaze slide over his body and read it, as logic dictated, incorrectly. He didn't intend to pass. He just let it happen.

The casting director, quite taken with this story, wept at the synergies. She contacted his manager to ask him back for a second reading, but she also asked for racial verification. "They want to make sure you are who you say you are," Miller was told. Proof came in the former of an old family photo, hastily copied in color at a corner Kinko's. The array of family members in the photo didn't change the way Miller looked. It didn't alter the way the casting director saw him. It merely served as historical evidence, proving through an accumulation of paper what couldn't be proven through sight alone. If the passing body is invisible, the ambiguous body is an object of racial mystery, demanding investigation. Through the surface manifestation of hidden clues, it provokes a second look, a questioning of the first glance. But it refuses, as well, any consequential clarity. The

more we look, the more we see something, but the less we understand it. As Miller put it, "if I were to wait only for roles that clarify
my racial makeup, I'd be waiting for a very, very long time."[12]

Miller's transcendent body set the racial tone of the film. To reconcile the ambiguity of Miller with the certainty of Hopkins, the two
men were brought together, to sit in a room with the film's director,
Robert Benton, and the department head of makeup, Donald Mowat.
Benton and Mowat hoped to find common features that could be
exploited to help the audience suspend its disbelief, enabling them
to see Hopkins on the screen as Wentworth Miller, grown old and
tired. "When I look at Tony Hopkins's face," Mowat recalled, thinking of that meeting, "if you just altered one or two things, you absolutely could see what his racial background could be." Hopkins would
keep his hair short, and so would Miller, but not too short, lest viewers focus on what was seen as a radically different skull shape, and
not too long, lest movie watchers note that Miller's hair was "wavy"
while Hopkins had "Caucasian hair." Hopkins would wear green contacts to match Miller's natural eye color, and so would the actors who
portrayed the rest of the Silk family. And Mowat would use makeup
to establish a common tone and sheen, again matching Hopkins to
Miller's physical template.

When we first meet the older Coleman Silk, he is at the front of
the classroom, inviting his students to debate. He has already been
introduced as Jewish by the voice-over narration of Nathan Zuckerman. But Benton pushes us to see beyond the backstory already provided—beyond Silk's status as "the first Jewish Professor of Classics"
at Athena. He saturates the screen with earth tones. He has Silk stand
before the class, wearing a black shirt and a dark-brown jacket, and
in front of a blackboard, rimmed with a deep brown wood. Though
the venerable professor is lecturing on Achilles and Greek literature,
Silk's body is the centerpiece, establishing a focal effect meant to
complement the makeup work in the film. Presuming that audiences
will know something of the plot before entering the film, and that
they will be looking at Hopkins differently, this introductory vignette
is meant to establish something else within Coleman Silk's body: the
proverbial one drop of black blood that corrupts and overwhelms, as
American political culture would have it, everything else. When Silk
utters the word "spook" at the close of the scene, his ruddy complexion and darkened backdrop—along with a brief, whimsical smile—

Hopkins as Coleman Silk. Images like this of Hopkins as Coleman Silk—where the actor is enveloped by dark browns and earth tones, clad in dark colors, and made up to correspond to Miller's palate—were meant to make it easier to see him, and to believe in him, as a passing figure. As a referent, a classical bust is placed in the background, standing in mute contrast to the profile of Hopkins-as-Silk. From *The Human Stain*, dir. Robert Benton (Miramax, 2004).

lets the audience know that no matter how much he might later protest, he knows full well the many meanings of that term.

The promotional paratext for the film served as a gateway reminder to prospective viewers that Hopkins-as-Silk was more than white, and more than Jewish, too. Some would have read about the film in the press or seen a review somewhere. Another subset would have read a profile of Wentworth Miller and come to understand his biography and its function in the movie. But the single most important piece of paratext was the common poster placed outside the movie theater and in the lobby (plate 10). Running left to right, the image fades from black to white. At the center is actress Nicole Kidman, who plays Coleman Silk's unlucky love interest, Faunia Farley, wearing nothing but a lacy black negligee, with one support strap dangling loosely. Kidman's skin is so pale that it blurs into the white backdrop on the right side of the poster. Hopkins's profile takes up the left side, and it is substantially, meaningfully darker than Kidman's. The black and white spectrum accentuates the differences in tone and color, but it also establishes race and romance as the central subjects of the film. Darkening the familiar face of Hopkins through lighting and juxtaposition, it does the work of blackface. It also creates, the filmmakers hoped, the potential for a suspension of disbelief, so that an audience that would normally and without a thought accept Hopkins as white might be able, within the film, to see him as a racially elusive passing figure.

With Miller, the film needed to use his body to highlight the younger Silk's African American past *and* make it plausible for the audience to see him after he had passed over into whiteness. In the East Orange of his youth, Silk is the lightest-skinned member of a very "high yellow" family, sharing the close-cropped hair and stiffly martial body language of his father and brother. We see the family together, and despite their minute variations, we understand that they are joined by blood and by race. Young Silk, we know, has occasionally passed as Jewish and often let people make the wrong assessment. During one such moment, while dating the Icelandic beauty Steena Pallson, he mistakenly brings her home for dinner with his mother, assuming that true love will trump racial prejudice. On the train ride home from dinner, lovely Steena rejects Coleman. "I can't do it!" she admits, with tears in her eyes. In Roth's novel, this is a momentary, if significant, dalliance, one of many recounted by the sexually avaricious Coleman Silk. The description of the dinner and its consequences is followed by Coleman's announcement to his mother that he has chosen to pass and her rejection of his "lily-white face." But in the film, the scene is drawn out and immediately followed with a boxing match pitting Coleman against a much darker skinned opponent. The contrast between the two men is accentuated once again by lighting, and Silk, angered by Steena's rejection, beats his visually blackened opponent mercilessly. When asked by his trainer why he didn't draw the fight out, he replies: "Because I don't carry no nigger."[13] The implication is not merely that he won't help out a brother but also that he doesn't carry any black blood within his veins.

Miller's casting implicitly also suggested a new narrative theme for the plot of The Human Stain, in which the visual whiteness of Coleman Silk grows harder and more certain the longer he passes. The film's presentation of the younger Silk, set in the busy urban landscape of midcentury New Jersey, confirms his interior blackness.

Coleman Silk played by Miller, whitened by his mute black referent and rendered pale by lighting and makeup. From *The Human Stain*, dir. Robert Benton (Miramax, 2004).

The unfinished version of Coleman is enveloped by a black family, with a black history, and lives in a place where people know—and see him—as black, and where that local knowledge has powerful, disturbing consequences. Only outside of this local environment, when boxing in Newark or settling in as a student at NYU, is he accidently mistaken for white. When he decides to pass, it is presented as a complete severing of these familial relations. But the escape from this environment, we are led to believe, also changes his exterior presentation. The farther away from black people he moved, the whiter he looked. By this perversely evolutionary logic, Silk would naturally grow whiter—and perhaps more Jewish looking—over the course of his life on the other side of the color line, a transformation that is assured, as well, by the wintry, rural surrounds of the Berkshires, where Athena College is located, and the relative absence of black bodies. Taking note of this progressive development, film reviewer Paumgarten suggested that casting Hopkins was risky because the actor was neither "mixed" nor "Jewish," just an ordinary Welshman wearing Jewface and, beneath that, some more rarified version of blackface. The narrative of Coleman Silk—from ambiguity to passing—joins Wentworth Miller's genealogical complications with Anthony Hopkins's racial certainties.

Hopkins's casting also changes the posthumous illumination of Coleman Silk's racial identity. When Zuckerman meets Silk's sister, Earnestine, at the funeral, his discerning eye can't see the link. He stands open-mouthed, unable to hazard a guess at what brings this darkly marked African American woman to the burial of the "first Jewish Professor of Classics at Athena College." In Roth's version, Zuckerman recognizes her after a prolonged stare, catching a certain something in her profile that is eerily reminiscent of Silk's daughter. But in the film, she has to reveal herself to Zuckerman, and in doing so, reveal Coleman Silk's racial secret. In the book, Zuckerman's narration helps us to understand the process of looking at and seeing difference, but there is no mechanism with which to decipher the racial mysteries of Anthony Hopkins's face. Except, that is, by offering up the "mixed-up" profile and dazzling genealogy of Wentworth Miller as his racial analogue.

Miller, like Jean Toomer, is a part of a growing archive that resists easy classification, an archive of pleasure and not of scientific concern. As Ruth La Ferla noted, the public delights in the ambiguous body, and state sanctioned science seems unconcerned with tracking the passage of ambiguous types any longer. Photographer Kip Fulbeck, the father of a racially mixed child, set out several years ago to contribute to this same archive, focusing on "mixed" as a comparatively new category of personhood. The resulting collection, *Mixed: Portraits of Multiracial Kids* (2010), is a follow-up of sorts to his earlier and related effort, *Part Asian, 100% Hapa* (2006). Like Ruth La Ferla, Fulbeck offers up the mixed body as neutral, or broadly appealing to multiple audiences. Though he writes that he hoped to push beyond "skin-deep" assessments, and though he rejects the fetish for "exotic"-looking bodies, he nevertheless suggests that mixed children are inherently "beautiful." Confirming this sentiment in the afterword, the performer Cher refers to children in the book as "magic potions," adding, "When I look at them, I see exotic spices, fragrant herbs, lovely flowers, and colors that can overwhelm the senses. I see a vision of the future." Echoing the language often used to describe adoptive families, Fulbeck also suggests that the children surveyed in his archive are proof of a potentially utopian future, adding that *Mixed* is meant to remind "half-breeds" everywhere that they aren't alone. "There is great value in seeing ourselves reflect in others," Maya Soetoro-Ng, President Obama's half sister, writes in the foreword, "and knowing that there is some shared experience between us and others." *Mixed*, then, is meant to be read by mixed people, or by people who think that mixed bodies are beautiful.

Beyond these introductory comments, Fulbeck's anthology of

DANIEL
Filipino
Chinese
Italian
English
Portuguese

One of the many children archived by Kip Fulbeck as "mixed" in his book *Mixed: Portraits of Multiracial Kids*. Reprinted here by permission of the author.

"mixed" types confirms the importance of a racial genealogy to the visual presentation of ethnic ambiguity. Though the photos are meant to capture more than the surface, they also beg us to attend to the relations of surface and depth. Listed alongside the photograph of each child are his or her background components, providing a geographical roadmap for anyone who wishes to conduct a close reading. The components, as usual, are misaligned, confusing race, nation, ethnicity, and region. One child is "Argentine, Jamaican," while another is "Korean, Slovakian, Ukrainian, Polish, Russian, Greek, Irish, Italian, German, Scottish, and English." We are asked, then, to look for these features on the faces of the children, to find a Jamaican chin, or an Irish eye, presented on a composite, tiny physique. The classifications are provided by the parents, and not by Fulbeck, and they reveal overlapping but not precisely matched vocabularies. They also highlight a surprising consensus about what sorts of things go into a racial mixture, emphasizing, beneath the finer points, a breakdown in the great divisions of the world. There are no inter-Asian "mixed" kids or inter-European "mixed" kids. Nor are there children with "American" or "South African," or "Australian" on their family trees, only those partially labeled "African American," an omission that suggests that predominantly white Anglophone settler societies either maintain pure physical types invented in Europe or invent new racial categories for nonwhite bodies. There is an old map of the world in play here in this tangle of challenging faces.

Like passing and masquerade and hybridity, the production of ambiguity calls the eye into action, forces it to look once, twice, three times for something, and finds evidence only at the bare edge of perception. To see the hidden details, we have to work harder. To produce the hidden details, to make them manifest on the body, or to teach us how to find them, we have to worker harder still. In all of these labors, the sightline—binding the seer and the seen—provides critically important guidance.

Coda

The discriminating look, I have suggested, is historically minded, drawing from centuries of representations to make sense of small details, but also fairly consistent and durable. Its consistency and durability encourage a set of familiar outcomes, allowing us to "see" bodies marked as racially different in common patterns, bodies that range from those boldly illuminated as simply "black" or "white" or "yellow" or "brown" to those on which the markings are much fainter and harder to discern. To make this plain, I've teased apart various sightlines and laid some of them out, side by side, to clarify how they each work, what they prescribe for us, and how we use them. These examples have been illustrative of the mechanics of racial sight, emphasizing close readings, or pairings, or the hidden truth.

In real life, the workings of sightlines aren't as neatly separated as the chapters and sections of this book. Unpredictable and interwoven, they come together and fall apart. A single detail—ripped out of its historical context—can fit a dozen different sightlines. A single event can be read in five different ways. And a single story can bring together sightlines that might seem discrete and opposed. When this happens, the simultaneous operation of sightlines can confirm racial sight even when their parallel appearance seems confusing. I want to end, here, by attending to the knotting and interplay of sightlines, to their overlapping, everyday racial refractions, and also by returning to the sordid topic of racial profiling that haunts this book.

A young African American man visiting his father decides to take a walk through the neighborhood, passing the time and giving himself a little privacy for a phone call. Because there is the hint of rain in the air, and because it is a cooler day in February, he wears a sweatshirt with a hood. Along his route, he stops and gets something to drink and something to eat—a bag of rainbow-colored candy, and an iced tea—casual purchases made, perhaps, by a slightly bored teenager compulsively snacking away the day. He calls his girlfriend and sets out, once again, for his dad's house. And at some point on his way back, he realizes that he is being followed. A local do-gooder, eager to police the boundaries of his neighborhood, has marked him as a probable criminal, is following him in a car, and has phoned the police to report a presumed transgression. By the time Trayvon Martin realizes that he has been marked, envisioned as a threat, he has minutes to live. His fate has been sealed by a racial look. What matters, in the end, is what the neighborhood watch captain believes, and what role racial sight has prescribed for him.

Like all of the examples in this book, racial profiling—a sightline that becomes policing strategy—can change what is seen dramatically, bending light and transforming color so that something ordinary or commonplace conforms to expectation or desire. In a poignant skit on police sketch artists, comedian Dave Chappelle calls attention to this aspect of racial sight, blaming the troubles of African American men on the perverse preoccupations of the police sketch artist, whose only function in society is to represent blackness as criminality. "Who is this generic man we all look like?" Chappelle asks, wondering why it is that he always, inevitably, fits a circulating description. Parodying a conversation between a sketch artist and a witness, the comedian imagines that once a perpetrator has been identified as black, the artist can "use a stencil" or "draw him from memory." "Big lips? Big nose? Dick hanging out? Say no more, sir!" Quickly, as Chappelle tells it, the description is broadcast over the police band, and the cops are on the lookout for "a black male between 4′7″ and 6′8″, 120 and 380 pounds; wearing Nikes."[1] This abrupt, half-thought focusing of the eye and immediate transfiguration of the object is what allows the black body in the urban cityscape to look like a mugger, or a rapist, or a hoodlum. It is what makes it possible for a gathering of neighbors on an Arizona street corner to be seen as menacing proof of illegal immigration, of a looming "brown" future that needs to be staved off. It makes a tattoo on the arm of an Asian body proof of gang affiliation. It makes a wallet, or a phone, or a set of car keys, or a candy bar look like a gun. On that late afternoon in Florida, such a sightline made it possible for Trayvon Martin to look troublesome.

When the story of Martin's shooting broke nationally, it took a few days for the visual themes of racial profiling to establish themselves. The first images of Martin, supplied by his family, showed a fresh-faced kid wearing a Hollister shirt, smiling innocently for the camera. So long as this respectable image held, the narrative was tragic, confirming a long-standing pattern of white shootings of black bodies. But this perfectly middle-class image—and others like it—was quickly supplemented, making room for a defense of the shooter, who, it was now claimed, had merely "stood his ground." Within days, right-wing websites and conservative news outlets began offering a new picture of Martin, seemingly older and provocatively shirtless, clutching a beer and giving the middle finger to the camera. These representations—later categorized as "fake Trayvon" once their authenticity was challenged—were implicit proofs of the accuracy of racial profiling. Imagine this other, more threatening Trayvon, one email circular urged, "dressed in a 'hoodie' (a disguise) stalking a neighborhood on a rainy night." These "more honest" portraits confirmed the initial threat assessment by the local do-gooder, the watch captain, George Zimmerman. They facilitated the translation of Martin's sweatshirt into a "disguise," his youthful stroll to a convenience store into an act of "stalking."[2] And they solved a bigger problem, too: the gap between what was seen on the ground that night—when George Zimmerman marked Trayvon Martin as a likely criminal—and what was being reported—an innocent young boy shot to death by a gun-happy white man—needed to be closed, with the logic of racial sight reconfirmed.

That reconfirmation required a parallel transformation of George Zimmerman. When the story first broke, Zimmerman was imagined as white. A older mugshot photo taken several years earlier and unearthed by a scrambling media showed a swollen, disheveled face, the sort of face that one might find in a trailer park, or a low-end housing complex, or a meth lab. A white-trash face, scarified by race and class. But then new photos emerged, photos of someone slimmer, cleaner, happier, and indescribably ethnic. "The images of Zimmerman," the Washington Post suggested, attempting to make sense of the man's classification, "can confound and confuse."[3] When

LEFT The first image of Trayvon Martin, shown here as a smiling young man. Associated Press. RIGHT The Zimmerman mugshot. Associated Press.

the *New York Times* described Zimmerman as a "white Hispanic," conservative commentators accused the newspaper of injecting race into the storyline. Just as many wondered about the cohesiveness of that categorization. And when PBS moderator Gwen Ifill, on an episode of PBS's *NewsHour*, referred to Zimmerman as "white," the outcry was even louder, prompting executive producer Linda Winslow to issue a new policy forbidding the racial identification of Zimmerman. "The thinking behind that policy," the *Post*'s media reporter, Erik Wemple, revealed, "is that the *NewsHour* furnishes photographs of both Martin and Zimmerman, thus providing enough information on their respective races."[4] In this way, by providing a range of images of George Zimmerman—sullen to smiling—the media encouraged viewers to trust their eyes, to infer the mixture of the man before them. As the saying goes, show, don't tell.

This manifest racial ambiguity helped to complicate Zimmerman's motives, and to provide cover for those who wished to find a rational act. It was easy to think that some white trash fellow might have gotten a little crazy with a gun and shot some poor black child. It was harder to demonize a hard-working Latino, or half Peruvian, or "white Hispanic," struggling to protect his precious property values against a hobgoblin like "fake Trayvon." "These photos look like four different people to me," one anonymous comment ran, calling attention to the shape-shifting nature of Zimmerman's peculiar body; "I find that kinda weird. He even looks like he's different ages in them."[5]

"If I had a son," Barack Obama said, "he'd look like Trayvon." A few simple words, the casual statement of a parent, parenthetically inserted into a news conference introducing the new head of the World Bank, were perfectly suited to the somber national mood in the wake of a young man's tragic, unnecessary death. The resulting conservative firestorm reached its peak intensity when conservative radio host Rush Limbaugh, in the middle of a long monologue about something else, joked that "if I had a daughter, she'd look like Ann Romney," a reference to the platinum-blond wife of an aspiring presidential contender. In the midst of all the manufactured fuss about a pretty bland statement, no one paused to think about what it meant for Obama—who looks quite unlike Trayvon Martin—to claim racial resemblance: the president had acknowledged a sightline and claimed his place within it as someone who, when viewed in profile, might be mistaken for a criminal.

A few years earlier, during the 2008 election, this claim might have been met with derision. Appearing on *The Colbert Report* in early February of that year, *Salon* magazine writer Debra Dickerson professed that Obama was definitely "not black," instead calling him an "African-African-American." Obama's Kenyan father, his Hawaiian and Indonesian upbringing, and his white mother had isolated him, she continued, from the "black experience" in America. Indeed, unlike Toni Morrison's earlier vision of the "first black president," Bill Clinton, the half-white Obama lacked any and all of the prevailing "trope[s] of blackness." "[T]he handsome Obama," Dickerson had written online in *Salon*, "looks like his white mother; not so subliminally, that's partially why whites can embrace him but blacks fear that one day he'll go Tiger Woods on us and get all race transcendent." Obama, Dickerson summed up critically, was "'black' but not black. Not descended from West African slaves brought to America, he steps into the benefits of black progress . . . without having borne any of the burden, and he gives the white folks plausible deniability of their unwillingness to embrace blacks in public life." "Obama," she concluded critically, "isn't black."[6] And by even calling himself such, she went on, he had forsaken his father's Kenyan past. The host of *The Colbert Report*—a popular and satirical cable show—was aghast. "Everybody," Stephen Colbert retorted with faux seriousness, "has a right to be black." When Colbert offered to call Obama "nouveau black," Dickerson instructed, as an alternative, "as-black-as-circumstances allow." "It sounds to me," Colbert caustically concluded, hearkening back to Martin Luther King Jr.'s words, "as if you are judging blackness not on the color of someone's skin, but on the content of their character."[7]

Such popular commentaries reflected a shared fascination with the physical history of Obama, then campaigning to be the symbolic head of the national family, and a child of mixed racial and national origins. Two days before Dickerson appeared on *The Colbert Report*, Obama was interviewed by journalist Steve Kroft for *60 Minutes*. "I am rooted in the African-American community," Obama admitted, in words that challenged over one hundred years of the "one-drop rule," "but I'm not defined by it . . . that's not the core of who I am." When Kroft, with great seriousness, noted that Obama "grew up white," it prompted a longer, more complicated response from the candidate. "I don't have the typical background of African-Americans," Obama began,

> not just because my mother was white, but because I grew up in Hawaii; I've spent time in Indonesia. There were all sorts of ethnicities and cultures that were swirling around my head as I was growing up. That's proven to be an enormous strength for me . . . the African-American community, which I now very much feel a part of, is itself a hybrid community. It's African. It's European. It's Native American. So it's much more difficult to define what the essential African-American experience is, at least more difficult than what popular culture would allow.

Blackness, as Obama describes it, is capacious, contingent, and hybrid; it circulates and changes over time and in different locations; it is not defined by any set of experiences or social factors beyond racism. But for Kroft, Obama's "decision" to call himself "black" was a rejection of whiteness. "I'm not sure I decided it," Obama replied once again, turning the question on its head. "I think if you look African-American in this society, you're treated as an African-American. And when you're a child in particular, that is how you begin to identify yourself."[8]

Despite Dickerson's concerns, evidence of Obama's blackness was everywhere. An avant-garde artist installed on the walls of a hastily assembled Manhattan gallery space a massive, fifty-foot-long dark phallus, along with the words, "Once you go Barack . . ."[9] "Obama has facial features," one blogger (randomly chosen for this book from many different possibilities) opined, "—prominent ears, thin lips, narrow chin—that are common in East Africa but rare in West Africa, and therefore in African-Americans."[10] And, most infamously, a low-browed barkeep in Marietta, Georgia—Mike Norman at Mulligan's Bar & Grill—made national headlines when he emblazoned on the front of a white T-shirt an image of H. A. Rey's Curious George peeling a banana. "Obama in '08," the shirt read. "Look at him," Norman told one newspaper, genuflecting before the long, viscous history of ascribing simian qualities to the profiles of black men, "the hairline, the ears, he looks just like Curious George."[11]

Still, if Obama's physical appearance was a popular text, readers came to very different conclusions after their readings. Fringe journalists and bloggers routinely noted his height, his ears, his lips, and his skin tone as evidence of his persistent Africanness, or as proof that he was born in Indonesia. "Those lying blue lips of Obama's," one "birther" site opined, "are indigenous to Equatorial New Guinea."[12] Investigating the depths of his foreignness, media outlets quested for look-alikes in Asia and Africa, hoping for a match that would authenticate Obama's globalism, and produced paired profiles to demonstrate the match. A look-alike, a carbon copy with foreign citizenship, would prove Obama's un-Americanness.[13] A satirical cover on the July 18, 2008, issue of the New Yorker dressed up Obama as a member of the Taliban, overemphasizing his lips, his ears, and his nose, and partnering him with a wife who seemed, in this caricature, to be the second coming of Angela Davis, complete with unruly Afro, darker skin, a bandolier, and an AK-47. Where she seemed like a homegrown radical, though, he seemed—and looked—like an alien. There was the oft-parodied image of Obama, biracial hero and harbinger of the future, astride a magical unicorn. And there was the famous silk-screen campaign poster—originally the creation of street artist Shepard Fairey—of a thoughtful Obama, suspended over

the word "Hope," the racial content drained away his body, all skin tones replaced with red, white, and blue.

Outside of the United States, Obama was read differently. In the spring of 2011, having only just publicly addressed the persistently annoying concerns about his supposed foreign origins and his sojourning youth away from the lower forty-eight states by releasing a copy of his official birth certificate, Obama claimed the mantle of "first black Irish president." Even more significantly, calling himself "Barack Obama of the Moneygall Obamas," he took possession of the Great Famine itself—the bitter wellspring of Irish emigrant identity—as the root of his family's exodus away from County Offaly. Unlike the rumors of Kenyan birth, this thrilling commitment to a foreign past simultaneously rendered him more familiar (the Irish diaspora being a standard feature of the American melting pot) and reestablished, once again, his undeniable and distinctive planetary pedigree, his determined hybridity. This claim about being black and Irish wasn't just a missing chapter in Obama's already extensive and thoughtful autobiographical musings. It wasn't merely an effort to woo the elusive white working-class voter. There was also something a little bit provocative and playful—in the very best meaning of the term—to be found in this embrace of Ireland by the man who once called himself a "mutt" but who checks "black" on his census form. This decision to wear "the green" (or, as one conservative commentator put it, to "chug a 40 ounce" of Guinness) fits a long-standing pattern in African American political culture, from Frederick Douglass to Roddy Doyle's *The Commitments*. And it was consequential, too. It altered, if briefly, the way that Obama was seen, because it set him in a different racial context. Shown a picture of one of his distant Irish relatives, one local said, "I think she's the one he got the ears from. It seems to be the family trait. They had similar ears, yes."[14] There, in a Dublin pub, with a Guinness in his hands, he looked just a little bit Irish.

Everywhere, in assessing the symbolic body of the nation, the public searched for the usual physical facts, for the old particularities, the subject of centuries of observational writing, thinking, and visualizing. Lips. Ears. Hair. Skin. Posture. By distilling down this vast trove of historic material, by repeating the same qualitative certainties, and by stressing the same sightlines, national popular culture made it easy to believe that everyone saw race commonly, that everyone attended to the same features on the body, that everyone noticed the same colors, shadows, slopes, and curls. It had created a simple, shared vocabulary, often implicitly stressed in representation but not always explicitly discussed, to structure conversations about race. It made it easy, in short, for anyone to see—and to de-

bate—the minutia of Barack Obama's body. There was genuine agreement that these fine markings could be universally seen, if only one
looked hard enough. And the variations of what was seen should be
familiar to readers of this book: black radical, untrustworthy alien,
hybrid superman.

And so it came to pass, then, that one of the nation's most popular obsessions—reading Barack Obama's body for racial clues—got
tangled up with George Zimmerman's shooting of Trayvon Martin.
"If I had a son, he'd look like Trayvon." Such a statement, coming
only a few years after the debate over Obama's blackness, suggests
a great distance from the heady, postracial days of 2008. Because
what Obama really meant, in truth, was that he—were he a little
younger—would look like Trayvon Martin to a cop, or to a neighborhood watch captain. And that if he, walking with Trayvon Martin,
had carried a bag of Skittles and a glass bottle of Arizona Ice Tea into
a strange Florida neighborhood in the rain, they would both have
looked like criminals. Their sweatshirts would have been simultaneously translated as "hoodies"; their parallel gaits read as "stalking." And what he also meant was that, in the end, it doesn't matter what you call yourself. What matters more is how you are seen,
whether your own self-identification can be revealed on the body,
and whether the person looking you over, and trying to place you in
the logical flow of racial sight, is holding a gun.

The challenge for those who write and think about race and race
relations is to recognize that the racial look of the beat cop—and the
tragic consequences that can sometimes attend it—is a part of something bigger, that what gets criticized as "racial profiling" is deeper,
flatter, and more ubiquitous. Discrimination is a shared practice of
racial sight, of finding evidence of race on the body, whether the
goal is to profile a criminal, to advertise a new soda line, or to make
a casting decision for a film. It structures the common conception
of criminality but also the sense of beauty and aesthetics encoded
within group identity. Through this common practice, the human
form is assessed, searched for details, hidden or obvious, and interpreted, set within a range of predictable possibilities. As was true
for Dave Chappelle's sketch artist, there are stencils already at hand,
templates for seeing and making sense of race, for fitting details into
a prescribed outline. Sometimes, when one uses this discriminating
gaze, the body is viewed singularly, microscopically, as if it were beg-

ging for a close reading. Sometimes it is viewed in an ensemble, because a comparative inspection might reveal or confirm something, not just of the individual racial character, but also of the interrelations of the races. And sometimes, when a close reading or a comparative inspection reveals only a confusion of details and uncertain conclusions, a deeper study is begun, an analysis of the subcutaneous facts, of the revealing performance, of shades and shadows. This bigger story highlights our racial sight, our own acknowledgment of difference in the everyday, our own sometimes unwitting work in making a world that saw Trayvon Martin—a boy and not yet a man—as a social peril worth shooting dead.

Notes

INTRODUCTION

1. James T. Campbell, *Middle Passages: African American Journeys to Africa, 1787–2005* (New York: Penguin, 2006).
2. Langston Hughes, *The Big Sea* (1940; reprint, New York: Hill & Wang, 1993), 102–3.
3. Ibid., 103.
4. Campbell, *Middle Passages*, xxii.
5. Michel Foucault, *The Order of Things: An Archaeology of the Human Sciences* (New York: Vintage, 1994), xvi.
6. On the notion of common sight and convention, see Michael Baxandall's discussion of the "period eye" in *Painting and Experience in Fifteenth-Century Italy* (New York: Oxford University Press, 1972), 29–41.
7. Formative works in the field of visual culture studies include Walter Benjamin, *The Work of Art in the Age of Its Technological Reproducibility* (Cambridge, Mass.: Harvard University Press, 2008); John Berger, Mike Dibb, Sven Blomberg, Chris Fox, and Richard Hollis, *Ways of Seeing* (New York: Penguin, 1990); Stuart Ewen, *All Consuming Images: The Politics of Style in Contemporary Culture* (New York: Basic Books, 1988); Margaret Dikovitskaya, *Visual Culture: The Study of the Visual after the Cultural Turn* (Cambridge, Mass.: MIT Press, 2005); and Marita Sturken and Lisa Cartwright, *Practices of Looking: An Introduction to Visual Culture* (Oxford: Oxford University Press, 2008).
8. W. J. T. Mitchell, *Seeing Through Race* (Cambridge, Mass.: Harvard University Press, 2012).
9. Michel Foucault, *Discipline and Punish: The Birth of the Prison*, trans. Alan Sheridan (1977; New York: Vintage, 1995), 139.
10. Linda Martín Alcoff, *Visible Identities: Race, Gender, and the Self* (New York: Oxford University Press, 2006), 196.
11. "LeBron James *Vogue* Cover Criticized for 'Perpetuating Racial Stereotypes,'" April 2, 2008, http://www.huffingtonpost.com/2008/03/25/lebron-james -vogue-cover-_n_93252.html (accessed April 15, 2012). In a sign of the cover's controversy, Condé Nast no longer allows the image to be reproduced.
12. Coco Fusco, "Racial Time, Racial Marks, Racial Metaphors," in *Only Skin Deep: Changing Visions of the American Self*, ed. Coco Fusco and Brian Wallis (New York: Harry N. Abrams, 2003), 23. For works that differentiate between the parallel histories of race relations and racialization, see Michael Omi and Howard Winant, *Racial Formation in the United States: From the 1960s to the 1980s* (New York: Routledge, 1986); David R. Roediger, *Wages of Whiteness: Race and*

the Making of the American Working Class (London: Verso, 1991); Matthew Frye Jacobson, *Whiteness of a Different Color: European Immigrants and the Alchemy of Race* (Cambridge, Mass.: Harvard University Press, 1998); and Nell Irvin Painter, *The History of White People* (New York: Norton, 2011).

13. Along these lines, if more narrowly, Martin Berger has recently worked through iconic civil rights–era photography for evidence of the white sympathetic gaze. See Martin A. Berger, *Seeing Through Race: A Reinterpretation of Civil Rights Photography* (Berkeley: University of California Press, 2011).

14. "Bronx Inspector, Secretly Taped, Suggests Race Is a Factor in Stops," *New York Times*, March 22, 2013.

PART I

1. "What makes a Mexican look Mexican?," http://answers.yahoo.com/question /index?qid=20090401130646AAwA6WR (accessed December 3, 2012).

CHAPTER ONE

1. Eva Dou, "See Something, Say Something Goes National," huffingtonpost.com, July 1, 2010 (accessed January 3, 2011).

2. "GOP House Candidate Runs TV Ad Calling for Racial Profiling," May 5, 2010, http://voices.washingtonpost.com/plum-line/2010/05/gop_house_candidate _runs_tv_ad.html?wprss=plum-line (accessed June 7, 2010).

3. World Free Press interview with Gabriella Saucedo Mercer, June 5, 2011, http:// www.youtube.com/watch?v=yUXiCjyGPbk&feature=youtu.be (accessed August 15, 2012).

4. Ann Fabian, *The Skull Collectors: Race, Science, and America's Unburied Dead* (Chicago: University of Chicago Press, 2010), 2. Fabian's eloquent discussion of Morton is not to be missed.

5. J. C. Nott and George R. Gliddon, *Types of Mankind; or, Ethnological Researches, Based on the Ancient Monuments, Paintings, Sculptures, and Crania of Races, and Upon Their Natural, Geographical, Philological, and Biblical History* (Philadelphia: Lippincott, Grambo, 1854), lvxvii.

6. Ibid., 67.

7. Ibid., 441.

8. Ibid., 448–49.

9. Najia Aarim-Heriot, *Chinese Immigrants, African Americans, and Racial Anxiety in the United States* (Urbana: University of Illinois Press, 2004).

10. Julie K. Peterson, *Understanding Surveillance Technologies: Spy Devices, Their Origins and Applications* (New York: CRC Press, 2000), 23–24.

11. Mark Twain, "John Chinaman in New York," *The Galaxy*, September 1870.

12. See, for instance, Erika Lee, *At America's Gates: Chinese Immigration during the Exclusion Era, 1882–1943* (Chapel Hill: University of North Carolina Press, 1997); Alexander Saxton, *The Indispensable Enemy: Labor and the Anti-Chinese Movement in California* (1971; reprint, Berkeley: University of California Press,

1995); and Aarim-Heriot, *Chinese Immigrants*; and Andrew Gyory, *Closing the Gates: Race, Politics, and the Chinese Exclusion Act* (Chapel Hill: University of North Carolina Press, 1998).

13. On the importance of technology to racial ideology, see Michael Adas, *Machiones as the Measure of Men: Science, Technology, and Ideologies of Western Dominance* (New York: Cornell University Press, 1990).

14. "3rd District Hopefuls Take Tough Stances on Immigration," thegazette.com, April 27, 2010 (accessed January 6, 2010); Dana Millbank, "Headless Bodies and Other Immigration Tall Tales in Arizona," *Washington Post*, July 11, 2010.

15. Comment by "Strobe74" on Christina Silva, "Sharron Angle Accuses Harry Reid of Helping Child Molesters Get Viagra," www.huffingtonpost.com, October 8, 2010 (accessed January 5, 2011).

16. "Brian Bilbray, GOP Rep., Claims Clothes Identify Illegal Immigrants," www .huffingtonpost.com, April 22, 2010 (accessed January 6, 2011).

17. "Statement by Governor Jan Brewer," April 23, 2010, http://azgovernor.gov /dms/upload/PR_042310_StatementByGovernorOnSB1070.pdf2010 (accessed January 6, 2011); "Police Training: Racial Profiling Not Allowed under SB 1070," www.tucsonsentinel.com, July 1, 2010 (accessed January 6, 2011).

18. Stephanie Zacharek, "Harold & Kumar Escape from Guantanamo Bay," www .salon.com (accessed January 24, 2009).

19. At a press conference held on November 7, 2008, president-elect Barack Obama suggested that his daughters, then searching for a new puppy, might get a "a mutt, like me." See Stephen M. Silverman, "President-Elect Obama May Get a Mutt 'Like Me,'" www.people.com (accessed January 24, 2009).

20. "Nevada Candidate Accused of Making Disparaging Remarks," *New York Times*, July 31, 2010.

21. "Angle to Hispanic Children: 'Some of you look a little more Asian to me,'" www.lasvegassun.com, October 18, 2010 (accessed January 6, 2011). Also see "Sharron Angle Tells Hispanic Students: 'Some of you look a little more Asian to me,'" www.washingtonpost.com, October 19, 2010 (accessed January 6, 2011).

22. "Sikh Protests Police Detention, Behavior," *Boston Globe*, September 16, 2001; Sabpreet Singh, "As You Were Saying," *Boston Herald*, September 15, 2001; "Under Attack, Sikhs Defend Their Religious Liberties," *Christian Science Monitor*, October 31, 2001.

CHAPTER TWO

1. Ida McLearn, G. M. Morant, and Karl Pearson, "On the Importance of the Type Silhouette for Racial Characterization in Anthropology," *Biometrika* 20B, no. 3/4 (December 1928): 390.

2. Ibid., 396.

3. Samuel Otter, *Philadelphia Stories: America's Literature of Race and Freedom* (New York: Oxford University Press, 2010), 95, 93, 92.

4. *Village Voice*, November 17, 1998.

5. Gwendolyn DuBois Shaw, *Seeing the Unspeakable: The Art of Kara Walker* (Durham, N.C.: Duke University Press, 2004).

6. Kara Walker, *After the Deluge* (New York: Rizzoli, 2007), author's note, front flap; 9.

7. Roberta Smith, "Kara Walker Makes Contrasts in Silhouette in Her Own Met Show," *New York Times*, March 24, 2006.

8. Those portraits are taken from John W. Barber, *A History of the Amistad Captives: Being A Circumstantial Account of the Capture of the Spanish Schooner Amistad, by the Africans on Board; Their Voyage, and Capture near Long Island, New York; with Biographical Sketches of Each of the Surviving Africans Also, an Account of the Trials had on their Case, Before the District and Circuit Courts of the United States, for the District of Connecticut.* (New Haven, Conn.: E. L. & J. W. Barber, Hitchcock & Stafford, Printers, 1840), 12.

9. Walker, *After the Deluge*, 9.

10. Walker's words taken from an interview posted at http://aoc.media.walkerart .org/dl/Walker_1202_1_Kara_Walker.mp3.

11. "Kara Walker," "Conversations with Contemporary Artists" (New York: Metropolitan Museum of Modern Art, 1999), http://www.moma.org /onlineprojects/conversations/kw_f.html (accessed November 16, 2011).

12. *Village Voice*, November 17, 1998.

CHAPTER THREE

1. James Silk Buckingham, *The Slave States of America* (London: Fisher, Son, & Co., 1842), 1:335.

2. Harriet Jacobs, *Incidents in the Life of a Slave Girl* (Boston, 1861), 11–12; Buckingham, *Slave States of America*, 1:335.

3. M. M. Manring, *Slave in a Box: The Strange Career of Aunt Jemima* (Charlottesville: University of Virginia Press, 1998).

4. Kenneth W. Goings, *Mammy and Uncle Mose: Black Collectibles and American Stereotyping* (Bloomington: Indiana University Press, 1994).

5. William C. Rhoden, *Forty Million Dollar Slaves: The Rise, Fall, and Redemption of the Black Athlete* (New York: Crown, 2006), 3.

6. Hank Willis Thomas, *Pitch Blackness* (New York: Aperture, 2008), 67, 69.

7. Vincent M. Mallozzi, "The Real Cagers: West 4th: Where Players Test Their Mettle," *Village Voice*, July 24, 2001.

8. Eric Konigsberg, "Find Cell-Phone Guy," *New Yorker*, December 17, 2001.

9. "Pepsi Looks to a New Drink to Jolt Soda Sales," *New York Times*, May 1, 2001.

10. "Code Red's Ads Present a New, Riveting Take on Reality," *Advertising Age*, October 22, 2001.

11. "Complete Marketer Helps Pepsi See Red," *Advertising Age*, June 4, 2001.

12. "BBDO Crafts Minority Alliance," *Advertising Age*, April 23, 2001.

13. Shannon Wilder, "Mountain Dew's Formula for Cool: Code Red," *Point of Purchase*, November 1, 2001.

14. Kathryn Lofton, *Oprah: The Gospel of an Icon* (Berkeley: University of California Press, 2010), 1, 6, 212.

15. Nicole R. Fleetwood, *Troubling Vision: Performance, Visuality, and Blackness* (Chicago: University of Chicago Press, 2011), 162–72.

16. "Cherry Coke to Debut New Can Designed by Jay-Z's Lifestyle Apparel Brand Rocawear," February 6, 2007, http://www.prnewswire.com/news-releases /cherry-coke-to-debut new-can-designed-by-jay-zs-lifestyle-apparel-brand -rocawear-54486117.html (accessed March 25, 2013).

17. "Jay-Z to Assist Cherry Coke's Relaunch," February 1, 2007, www.spin.com /articles/jay-z-assist-cherry-cokes-relaunch (accessed November 16, 2011).

18. Video of Cherry Coke unveiling, http://www.youtube.com/watch?v= _fwErLndqs4 (accessed November 16, 2011).

19. "Cherry Coke Now Available for Coloreds, Hipsters, and Ghetto Party Attendees," February 8, 2007, http://biochemicalslang.blogspot.com/2007/02 /cherry-coke-now-available-for-coloreds.html (accessed November 16, 2011).

20. Sasha Frere-Jones, "Hip Hop Is a Guest at the Indian Wedding," *New York Times*, August 3, 2003.

21. Alona Wartofsky, "Rap's Fresh Heir: Panjabi MC, Making Some Noise on the Hip Hop Scene with a South Asian Sound," *Washington Post*, July 13, 2003; Panjabi MC, *Beware*, Sequence Records (New York), 2003. The quotes are from Tina Chadha, "Mix This," *Village Voice*, July 2–8, 2003.

22. "Jay-Z Remix Spices Interest in Panjabi MC," *USA Today*, May 21, 2003.

23. "Hip Hop by Way of India," *Los Angeles Times*, June 8, 2003.

24. Thomas C. Holt, "Marking: Race, Race-making, and the Writing of History," *American Historical Review* 100, no. 1 (February 1995): 8.

CHAPTER FOUR

1. Linda Gordon, *The Great Arizona Orphan Abduction* (Cambridge, Mass.: Harvard University Press, 1999).

2. Ellen Herman, *Kinship by Design: A History of Adoption in the Modern United States* (Chicago: University of Chicago Press, 2008); Barbara Melosh, *Strangers and Kin: The American Way of Adoption* (Cambridge, Mass.: Harvard University Press, 2002).

3. Toby Alice Volkman, ed., *Cultures of Transnational Adoption* (Durham, N.C.: Duke University Press, 2005), 1–19.

4. Ann Anagnost, "Scenes of Misrecognition: Maternal Citizenship in the Age of Transnational Adoption," *positions* 8, no. 2 (2000): 389.

5. Ibid.; David Eng, "Transnational Adoption and Queer Diasporas," *Social Text* 76, 21, no. 3 (Fall 2003): 1–37; Jodi Kim, "An 'Orphan' with Two Mothers: Transnational and Transracial Adoption, the Cold War, and Contemporary Asian American Cultural Politics," *American Quarterly* 61, no. 4 (2009): 855–80.

6. "*Life* Visits a One-Family U.N.," *Life*, November 12, 1951, 157.

7. Ibid.

8. Ibid.

9. Helen Doss, *The Family Nobody Wanted* (1954; reprint, Boston: Northeastern University Press, 2001), 3.

10. Ibid., 29.

11. Ibid., 40, 51, 59, 82, 85, 148. Doss's comments here recall Andrea Louie's essay on "China Dolls" and the white construction of Chineseness in adoptive families. See Andrea Louie, "'Pandas, Lions, and Dragons, Oh My!': How White Adoptive Parents Construct Chineseness," *Journal of Asian American Studies* 12, no. 3 (2009): 285–320.

12. Doss, *The Family Nobody Wanted*, 208–9.

13. Ibid., 225.

14. Ibid., afterword to the 2001 edition.

15. Lynn Thomas, "Karen Finds Love," *Ebony*, February 1974, 62.

16. Ibid., 62, 64.

17. Ibid., 64.

18. Joseph P. Blank, *19 Steps Up the Mountain: The Story of the DeBolt Family* (New York: Jove, 1982). John Korty, dir., *Who Are the DeBolts? And Where Did They Get 19 Kids?* (1977).

19. "Close to the Divine," *Washington Post*, April 23, 1975; Shales, "Joy and Valor of '19 Kids,'" *Washington Post*, December 23, 1978.

20. "They Find Children in Need—And Ask Them to Join the Family," *New York Times*, January 22, 1974.

21. The description is Ishmael Reed's, in "Remembering Josephine Baker," in *Shrovetide in Old New Orleans* (New York: Atheneum, 1989), 287.

22. "The Tempest; Angelina Jolie, Actress, Tabloid Siren," *Vanity Fair*, March 1, 2006.

23. J. Hoberman, "Mighty Heart, Mightier Spotlight," *Village Voice*, June 12, 2007.

24. For a useful summary of the tropes of "rescue" and "kidnap" in adoption literature, see Karen Dubinsky, "Babies Without Borders: Rescue, Kidnap, and the Symbolic Child," *Journal of Women's History* 19, no. 1 (2007): 142–50.

25. "World's Most Beautiful Family," *People*, May 8, 2006.

26. "And Babies Make Eight!," *People*, July 28, 2008.

27. The image is in the June 19, 2006, issue of *People*.

28. *Blessed Art Thou*, http://katekretz.blogspot.com/2006/12/blessed-art-thou -2006-88-x-60-oil.html (accessed January 31, 2010).

29. "I Want to Adopt Again—Angelina Jolie," *People*, October 26, 2005.

CHAPTER FIVE

1. Horace M. Kallen, "Democracy versus the Melting Pot: A Study of American Nationality," *The Nation*, February 25, 1915.

2. Ibid.

3. Richard Slotkin, *Gunfighter Nation: The Myth of the Frontier in Twentieth-Century America* (New York: Atheneum, 1992), 326.

4. Ibid.

5. See, for instance, Susan Faludi, *Backlash: The Undeclared War Against American Women* (New York: Broadway, 2006), 150–51.

CHAPTER SIX

1. Richard Dyer, *White: Essays on Race and Culture* (London: Routledge, 1997), 156.
2. Ibid., 161.
3. Ibid., 163.
4. Susan Jeffords, *Hard Bodies: Hollywood Masculinity in the Reagan Era* (New Brunswick, N.J.: Rutgers University Press, 1994), 33.
5. Ibid., 34.
6. "Interview: Stallone," January 25, 2008, http://movies.ign.com/articles/847 /847798p1.html.
7. David D. Kirkpatrick, "Wrath and Mercy: The Return of the Warrior Jesus," *New York Times*, April 4, 2004.
8. Martin Marty, "Rambo Jesus," *Christian Century*, May 4, 2004.
9. Gail Bederman, *Manliness and Civilization: A Cultural History of Gender and Race in the United States, 1880–1917* (Chicago: University of Chicago Press, 1996), 227.
10. Edgar Rice Burroughs, *Tarzan of the Apes* (New York, 1914), 167, 184.
11. Madison Grant, *Passing of the Great Race; or, The Racial Basis of European History* (New York: Charles Scribner's Sons, 1916), 150.
12. Vijay Prashad, *Everybody Was Kung Fu Fighting: Afro-Asian Connections and the Myth of Cultural Purity* (Boston: Beacon, 2001), 129; Robert G. Lee, *Orientals: Asian Americans in Popular Culture* (Philadelphia: Temple University Press, 1999), 145–203.
13. The episode is titled "Dark Angel."
14. The episode is titled "The Brothers Caine."

CHAPTER SEVEN

1. Robert Toll, *Blacking Up: The Minstrel Show in Nineteenth-Century America* (New York: Oxford University Press, 1977); Eric Lott, *Love and Theft: Blackface Minstrelsy and the American Working Class* (New York: Oxford University Press, 1995); W. T. Lhamon, *Raising Cain: Blackface Performance from Jim Crow to Hip Hop* (Cambridge, Mass.: Harvard University Press, 2000); W. Fitzhugh Brundage, ed., *Beyond Blackface: African Americans and the Creation of American Culture, 1890–1930* (Chapel Hill: University of North Carolina Press, 2011).
2. "Celebrating Robert Downey Jr.'s blackface at the Oscars? (The week we inaugurate Obama?)," http://latimesblogs.latimes.com/files/2009/01/blackface -at-th.html (accessed March 15, 2010).
3. In addition to Toll, Lott, and Lhamon, David Roediger's *Wages of Whiteness: Race and the Making of the American Working Class* (London: Verso, 1991) is especially good on this connection between whiteness and minstrelsy.
4. Famously, in Michelle Wallace, *Black Macho and the Myth of the Superwoman* (London: Verso, 1999).

5. James Hannaham, "Beyond the Pale," *New York Magazine*, June 28, 2004, http://nymag.com/nymetro/arts/features/9325/.
6. Marvin McAllister, *Whiting Up: Whiteface Minstrels & Stage Europeans in African American Performance* (Chapel Hill: University of North Carolina Press, 2011).
7. Hannaham, "Beyond the Pale."

CHAPTER EIGHT

1. George Schuyler, *Black No More* (New York: Macaulay, 1931).
2. On passing, generally, see Elaine Ginsberg, *Passing and the Fictions of Identity* (Durham, N.C.: Duke University Press, 1996); Gayle Wald, *Crossing the Line: Racial Passing in Twentieth-Century U.S. Literature and Culture* (Durham, N.C.: Duke University Press, 2000); Stephen Belluscio, *To Be Suddenly White: Literary Realism and Racial Passing* (Columbia: University of Missouri Press, 2006); Gerald Horne, *The Color of Fascism: Lawrence Dennis, Racial Passing, and the Rise of Right-Wing Extremism* (New York: New York University Press, 2009); and Marcia Alesan Dawkins, *Racial Passing and the Color of Cultural Identity* (Waco, Tex.: Baylor University Press, 2012).
3. Wald, *Crossing the Color Line*, introduction.
4. Peter Irons, *Justice at War: The Story of the Japanese American Internment Cases* (Berkeley: University of California Press, 1993), 95–96; Susan Dudley Gold, *Korematsu versus United States: Japanese American Internment* (New York: Benchmark Books, 2005), 54; Paul Spikard, *Japanese Americans: The Formations and Transformations of an Ethnic Group* (New Brunswick, N.J.: Rutgers University Press, 2009), 111.
5. The surgery Korematsu sought is now one of the more popular, if politically charged, bodily "improvements" offered to Asians and Asian Americans, guaranteeing enhanced "prettiness," or whiteness, to those who loathe "the monolid." Through a procedure known as blepharoplasty, or double eyelid surgery, a supratarsal fold is created below the eyebrow, adding a crease to the eyelid that is, as numerous websites will tell you, routinely absent in Asians. The surgery is popular in Asia but disputed in the United States, where it has been labeled, at different times, as "self-mutilation," as an effort to "look white" or to ape white fashion and aesthetics, as a marker of privilege and luck, and as transformation of the very definition of an "aesthetically pleasing" Asian eye. See the Asian Eyelid Surgery Center's website, http://www.asianbleph.com/faq.html (accessed March 9, 2010). See also Anupreeta Das, "The Search for Beautiful," *Boston Globe*, January 21, 2007.
6. Martha A. Sandweiss, *Passing Strange: A Gilded Age Tale of Love and Deception Across the Color Line* (New York: Penguin, 2009).
7. Gwendolyn Audrey Foster, *Class Passing: Social Mobility in Film and Popular Culture* (Carbondale: Southern Illinois University Press, 2005).
8. Janet Maslin, review of "Trading Places," *New York Times*, June 8, 1983.
9. Christopher Lasch, *The Revolt of the Elite and the Betrayal of Democracy* (New York: Norton, 1996).

CHAPTER NINE

1. Ruth La Ferla, "Generation E.A.: Ethnically Ambiguous," *New York Times*, December 28, 2003.
2. "100 Most Beautiful People," *People*, May 11, 2009, 11.
3. "Jennifer Lopez Plays Italian in *The Wedding Planner*," *New York Press*, http://nypress.com/jennifer-lopez-plays-italian-in-the-wedding-planner/.
4. Philip Roth, *Human Stain: A Novel* (New York: Vintage, 2001), 15–16.
5. Ibid., 139.
6. Ibid., 132.
7. Ibid., 316.
8. Philip Roth "An Open Letter to Wikipedia," *New Yorker*, September 7, 2012.
9. Henry Louis Gates Jr., *Thirteen Ways of Looking at a Black Man* (New York: Random House, 1997), 180–214.
10. Lorrie Moore, "The Wrath of Athena," *New York Times*, May 7, 2000.
11. Nick Paumgarten, "Central Casting: The Race Card," *New Yorker*, November 10, 2003; Christopher Chambers, "Stranger than Fiction: Wentworth Miller's Real-Life 'Human Stain' Experience," racialicious.com, December 7, 2006; J. Hoberman, "Telling Lies in America," *Village Voice*, October 28, 2003.
12. "Up-'n'-comer Wentworth Miller talks about *The Human Stain*," thefilmfreakcentral.com, November 2, 2003.
13. Roth, *Human Stain*, 116, 125.

CODA

1. David Chappelle, "Sketch Artist," http://www.youtube.com/watch?v=IryflAS6mpY (accessed April 15, 2012).
2. "When in Doubt, Smear the Dead Kid," http://www.slate.com/blogs/weigel/2012/03/27/when_in_doubt_smear_the_dead_kid.html (accessed May 16, 2012); "In Trayvon Martin Case, Plenty of Misinformation," http://www.washingtonpost.com/blogs/blogpost/post/in-trayvon-martin-case-plenty-of-misinformation/2012/03/28/gIQAxaPhgS_blog.html (accessed May 17, 2012); "Pictures of Trayvon Martin Are Fakes," http://www.politicalforum.com/political-opinions-beliefs/240554-pictures-trayvon-martin-fakes.html (accessed May 17, 2012).
3. "Who is George Zimmerman?," http://www.washingtonpost.com/lifestyle/style/who-is-george-zimmerman/2012/03/22/gIQAkXdbUS_story.html (accessed May 16, 2012).
4. "Why Did *New York Times* Call George Zimmerman 'White Hispanic'?," http://www.washingtonpost.com/blogs/erik-wemple/post/why-did-new-york-times-call-george-zimmerman-white-hispanic/2012/03/28/gIQAW6fngS_blog.html (accessed May 17, 2012); "Why Did PBS call George Zimmerman 'White'?," http://www.washingtonpost.com/blogs/erik-wemple/post/why-did-pbs-call-george-zimmerman-white/2012/04/11/gIQAZsC4AT_blog.html (accessed May 16, 2012).

5. "George Zimmerman Looks Like a Different Person in Each of His Photos," http://www.democraticunderground.com/1002557370 (accessed November 19, 2012).

6. "Colorblind," *Salon*, January 22, 2007, http://www.salon.com/opinion/feature/2007/01/22/obama/ (accessed December 18, 2007).

7. February 8, 2007, episode of *The Colbert Report*. http://www.comedycentral.com (accessed December 18, 2007).

8. Transcript excerpt of *60 Minutes* interview with Barack Obama, http://www.cbsnews.com/stories/2007/02/11/60minutes/main2458530_page5.shtml (accessed December 18, 2007).

9. "Secret Service Shuts Down 'Assassination of Obama and Clinton' Art Exhibit," http://gothamist.com/2008/06/04/secret_service.php (accessed May 17, 2012).

10. James Wimberley, "Is Barack Obama Black?," http://www.samefacts.com/2008/02/race-related-isms/is-barack-obama-black/ (accessed November 19, 2012).

11. Erinn Haines, "Obama/Curious George T-Shirt Draws Protests," http://articles.washingtonpost.com/2008-05-15/news/36847738_1_t-shirts-curious-george-illinois-senator (accessed March 26, 2013).

12. "Obama's Lying Blue Lips," http://wtpotus.wordpress.com/2010/02/21/obamas-lying-blue-lips/ (accessed May 16, 2012).

13. Michael D. Shear, "In Indonesia, an Obama Look-Alike," http://voices.washingtonpost.com/44/2010/03/in-indonesia-an-obama-look-ali.html (accessed May 16, 2012).

14. Huma Khan, "President Obama's Irish Eyes—and Ears?—Smile in Ancestral Hometown," http://abcnews.go.com/blogs/politics/2011/05/president-obamas-irish-eyes-and-ears-smile-in-ancestral-hometown/ (accessed May 15, 2012).

Index